Far-Right Politics in Europe

Far-Right
Politics
in Europe

Jean-Yves Camus

Nicolas Lebourg

TRANSLATED BY JANE MARIE TODD

The Belknap Press of Harvard University Press

Cambridge, Massachusetts
London, England

2017

First Printing

This book was originally published as *Les droites extrêmes en
Europe* © Éditions du Seuil, 2015

Library of Congress Cataloging-in-Publication Data

Names: Camus, Jean-Yves, 1958– author. | Lebourg, Nicolas, 1974– author.
Title: Far-right politics in Europe / Jean-Yves Camus and
Nicolas Lebourg ; translated by Jane Marie Todd.
Other titles: Droites extrêmes en Europe. English
Description: Cambridge, Massachusetts : The Belknap Press of
Harvard University Press, 2017. | "This book was originally published
as Les droites extrêmes en Europe © Éditions du Seuil, 2015"—
Title page verso. | Includes bibliographical references and index.
Identifiers: LCCN 2016042033 | ISBN 9780674971530 (hardcover : alk. paper)
Subjects: LCSH: Right-wing extremists—Europe. | Political culture—Europe. |
Europe—Politics and government—21st century.
Classification: LCC JC573.2.E85 C3613 2017 | DDC 320.53/3094—dc23
LC record available at https://lccn.loc.gov/2016042033

Contents

Far-Right Politics in Europe

Introduction: How the Far Right Came into Being

The expression "far right" has dominated commentary and analysis of the French political scene ever since the Front National (FN; National Front) began to have success at the polls in the mid-1980s. Outside France, events as diverse as the inclusion in the Austrian government of the Freiheitliche Partei Österreichs (FPÖ) under the leadership of Jörg Haider (2000), the race riots in Burnley, Bradford, and Oldham in the United Kingdom (2001), and the attacks committed by Anders Behring Breivik in Norway (2011) have made the term even more familiar. Its fundamental ambiguity lies in the fact that it is generally used by political adversaries of the "far right" to disqualify and stigmatize all forms of partisan nationalism by reducing them to the historical experiments of Italian Fascism, German National Socialism, and national variations more or less close to them from the first half of the twentieth century. The label "far right" is practically never used by those who belong to it:[1] they prefer to call themselves a "national movement" or the "national right."

All the scholarly literature concurs that a family of far-right parties does exist, however. Nonetheless, belief in the universality of democratic values does not automatically entail the idea that the split between right and left is atemporal or universal. The "far right" remains a category of analysis suited primarily to the Western European political context. In a pinch, the label can be attached to the Australian One Nation Party, a few marginal groups in the United States (the American Party), and even South African organizations nostalgic for apartheid (Vryheidsfront, Herstigte Nasionale Party), but not to the various "caudillist,"[2] reactionary, and clerical parties in Latin America's history (Pinochet's Chile, Videla's Argentina). Furthermore, the term "far right" sheds little light on the specific situation of the new democracies in Central and Eastern Europe, where nationalist, populist, and xenophobic parties are thriving: the Samoobrona in Poland, the LNNK (For Freedom and Fatherland) in Latvia, and the SRS (Serbian Radical Party). They, much more than Western far-right groups, are linked to authoritarian ethnicist and nationalist tendencies, which in the first thirty years of the twentieth century went hand in hand with the achievement of independence in those countries. To understand the far right in Europe as it now exists, we must in fact begin with French history. We will then be able to elaborate a general theory of the far right.

Reactionary Movements and Counterrevolution

The first political parties came into existence in the French Constituent Assembly, the name adopted by the Estates General on July 9, 1789. At the time, the aristocrats (Blacks), that is, the supporters of the ancien régime who rejected the revolution outright, were located farthest to the president's right in the spatial organization of the meeting hall. Then, from right to left, came the monarchists, advocates of an English-style bicameral parliamentary monarchy; the patriots or constitutionalists, who sought to reduce the king's power to a minimum and wanted a single legislative chamber; and, farthest to the left, the democrats, proponents of universal suffrage. That division within the Salle du Manège (Riding Hall) at the Tuileries Palace in Paris seems to date to September 11, 1789, when the proponents of a royal veto power sat to the right of the president and the adversaries of the veto to his left. The faction farthest to the right, located outside the Assembly in the Salon Français, was led by Vicomte de Mirabeau, known as "Mirabeau-Tonneau" (Barrel Mirabeau), the brother of Honoré Gabriel de Mirabeau and an officer who had served under Jacques Antoine Marie de Cazalès and Abbé Maury. That faction rapidly deserted the scene. By late 1789, about 200 of its members, the majority of them nobles, had emigrated, and 149 others had retreated to their lands. For the duration of the French Revolution, then during the Consulate and the Empire—generally as part of the emigration—the Restoration and the July Monarchy, and finally, the Second Empire, the heterogeneous counterrevolutionary camp embodied what would become the far right. The words and ideas were already in existence, but their dissemination was another matter. Although the political categories (far right, right, and so forth) were in place from the early nineteenth century on, until World War I citizens rarely classified themselves along the right-left axis: it was still primarily members of the legislature who positioned themselves in that way.[3]

The first taxonomies are not without interest. In a lampoon that circulated under the reign of Charles X (1824–1830), those on the "far right" are portrayed as hostile to the status quo and the ruling elites, skeptical, in favor of starting all over from scratch in order to reestablish order, contemptuous of politicians but laudatory of action and force, and fearful of a coming revolution.[4] That is a description of character more than of an orthodoxy, but the approach is not misguided, and at least the portrait is coherent. The current heirs of those counterrevolutionaries are the legitimists, the small group of royalists who embrace the Spanish branch of the Bourbons and traditional (also called "integral" or "integrist") Catholicism—the disciples of Monsignor Marcel Lefebvre, for example. Counterrevolutionary doctrinaires have a politico-theological worldview based on the notion of order: historically, Joseph de Maistre, Louis de Bonald, and Antoine de Rivarol, proponents of the ancien régime, are the best-known examples. In their view, the natural order, as defined by Catholicism, imposed a mode of government (monarchy) and a mode of social organization that assigned to each "order," precisely, an established and immutable function. They were French, but nationalism, as that concept was understood beginning in the 1870s, was not the cornerstone of their ideas. In fact, their intellectual views were borrowed in part from the Englishman Edmund Burke and the Swiss thinkers Mallet du Pan and Karl Ludwig von Haller—and Maistre, a native of the Savoy region, was a subject of the king of Sardinia. They were wary of progress and even more suspicious of what the Enlightenment had ushered in: free inquiry, skepticism, even atheism. According to them, disregarding the lessons of history was out of the question: like Charles Maurras at a later date, they were traditionalists. They had a strong inclination to idealize the past, to adopt the posture of a minority faithful to the end, even when all hope was gone. That ideology of the "remnant," of the sole survivors, also turned their romanticism into a form of politics. For some, such as Abbé Augustin Barruel, their loathing of the revolution, considered a subversion first and foremost, gave rise to conspiracy theories, which have flourished on the far right. In his *Mémoires pour servir à l'histoire du jacobinisme* (1797; Memoirs illustrating the history of Jacobinism), which continues to be reissued to this day, Barruel denounces the supposed efforts by the Masonic lodges, the "Illuminati," the Philosophes, and, to a lesser extent, the Jews, to overthrow the ancien régime. The revolution—not the event but its *principle*—is in this view Satanic in its essence, an emanation of the dark forces seeking to destroy both religion and France. Barruel invents a new word to describe his adversaries' ideology: "nationalism," which supposedly destroyed the old provinces and left universal friendship in tatters.[5]

As René Rémond has aptly written,[6] in the period running from the Restoration of 1814 to the Revolution of 1830, the only political family that merited the designation "right" was the one that advocated the return to absolute monarchy. Its members adopted the label "ultraroyalists." The adjective "ultra" is appropriate, because what they embraced went beyond the mere principle of monarchy consecrated with Louis XVIII's accession to the throne. The "ultras" were mystics who had a providentialist notion of history, believing that France and the Bourbon dynasty were the repositories of divine will (*Gesta Dei per Francos,* "the deeds of God through the Franks," in a medieval formula). Counterrevolutionary émigrés, cut off from their country for two decades, clung to a myth: the return of the ancien régime in its integrity. They became increasingly bitter, so that even the comte de Provence, now the new king, seemed liberal to them. In the Chambre Introuvable (Unobtainable Chamber), they opposed the Charter of 1814 and even their own sovereign. They expressed their views in newspapers such as *Le drapeau blanc* or in pamphlets, for example, Chateaubriand's *De la monarchie selon la Charte* (The monarchy according to the charter). Victory came to them only in 1824, with the accession to the throne of Charles X, who supported their cause. They became the minority again in 1830, with the advent of the July Monarchy, and never again returned to power. At that time, the monarchist camp divided into two families: the Orleanists behind Louis-Philippe, who supported a liberal monarchy, and the ultraracist legitimists. The Orleanists, who favored a parliamentary monarchy, were in some sense the precursors of liberalism, of a centrism that privileged the balance between social conservatism and the economic progress resulting from industrialization, the rise in power of the bourgeoisie, and the financialization of the economy. The legitimists, by virtue of their ideological intransigence, were already on the losing side of history.

According to the jurist Stéphane Rials,[7] the legitimists elaborated ideas throughout the nineteenth century based on a reaction to what they perceived as decadence, on an intransigent Catholicism, and on a form of providentialism, which authors such as Blanc de Saint-Bonnet and Louis Veuillot readily expressed as a tremendous pessimism. The legitimists scarcely believed that their ideas could prevail by human means. They placed their hopes in the "miracle," the supernatural, a view later found in writers close to them, such as Léon

Bloy, Jules Barbey d'Aurevilly, and Ernest Hello. That mystic pessimism is a salient trait of the far-right mind-set, from which, however, Fascism takes its distance, through its vitalism and the value it places on progress.

The definitive marginalization of the counterrevolutionary tendency occurred in the last quarter of the nineteenth century. Granted, the by-elections of July 2, 1871, which followed the National Assembly election of February 8, ushered in a monarchist majority. Paradoxically, it was a liberal Catholic, Monsignor Dupanloup, who now sat on the far right of the Assembly. Beside him were the Chevau-Légers, the most intransigent of the legitimists, under the leadership of Armand de Belcastel, Cazenove de Pradines, and Albert de Mun. They took their name from the Versailles walkway where they assembled. Unable to restore the ancien régime in its integrity, they supported a monarchy absolutely faithful to its symbols. They were imbued with a rigid Catholicism, which made them quick to view France's 1870 defeat to Prussia as divine punishment. The legitimists represented a provincial petty nobility and their obligees among the common people, groups that were losing ground. They were thwarted in their aims in 1873, with the "failed restoration" of their pretender, the comte de Chambord; they had fallen victim to a leader with no real desire for power. In 1892, they obeyed the pope's instructions to accept the legitimacy of the French Republic. Henceforth, the only royalist form of expression with a certain visibility would occur within the context of Action Française, the far-right, anti-Semitic group spearheaded by Charles Maurras in the first half of the twentieth century.

At the time of the counterrevolution, when the nation-state was only barely constituted, and the nobiliary and intellectual elites lived throughout Europe, both the liberal and the counterrevolutionary camps transcended borders. For example, with the start of the Peninsular War against Napoleon's troops (1808), there was in Spain an absolutist group with a strong aristocratic and clerical component. It manifested itself especially at the Cádis Cortès, the first national assembly to claim sovereignty in Spain. In 1810, that group opposed any acknowledgment on the part of the Council of Regency that the principle of national sovereignty was embodied in the Chamber. The absolutists became further radicalized after Ferdinand VII returned to the throne in 1813. From 1833 on, their philosophy was incarnated in "Carlism," which, like legitimism, was based on both a dynastic claim and an ideology. The absolutist movement invented the theory of the "two Spains" and the theme of a "Crusade," which would be found again in Francoism in 1936. Carlism produced several important thinkers: Jaime Balmes (1810–1848), but especially Juan Donoso Cortés (1809–1853), Juan Vázquez de Mella, and Félix Sardá y Salvany, whose *Liberalism Is a Sin* (1886) provides a good summary of the doctrine. In Mexico, the golden age of the Spanish Viceroyalty and counterrevolutionary thought (integrist Catholic mysticism) inspired the literary writings and political actions of Salvador Abascal Infante (1910–2000) and the Sinarquista movement. This was a late offshoot of the popular revolt of the Cristeros (1926–1929) against the secular republic, which was established by the Mexican Constitution of 1917.

In short, what historians call "the first globalization" (i.e., of Europe) allowed the circulation of ideas as well as people. During this period, which produced 180 million migrants between 1840 and 1940,[8] nations were superseded by empires with discriminatory legal theories and practices. A number of the ideas that currently constitute the foundation of far-right ideology (nationalism, populism, and anti-Semitism in particular) were defended at that time by the revolutionary *left*.

Nationalism and Socialism

The lexico-ideological confusion was only the greater in that the leaders of the far right did not call themselves "nationalists," but rather "patriots." Above all, they made great use of the term "Socialism," a word that, though imprecise, had been in vogue since the

1820s. Maurice Barrès (1862–1923), an intellectual and political figure on the far right, wrote plainly in 1889: "Socialism! That is the word in which France has placed its hope. Let us therefore be Socialists."[9] That dynamic persisted. In Italy, Fascism had its roots in the revolutionary Socialist movement, to which Benito Mussolini belonged, and in revolutionary syndicalism under the leadership of Antonio Labriola, which between 1902 and 1918 gradually moved away from the Socialist Party, eventually splitting along nationalist lines. Like many figures in German far-right politics, Mussolini was a devoted reader of Georges Sorel, whose *Réflexions sur la violence* (1908; Reflections on violence) was also a text of reference for anarcho-syndicalism. Sorel himself had gone back and forth between the two extremes, Fascism and Socialism—so much so that Lenin saw him as "muddle-headed" and Mussolini claimed: "I owe my greatest debt to Sorel."[10] In addition, the Russian Revolution of 1917 provided a model for seizing power through a revolutionary organization. Fascism was thus in part "an acculturation by the right of the lessons of the October Revolution."[11] In Germany, the philosopher Arthur Moeller van den Bruch expressed the position of the "Konservative Revolution" network, which opposed the Weimar Republic. In his view, nationalists and Communists were in a race to "win the revolution" to come and, in every country, revolutionaries were seeking to establish a "national Socialism," such as Bolshevism in Russia or Fascism in Italy. The far right therefore needed to take a "revolutionary detour" to establish a Socialist Third Reich: Socialism, in that sense, "is when a nation in its entirety feels it is living together."[12] That tendency may have sometimes led to a slavish imitation of far-left politics—the German, Italian, and French neo-Fascists borrowed aspects of leftist discourse after 1968, for example—but its interclassist conception of Socialism never changed. The ideal was national unity, not class struggle. For the far right, Socialism was always the remedy for Communism and anarchism. The reason that the congruence between the national and the social could occur on the far right was that the years between the Franco-Prussian War and World

War I completely changed the French and European political and ideological landscape.

The military defeat of 1870 put an end to the Second Empire, which was a Caesarism of the people. In 1840, Louis-Napoléon Bonaparte, before he became Napoleon III, had declared that "the Napoleonic idea consists of reconstituting French society, shattered by fifty years of revolution, of reconciling order and liberty, the people's rights and the principles of authority."[13] According to the historian Philippe Burrin, that version of Bonapartism belongs to the political family of "national unity," which transcends the split between right and left. Current members of that family would include Jean-Pierre Chevènement on the left, Nicolas Dupont-Aignan on the right, and Florian Philippot on the far right. In fact, Napoleon III's Bonapartism, as the historian André Encrevé writes, borrowed some "elements from the left (the principles of 1789, the promotion of economic progress, social legislation, and the defense of nationality), others from the right (the lack of respect for the major public liberties, clericalism, authoritarianism, the defense of order and property)."[14] Burrin's model allows us to understand what sometimes links the far right to other political spheres *and* what sometimes causes confusion among observers. Indeed, if Fascism is the "radical" form of the political family of "national unity" ideologies (Bonapartism, Caesarist authoritarianism, and so on), Nazism, according to the Swiss historian, would itself be a "radical Fascism." We thus arrive at a continuum that preserves specificities: Fascism is autonomous vis-à-vis "fin de siècle nationalism," but without being disconnected from it, and the comparison between Nazism and Fascism moves in only one direction (Nazism goes further than Fascism).[15] It is easy to understand what separates the factions from each other, what allows individuals to move from one to the other, but also what leads to so many excesses in the efforts to amalgamate the two.

The primary factor explaining the importance of the articulation between the national and the social was clearly the inrush of the masses into the system of production with the industrial revolution and into political debate with the spread of universal suffrage. Just as the French republic was being consolidated in the 1880s, a cross-pollination of ideas occurred, leading to the constitution of a new right wing, what Zeev Sternhell calls the "revolutionary right," which he sees as the prefiguration of Fascism. The first ideological belief to migrate from left to right was nationalism. Until that time, it was the republican camp that had displayed its attachment to the nation. The soldier Bara, the battles of Valmy and Jemmapes, the people in arms, and later Louis Rossel, an officer involved in the Paris Commune, were symbols of the patriotic left, which embraced the idea that citizenship and equality achieved their natural state of perfection within the framework of the sovereign nation. The personification of that Socialist nationalism was Louis-Auguste Blanqui (1805–1881). During his lifetime, he divided his time between prison and participation in conspiracies. Blanquism is much more an attitude than a doctrine, a style that influenced both Italian Fascism and the radical French movements on the far right and ultraleft. It glorified insurrection and the barricades (Blanqui wrote in 1868: "The duty of a revolutionary is struggle always, struggle nonetheless, struggle to the point of extinction"). The movement denounced Jewish capitalism; it participated in the Commune, calling the bourgeois regime, which was ready to abandon Alsace-Lorraine, "Prussian at its heart."[16] The Blanquists later rallied behind General Ernest Boulanger, a nationalist figure nicknamed "Général Revanche," at a time when the left was also deep in the process of producing an ideology.

A rift between the left and nationalism appeared with Marx and Engels, according to whom "the working men have no country."[17] The Dreyfus Affair and the massacre at Fourmies (where, on May 1, 1891, the French army fired on demonstrators) exacerbated antimilitarism on the left. The Confédération Générale du Travail (CGT; General Labor Federation) staged a general strike against the war in Morocco on December 16, 1912, and a demonstration against the three-year military service proposal on February 25, 1913. An antipatriotic faction had developed in the late nineteenth century, especially among anarchists and syndicalists. Their leading figure was Gustave Hervé (1871–1944), who advocated putting the "flag in the dung heap." Antipatriotism was inseparable from antimilitarism. In 1906 Hervé wrote: "We agree to only one war, civil war, social war." Likewise, he called for a boycott of the elections, so that the people would not compromise themselves in the parliamentary circus. That antipatriotic agitator, however, rallied behind the Sacred Union in 1914. His Socialism now took Blanqui and Proudhon as its points of reference. Hervé was a pacifist during the 1920s, then joined the ranks of the Fascists in 1932. Convinced that the Sacred Union had to be recreated, in 1936 he published a book with a famous title, *C'est Pétain qu'il nous faut* (Pétain's the one we need), an allusion to the old popular song "Boulanger's the One We Need." But in 1941 Hervé refused to follow Vichy any further and put an end to his militarism.[18] This brief biography of Hervé highlights only the paths that seem at present to be on the radar screen. They indicate the coherence of a past age, running from the post-1870 period to the aftermath of World War I. Those years were the turning point for the far right in Europe.

After 1870, the right, fired up by the imperative to seek revenge on Germany, constructed a nationalist mysticism entirely different from that on the left. It can be seen at work during the Dreyfus Affair, both in Hubert-Joseph Henry's "patriotic forgery" and in the text that accompanied the writer Paul Léautaud's subscription to the "Henry monument": "For order, against Justice and Truth." Anti-Semitism spread on the right: affirmed on the left by Proudhon and Rochefort, it also became the credo of the nationalists around Édouard Drumont and Maurice Barrès, the Ligue des Patriotes and the Ligue de la Patrie Française, then Charles Maurras and Action Française, who made the Jew public enemy number one, the embodiment of anti-France, the efficient cause of all society's ills.

The leagues had first appeared in the 1860s, during a more liberal phase of the Second Empire. These were political organizations that emphasized action over elections (though there were also electoral leagues from the 1880s onward): they focused on an objective and not a political program. Their aim was "unity"—truly the essential word in their vocabulary—around a key idea, as a way of moving beyond notions of class. The leagues were the first instruments by which the masses joined the political process.[19] Under the leadership of Paul Déroulède, the Ligue des Patriotes revered the French Revolution as well as the nation. Its motto, often imitated, was "Republican, Bonapartist, legitimist, Orleanist: for us, those are only given names. The family name is patriot." The league nevertheless moved away from the idea of liberating Alsace-Lorraine to embrace that of liberating the country: national regeneration took precedence over revenge. Although Déroulède criticized parliamentary institutions, he remained in the republican camp with the Blanquists and former Communards. Déroulède spoke of a "plebiscitary republic," in which the president of the republic would be elected by universal suffrage, and the popular will would be expressed through "legislative plebiscites," another name for referendums. With Déroulède, an extreme republican and social right made inroads. The formula long used by Jean-Marie Le Pen, "national, social, and popular right," is altogether true to that spirit.[20] Déroulède offered his strike force to General Boulanger, who seemed unstoppable in 1887–1889. Criticism of parliamentarianism and odes to the people and the nation allowed Boulangism to unite royalists and former Communards. But Boulanger's refusal to use force sealed the fate of the movement, which was liquidated by judicial repression, then by the suicide of the supposed savior on his mistress's grave. Boulangism shows how one far-right tendency, national populism, can crystallize; it also demonstrates why it makes no sense to define extremism by the criterion of violence. To do so would be to confuse Fascism with the far right, to deduce from far-right *regimes* the nature of far-right *movements*.

National populism has remained the main tendency of the French far right, thanks especially to the election results of the National Front, which, though founded in 1972, did not have any success at the polls until a decade later. In fact, it was in an effort to understand the FN's first electoral successes that the political scientist Pierre-André Taguieff imported the expression "national populism" to France.[21] That movement conceives of political change as decadence, from which only the healthy common people can extract the nation. National populism, privileging a direct relationship between a savior and the people, beyond the divisions and parasitical institutions said to pose a death threat to the nation, claims to defend the little guy, the "average Frenchman," "common sense," against the betrayal of inevitably corrupt elites. The apologist of a closed nationalism, it seeks a mythical national unity. It is alterophobic (that is, it fears "the other," which is assigned an essentialized identity through permutations of the ethnic and the cultural, generally by way of religion). It combines the social values of the left and the political values of the right (order, authority, and so on). Although its verbal aesthetic leans toward Socialism, its wish for the union of all, after the exclusion of the tiny stratum of profiteers disloyal to the nation, marks a total rupture with the ideology of class struggle. To make nation and people coincide, national populism introduces permutations in the meaning of the word "people." The people are the *demos,* political unity; they are the *ethnos,* biological unity; they are a social body, the "working classes"; and they are the "plebs," the masses. The national populist far right plays on the confusion between these first three meanings: a provision such as "national preference" (a policy that would restrict social benefits to French citizens) must unify the people socially, ethnically, and politically. The plebs hand themselves over to a savior, so that he will break their shackles and allow the people and the nation to exercise their sovereignty. The masses, rid of parasites, become the people united. National populism is therefore an interclassist ideology that vaunts "rural" values against "false intellectualization." It has occupied a place in our political life for the last 130 years. There is thus no more sense in linking it to the image of Nazism than there is in separating it from the history of the French far right, and no logical possibility that it will disappear with the wave of a magic wand. It is part of the structure of the French political system.

In addition, national populism became a phenomenon of European scope with the formation of a number of parties during the 1970s. That dynamic had three dimensions: first, voters' rejection of the welfare state (generally modeled on the Scandinavian system) and of the tax system, which is judged to be "confiscatory"; second, the rise of xenophobia against the backdrop of immigration movements that, because they originate outside Europe, are considered to be of a new kind; and finally, the end of the prosperity that had reigned since the post–World War II era, a shock registered with the oil crisis of 1973. The two precursory parties typical of the first dimension are, in Denmark, the Fremskridtspartiet (Progress Party), under the leadership of Mogens Glistrup, and, in Norway, the Anders Lange's Party, which bears the name of its founder. Two other parties embody the mobilization of voters against immigration, while at the same time opting for ultraliberal economic positions: the French National Front, which finally managed to gain a foothold in the elections of 1983–1994; and a revitalized and radicalized party, the FPÖ in Austria, which, under Jörg Haider's banner from 1986 on, began a slow and continuous advance that peaked in 1999. During the same period, the Flemish Vlaams Blok was beginning to make its mark in Belgian politics, symbolizing—better than all the other European organizations no doubt—both historical continuity with the nationalism of the first half of the twentieth century and a thorough modernization of the methods of political action.

During the period when national populism was taking shape, however, it was far from the only case of political ferment. Within the constellation of right-wing politics at the time, one movement set itself apart, both by the coherence of its doctrine and by the intellectual authority it exerted (until its dissolution in 1944): Action Française.[22] The review *L'Action française* emerged from the Dreyfus Affair in 1898: at the time, it was nationalist, antiparliamentary, anti-Dreyfusard, and republican. It underwent an evolution in 1899 when Charles Maurras (1868–1952) joined on, and it spread the word about that theorist's "integral nationalism." The review gave its name to the movement it founded in 1905 and became a combative daily newspaper in 1908.

Action Française was a neoroyalist movement far more attached to the institution of kingship than to the royals themselves—who would disavow it. At the time, neither the league nor its intellectual guide, Maurras, was categorized as being on the "far right." Action Française's integral nationalism was authoritarian but decentralizing, and placed the notion of order above everything else, even if that meant reducing the Catholic religion—to which it attached great importance—to a mere instrument in the submission of individuals to the natural order, which Maurras defined in terms of reason (taxonomic empiricism) and not mysticism. The matter at hand was to make the "real country" coincide with the "legal country" and to put an end to individualism, in favor of natural communities and hierarchies (family, métier). The Jacobin state would disappear, and the ancient provinces would be reestablished. Action Française was on the far right by virtue of its irrevocable condemnation of democracy, its utopian dream of an organic community, its exclusivist definition of who belonged to the nation, and its fierce anti-Semitism, which culminated in the anti-Jewish laws implemented by the Vichy government (1940)—and written by a Maurrassian, Minister of Justice Raphaël Alibert. But Action Française and Maurras had an influence and a posterity well beyond the far right. In the French Resistance, the philosopher Pierre Boutang, the academic Pierre Renouvin, Navy Lieutenant Honoré d'Estienne d'Orves, and "Colonel Rémy" placed Maurras's and Bainville's anti-German nationalism in the service of the nation's independence, not its submission. Later on, in the 1970s, royalists updated Maurras's thinking with the Nouvelle Action Française, which in 1981 supported the left. And, as Eugen Weber reminds us, politicians as diverse as François Mitterrand, René Pleven, and Robert Buron "were affected by their brief acquaintances with Action Française circles."[23] So too were a number of writers with no involvement in political action or extremism (some of the "Hussards," such as Michel Déon and Michel Mohrt). Internationally, the influence of Maurras was in evidence from the post-1919 period to the 1960s. He probably received his most enthusiastic welcome on the Iberian Peninsula. General Francisco Franco, leader of Spain from 1939 to 1975, and António de Oliveira Salazar, prime minister of the Estado Novo of Portugal from 1933 to 1968, knew and appreciated his doctrine—and integral nationalism was also an inspiration in Belgium, Switzerland, French Canada, Brazil, and Argentina.[24]

These antiliberal modes of thought were able to flourish in the late nineteenth century because they entailed a transformation of representations. In France, pacifism was clearly on the wane as of the Second Moroccan Crisis of 1911, which spread the idea of the ineluctability of a new war between the French and the Germans. A book published the same year, *Enquête sur les jeunes gens d'aujourd'hui* (Survey of today's young people), showed that the ascendant values were order, discipline, nation, religious practice, sports, and the will to act. The book was signed "Agathon" (the pen name of Henri Massis and Alfred de Tarde), and the expression "Agathon generation" was used to describe this cohort of young people ready for war, who had broken away from both the liberal system and the revolutionary Socialist fringe.[25]

In these years prior to World War I, an exacerbation of tensions occurred between France and Germany and within the French population itself. Across the Rhine, German Romanticism played a fundamental role at the time: reason and scientism were being rejected in favor of legendary folklore and the myth of a Golden Age, namely, the Roman Holy Empire of the German Nation (962–1806). The medieval Reich, with its feudal principalities and trade guilds, represented an ideal Germany in which society as a whole was supposedly organized into a harmonious hierarchical order. Pan-Germanism founded its legitimacy on the idea of uniting in the second Reich (1871–1918) all German speakers, who would lend their full strength to Germany in the face of the Western nations. A new passion was sparked in that country with the spread in 1879 of the neologism "anti-Semitism," marking a break from "anti-Judaism" in favor of a racial and scientific notion. Blood, soil, and language were the trinity the Völkischen erected to oppose the nationalism of the social contract. The term *völkisch* is reputed to be untranslatable. In addition to its mystic, populist, and agrarian dimensions, it means "racist" (the French *raciste* is the root of the German word) and, as of 1900, came to signify "anti-Semitic." The Völkischen were believers in the ideal of *Blut und Boden* (blood and soil). The root *Volk* means "people," but its connotations are broader, fundamentally ethnic in scope. The term may be understood as expressing a racist nostalgia, one based in folklore, for a largely mythified German prehistory. That variegated movement drew its inspiration from Romanticism, occultism, the first "alternative" doctrines (alternative medicine, naturism, vegetarianism, and so on), and finally, from racist doctrines. The reconstitution of a largely mythical Germanic past distanced the Völkischen from monotheism, as they attempted to recreate a pagan, purely German religion. That tendency strongly fueled Nazism, but it was also the basis for many nationalist reorientations in Europe after World War II, in factions as varied as revolutionary nationalism, the New Right, and neo-Nazism.[26]

As the notions associated with "Blubo" (short for Blut und Boden) spread, France saw the development of new sciences, such as anthroposociology and social psychology, pervaded with a racism—a sort of commonplace at the time—that long shaped the belief in a racial essence of the French nation. Arthur de Gobineau and Georges Vacher de Lapouge, using and distorting Darwin's theory of evolution with a view to the "race struggle," theorized the importance of species selection. Their hygenicist perspective was adopted by Alexis Carrel and was combined with the Aryan myth, which also owes a great deal to the Englishman Houston Stewart Chamberlain and his vision of the possibility of a new race. The myth of the two French races (according to which the Third Estate was descended from the Gauls, the nobility from the Franks), in place since the early eighteenth century, faded away in favor of the idea—central to the writings of Maurice Barrès and Édouard Drumont—of one pure French race, which was being corrupted by foreign elements, Jewish in particular. That doctrine considered inheritance based on blood the sole criterion for being part of the nation; it was absolutely at odds with the notion of contractual and voluntary citizenship on which the republican nation was founded. Racism was now cloaked in the mantle of science. At the same time, when racist doctrine decreed the natural inferiority of peoples of color or Arabs, it came to legitimize the colonization policy being conducted with the support of the parliamentary left. It reduced the "natives" to the rank of subjects unequal before the law, within the context of the French empire and the administrative departments of Algeria. Here as well (and this too was an important change), racial anti-Semitism gradually supplanted theological anti-Judaism, which, however, the newspaper *La Croix* disseminated efficiently and virulently during the last twenty years of the nineteenth century. That anti-Semitism could also be found among leftist revolutionaries of all stripes, fueled by a permanent identification of the Jews with capitalism, money, and usury. The result was a synthesis of Socialism and the old fount of religious hatred.

The Israeli political scientist Zeev Sternhell is therefore quite right in claiming that, beginning at this time, the distinction that René Rémond has established among the three right-wing factions (counterrevolutionary, Orleanist, and Bonapartist) no longer held: a synthesis was occurring. This "revolutionary right," to use Sternhell's expression, continued with the antidemocratic movements of 1918–1940, then the Vichy ideology of National Revolution, and, according to Sternhell, Fascism as well. That "revolutionary right" was based on the modernization of the European continent, the technological revolution, and the access of the working classes to the electoral market. The "revolutionary right" sought to respond to the demands regarding status and working conditions being made by these sectors. But it was also responsive to the strong opposition to Marxism among a good part of the working classes. That opposition could also be found in other components of society, where Barrès's beloved cult of "the earth and the dead" became a French equivalent of sorts to the German Blut und Boden. The predominant features of that movement, which proclaimed itself to be "neither on the right nor on the left,"[27] were: an intellectual crisis; a rejection of the established social order, with revolutionary tendencies and anticapitalist overtones; a populist dimension that adopted the plebiscitary tradition; the vindication and even advocacy of violence as a means of action; and a call for individual and collective regeneration. In the early twentieth century, along with the anti-Dreyfusards, the Maurrassians, Georges Valois, Georges Sorel, and other figures, that right wing came to embody a radicalization that Sternhell believes to be a form of Fascism, even its first form.

Forms of Fascism

Since the late 1970s, Sternhell has opposed the widely accepted view that Fascism came out of Italy in the aftermath of World War I and is to be distinguished from the "holy trinity" of rightist movements in France. Far from being absent from France, he argues, Fascism arose in that country in the late nineteenth century. His writings both reposition the debate on French Fascism and break free of the constraints of what Ernst Nolte calls "the Fascist epoch," which would run from the aftermath of World War I to World War II. Sternhell's research sheds light on the particular alchemy of Fascism and the important role played in its foundation by both the revision of Marxism and the fin-de-siècle rejection of the legacy of the Enlightenment. In so doing, it has contributed toward de-Marxifying and de-Italianizing the history of Fascism. Sternhell does not view World War I as the mother of Fascism, which he considers a coherent and organized ideological system. For him, the Fascist state is "the totalitarian state par excellence, and totalitarianism is the essence of Fascism."[28]

Historically, Georges Valois (1878–1945), an important figure in Sternhell's thinking, did acknowledge that Italy had given Fascism its name and its modes of operation. But he continually claimed that, in France, Fascism was the ideology of fin-de-siècle nationalism and that its founder was Barrès, a republican and antiparliamentarian nationalist Socialist who attracted men on both the left and the right. There are, however, many factual arguments to refute the idea of a Fascism indebted to Barrès. More than that, however, such a quest for a primal essence of Fascism ought not to leave out its "plasticity" (to borrow Pascal Ory's characterization),[29] a dimension that allows it to incorporate a large number of contradictory elements. For example, Georges Valois said both that the source of Fascism could be traced back to the Jacobins and that the experience of World War I made the Fascists what they were. Furthermore, just because the French Fascist vanguard came from Action Française does not mean that Action Française was a "Fascist" movement—that would be turning chronology into causality. Valois, Brasillach, and Drieu La Rochelle were Fascists because they broke away from Maurras's way of thinking, not because they were indebted to it. What was Valois saying when he told French Fascists to remain faithful to their sources, arguing that the "Jacobins forged the notion of the totalitarian state"? What was the French Communist-turned-Fascist Jacques Doriot saying when he exclaimed that "we did not wait for Germany's victory over France to discover National Socialism and to propose National Socialist solutions for our country"?[30] They were legitimizing themselves by producing a set of signs in which the importation of extranational elements intermingled with the assertion of a specific national tradition, over a longer time span than that of the Italian and German models. These perspectives lead us to George Mosse, who paved the way for an analysis of Fascism as culture, "style," and not merely as a negative reaction. Mosse propounded the view that Fascism resulted in great part from the brutalization of societies in 1914–1918, and he understood the relationship between the French Revolution and Fascism within the context of a mass ideology that may well be a civil religion.[31]

It was truly the experience of total war that radicalized the fringe elements and that allowed them to come in contact with the masses. In Italy, Germany, and France, the desire that society live as a "combat community," with the same unity in peacetime as in war, was realized politically in Fascism.[32] It was after 1918 that the right wing learned to call itself "revolutionary": in that respect, Sternhell's "revolutionary right" is a quirk in the history of language. It would have been better to say not "revolutionary" but "reactionary," a term that does not inevitably signify a mere conservative protest. What in 1795 was called "the Reaction" was an episode of counterrevolutionary violence, also known as "the White Terror."

This interpretive debate is particularly rich because of the burgeoning of ideologies and taxonomies that occurred within a limited span of space-time. Indeed, the word *extrémiste* (extremist) appeared in French public debate in 1917: the French press used it to lambaste the Bolsheviks, who had just taken power in Russia. The "far right" (*extrême droite*) camp was now positioned in reaction to the "far left" (*extrême gauche*).[33] And that designation appeared at almost the same moment as an actual bipartition of the field. As a field, the far right was certainly coherent. The core of the far right's worldview was organicism, that is, the idea that society functions as a living being. The far-right movements disseminated an organicist conception of the community they wished to constitute (whether based on ethnicity, nationality, or race), or that they said they wanted to reconstitute. That organicism entailed the rejection of every form of universalism, in favor of autophilia (the valorization of the "we") and alterophobia. Extremists on the right thus absolutize differences (between nations, races, individuals, cultures). They tend to conflate inequalities and differences, which creates a climate of anxiety, since differences disrupt their efforts to organize their community homogeneously. They cultivate the utopian dream of a "closed society" able to ensure the rebirth of community. Far-right movements challenge the political system in place, both its institutions and its values (political liberalism and egalitarian humanism). They feel that society is in a state of decay, which is exacerbated by the state: accordingly, they take on what they perceive to be a redemptive mission. They constitute a countersociety and portray themselves as an alternative elite. Their internal operations rest not on democratic rules but on the emergence of "true elites." In their imaginary, they link history and society to great archetypal figures (the golden age, the savior, decadence, conspiracy, and so on) and glorify irrational, nonmaterialistic values (youth or the cult of the dead, for example). And finally, they reject the geopolitical order as it exists.

That definition covers the broad field of the far right. It therefore includes those who aspire more to an authoritarian reformulation of institutions than to a total (anthropological and social) revolution that would destroy everything inherited from political liberalism. This last aspect characterized the radical far right that emerged from World War I, which had a Fascist structure and frame of reference but also drew from other movements. Granted, renegades escaping Socialism—an element Sternhell particularly emphasizes—played a role in its construction, but they had all adopted that worldview and that political sociability beforehand.

The experience of World War I and the repercussions of the Russian Revolution were the matrix for the classic form of Fascism and its self-representation. The result was a hierarchized and militarized mass party, destined to enter into osmosis with society and the state, and a new man, forged by the imperialist war abroad and a domestic totalitarian state. That state was taken in hand by a militia-party that imposed its worldview as a political religion, permanently mobilizing its population. Although ultranationalist, Fascism did not overlook the European question, appropriating the notion of "proletarian nations" invented by Enrico Corradini (1865–1931) in 1909. Corradini was a social Darwinist, antiliberal and antisocialist, who said that the battle was not between classes but between plutocratic nations on one hand (Great Britain and France, for example) and proletarian nations on the other (Italy included). Italy should therefore wage war to regenerate itself and to build an empire. In 1910 he founded the Italian Nationalist Association, which played a notable role in agitating for Italy's entry into the war in 1914. It merged with the National Fascist Party in 1923. Corradini had a major influence on Mussolini, who believed that Europe, suffering a civilization crisis, could save itself only through the imperialist actions of the proletarian nations, Italy in the first place. Fascist imperialism was thus an instrument in the service of Europe as a whole. Revitalized by Fascism, Europe would recover the greatness of its civilization. The newspaper of Mussolinianism, *Il popolo d'Italia,* was in fact symptomatic in this respect. Its masthead was framed by a quotation from Blanqui and another from Napoleon, clearly indicating that, though Fascism was an Italian nationalism, its perspective Socialist, nationalist, and imperialist, it was not afraid of foreign contact. In fact, Mussolini's positions on the universality of Fascism evolved over time. In 1928 he declared that Fascism was not exportable. In 1929 he wrote a preface to *The Universal Aspects of Fascism,* by the English Fascist Major James Strachey Barnes (1890–1955), in which he said that Fascism was a purely Italian phenomenon in its historical expression, but that its principles were universal. In 1932 he affirmed that Fascism was the ideology of the twentieth century. That same year, the regime launched *Ottobre,* subtitled "Review of Universal Fascism." The newspaper, which sold very well, received contributions from the Englishman Oswald Mosley, the German Alfred Rosenberg, and from Léon Daudet of Action Française. It supported Jeune Europe (Young Europe) and the "Fascist International," which was supposedly destined to sweep away "old Europe." In summer 1933, Il Duce hailed the construction of what he called a "Fascist state" in Germany. But the Fascist regime did not confine itself to intellectual combat: it also financed Fascism across Europe. In particular, in 1935–1936 Rome gave its money to Oswald Mosley in Great Britain; to Marcel Déat,

Marcel Bucard, Eugène Deloncle, and Doriot in France; and to the Falange in Spain.[34]

Non-Italian movements did not hesitate to make overt references to Mussolini's state, as indicated by the case of Mosley, leader of the British Union of Fascists. With the twilight of Italian Fascism, the banner of internationalism was once more brandished, as a return to a program of revolution and mobilization. In November 1943, the Congress of Verona established, as the geopolitical goal of the Italian Social Republic, the constitution of a European federation of nationalist states that would undertake the struggle against "global plutocracy" and organize the exploitation of Africa with the support of Muslim nationalists.[35] That program was later the core of European neo-Fascism.

It is noteworthy that this Europeanism was exclusively doctrinal: the Fascists sought power for themselves, not for foreigners. The Fascist movements in the various European countries were an expression first and foremost of their own national contexts: in Western Europe, they set out to regenerate individuals and the systems of government emerging from World War I; in Central and Eastern Europe, to resolve the difficult national question following the dismemberment of the Central Powers and the imposition of regulations by the treaties following on the Treaty of Versailles. Contrary to a widespread myth, there was never a "Fascist international," not even after December 16 and 17, 1934, when a "congress of European nationalist movements" was held in Montreux, Switzerland—it was actually just a propaganda operation of Mussolini's Italy. The reason is that Fascism, unlike Communism, had no centralized international organization, no single headquarters, no unified doctrine, no convergence of interests by its various parts and parties. There were, however, individual Fascist movements with a common foundation: the rejection of democracy, an aversion to Communism, the promotion of violence, a cult of personality devoted to a leader, along with racism, anti-Semitism, and ethnic chauvinism. Each possessed a national specificity, however, and, to varying degrees, continued to enrich the greater movement with new ideas.

The Diversity of the Radical Movements

Fascism is far from the only movement on the radical far right. Indeed, there are political offerings farther to the right than Fascism. In Italy, the philosopher Julius Evola (1898–1974), author of *Il Fascismo visto della destra* (Fascism seen from the right), established a so-called traditionalist doctrine, which in the 1960s to 1970s spread to the Western European far right. In Germany, the "National Bolshevism" of Ernst Niekisch (1889–1967) constituted "the most extreme right."[36] The history of the Nazi Party has tended to overshadow the pluralism of German nationalism, in both its ideologies and its organizations. That nationalism cannot be reduced to the cursory doctrines of Adolf Hitler, Alfred Rosenberg, and Walter Darré. Its source lies in the Deutsche Bewegung (German Movement), a vast current of ideas going from Johann Gottfried Herder to Romanticism, which arose in reaction to French rationalism and English empiricism. That entire intellectual family was structured around a worldview (*Weltanschauung*) rather than an ideology. The concept of Germanness occupied a central place, as did the idea of Reich, which was much closer to the notion of the ancient Roman *Imperium* than to that of a nation-state. Before National Socialism, then, there was Paul de Lagarde and Julius Langbehn; the völkisch movement and the Wandervogel youth movement (in its two distinct phases, one running from 1895 to 1914, the other up to 1933, when it was "brought to heel," constrained to join Hitlerjugend [Hitler Youth], though some of its members refused to do so). And, alongside Nazism, participating in it to a certain degree but often— as in Ernst Jünger's case—maintaining a critical distance, was another major movement: the Conservative Revolution, whose intellectual history the Swiss political writer Armin Mohler recorded in all its richness and complexity.[37] Like Mohler, we can no doubt find foreign equivalents of the Conservative Revolution in the Russians Dostoevsky and Aksakov, in the Spaniard Miguel de Unamuno, in the Italians Vilfredo Pareto and Julius Evola, in the Englishmen D. H. Lawrence and G. K. Chesterton, and even in the thinking of the theorist of Revisionist Zionism, Vladimir Ze'ev Jabotinsky, who, one could argue, transposed to Jewish nationalism the Polish nationalist philosophy of his Endecja (National Democracy) contemporary Roman Dmowski. These various factions competed intellectually, and they all also sought to put their stamp on the race for power. They felt the effects of the split within the far right: as of 1928, the conservative revolutionary Hartmut Plaas proposed making a distinction between the "nationals," who were conservative, and the "nationalists," who were revolutionaries.[38] In France, that distinction became dogma after the Algerian War, thanks to the publication of Dominique Venner's *Pour une critique positive* (For a positive critique). Just what dynamic that plurality would entail was still an open question.

The "antisystem" dimension of the far right tends to be the minimalist argument used to champion its unification. In 1927 the German cadres of various tendencies on the far right—the National Socialist Joseph Goebbels, the National Bolshevik Ernst Niekisch, and the neonationalist Ernst Jünger—denounced the Weimar Republic's "Systemzeit," which they considered politically harmful and culturally degenerate. Against that behemoth, they called for the union of its opponents, members of the "Periphery," extremists striking at the "Center," an image borrowed from Werner Sombart, the theorist of a German form of Socialism and a man highly appreciated by the European far right. The concept was also current among German geopoliticians, who used it in the elaboration of the notion of *Lebensraum* ("living space," the policy of colonizing or conquering territories for settlement). For the Nazis, the "System" went hand in hand with *Kulturbolschewismus* (cultural Bolshevism). Rosenberg saw it as the source of disintegration of the people's soul. For

Hitler, its agents were the Jews, who wanted to make the Germans lose their "roots"; for Goebbels, it was associated with those who were themselves rootless, cosmopolitans.[39]

The concept of "system" made inroads in French neo-Fascist circles beginning in 1951.[40] It served as a point of reference for Jean-Louis Tixier-Vignancour and Maurice Bardèche, in their rationale for the Rassemblement National (National Unity), founded in 1954 to unify about twenty small groups. Once again, as always, the matter at hand was to figure out how to bring together a Balkanized political force at a particularly intense moment in France's history. In light of the split within the far right, Maurras proposed in 1934 that the right wing should form a "National Front" by means of a "nationalist compromise."[41] The process failed because, among other reasons, the radicals feared that this National Front would be in the service of reactionaries. Nonetheless, between 1934 and 1940, under the leadership of the Parisian politician Charles Trochu, the National Front assembled militants from Action Française, Jeunesses Patriotes, and Solidarité Française, though it did not incorporate the Croix de Feu, the Parti Populaire Français (PPF), or the Francistes. In 1937 Doriot attempted to launch his own united association around his PPF, even appealing to the reformist left. The far-right Vichy regime was faced with a pluralism of far-right movements and with many futile calls from radicals to establish a single party.

The difficulties raised by the far-right movements in France lie in the complexity of the forms they take. Few historians have questioned Raoul Girardet's 1955 analysis, namely, that the French interwar period, for lack of a true "Fascist movement," was marked by a "Fascist permeation."[42] Burrin, for example, situated France within the "magnetic field" of Fascism.[43] The possibility arises, however, of a third way—analytically speaking—between the idea that Fascism was nonexistent in France and the notion that the country was saturated by Fascists. In Germany and Italy, Fascism was under the control of a militarized and hierarchized party that had come to power. But that was not the form it took in France. During the interwar period, a powerful antiliberalism took hold there, based in great part on its national history and on the spread of pre-Fascist ideas (those analyzed by Sternhell). On the whole, however, the Fascist phenomenon in France remained on the order of small groups and consisted of the acculturation of foreign elements by way of fin-de-siècle nationalism. Hence, as Jean-Louis Loubet del Bayle has shown, nonconformists were not Fascists, but they contributed to "the spirit of the 1930s" and "Fascist permeation."[44]

Was the Vichy regime on the far right? Indisputably so, provided we understand that the National Revolution succeeded in rallying behind it a minority of intellectuals and politicians on the left, whether neo-Socialists or "planists," that is, proponents of a planned economy. It even incorporated Communist defectors and former pacifists from the revolutionary Socialist camp, at the end of a trajectory that, in some cases, had taken them from Dreyfusism to collaboration.[45] But Marshal Philippe Pétain's regime abolished the republic, political parties, and democratically elected institutions, not only in response to the extraordinary circumstances but also in a spirit of revenge against the values of 1789 and more recent republican gains, such as secularism. Vichy's actions can no doubt be best understood in terms of state anti-Semitism. Without it, according to the proponents of the "new order," the regeneration of the French nation would be incomplete. Yet we cannot overlook the fact that some on the nationalist or revolutionary right opposed Vichy. Such was the case for Georges Valois, who joined the Resistance and died in the deportation, and of Colonel de La Rocque, who was also deported. Charles Vallin, the leader of the Parti Social Français, a right-wing party formerly close to the (now dissolved) leagues, left for London in 1942. And representatives of conservative groups, such as Louis Marin of the Fédération Républicaine, as well as Georges Mandel and Paul Raynau, also opposed the regime. In fact, it was that opposition by part of the right wing that gave the expression "far right" a certain consistency after 1945. At that time, it came to designate the political forces that had compromised themselves during the Occupation and the groups that later embraced Pétainism, in contrast to the rightists who acquired legitimacy because they had been part of the Resistance.

Under Vichy, Pétain's refusal to set in place a single, unified party, as well as the rivalries among groups and personalities, led to the situation described by Pierre-Antoine Cousteau (1906–1956) in the September 17, 1943, issue of *Je suis partout:* "French Fascism exists. It is not a party (it is, if you will, a pulverization of parties); above all, it is a state of mind, a set of reflexes, a heroic manner of conceiving life, it is a great deal of harshness and exigency, a constant will for grandeur and purity, the acceptance of Europe without the renunciation of the nation, it is Socialism without the Jews, reason and faith."[46] In short, Cousteau tells us, to define French Fascism, there is no need for a party structure: what is at issue first and foremost is a "Fascist style." Fascism in France is composed of a plethora of groups, each with only a few members. Burrin points out that, "even with the inclusion of de La Rocque's movement, which is problematic, the troops of [French] Fascism would approach the million-member threshold, which is to say, far less than 5 percent of the adult population."[47] Not only does French Fascism not recognize the key importance of a *Duce* or *Führer,* but that leaderless aspect was even theorized by those in the violent Fascist group known as "La Cagoule," active in France in the late 1930s. In 1941 its founder, Eugène Deloncle, argued that "secret societies, suitably fragmented, separated from one another: [such is] the main point." And the Mouvement Social Républicain from the end of the Vichy regime held that Fascism was "a 'new knighthood,' but without a leader, which ought to favor the regrouping of the collaborationist forces."[48]

Both the split in the French far right and the network structure of its radical wing persisted in the postwar period. Other European countries were experiencing the same phenomenon. After the war, the Danish and French intelligence services noted in similar terms the existence of a vast network of groups: in several cases, one association was merely a front for another; and militants were connected to one another in movements that, though diverse, constituted a common space whose fragmentation was partially desired and constructed. According to the French intelligence services, in 1946 former members of the French Waffen-SS formed a network that sought to plant cadres in anti-Communist movements, in order to introduce a subversive dynamic into countersubversive activities. Among them was a veteran of the Charlemagne Division, Pierre Bousquet, who would become part of Jeune Nation (JN), Europe-Action, and *Militant,* and would be the first treasurer of the National Front founded in 1972.[49] In 1947 the underground Comité National de Coordination indicated in a memorandum that cadres needed to infiltrate the anti-Communist movements, in order to shape political life through that secret network, and concluded: "We are the new resistance." In 1951 the opposition between Pétainists and collaborationists crystallized anew, with the collaborationists assembling around the weekly *Rivarol* (which is still being published).[50] After the dissolution of Pierre Sidos's Jeune Nation in 1958, the Parti Nationaliste was launched, in the hope (official, not real) of gathering together all the movements into a Comité d'Entente (Entente Committee), but it too was dissolved.[51] Attempts by the former JN and the former PPF to maneuver the Poujadist tax protest movement produced no results, though the militants had hoped to provoke a crisis like the antiparliamentarian street demonstration in Paris of February 6, 1934, one that, this time, would be successful. A short time later, the hope that the Organisation de l'Armée Secrète (OAS; Secret Army Organization), a paramilitary organization that opposed Algerian independence, might be a winning nationalist compromise also proved vain. It was with that in mind that Dominique Venner wrote *Pour une critique positive,* in which he said he would reject the Maurrassian nationalist compromise, unless it was supported by a Leninist praxis on the part of nationalists: "Zero plus zero is still zero. . . . The tactic of the front cannot be envisioned without a powerful nationalist organization capable of giving it momentum and imposing a political line on it."[52] For Venner, it was not illogical to conceive of union in terms more similar to Doriot than to Maurras. The distinction between "nationals" and "nationalists" took root, parallel to attempts at a horizontal organization of the two camps. In that respect, the review *L'Esprit public,* a screen for the OAS, served as a trial run, albeit a failed one: its coeditor, Raoul Girardet, saw nothing but confusion and ethnic hysteria in the thinking of one of its contributors, Jean Mabire, who extolled the virtues of revolution and of the white man's world.[53]

The Third Reich's New European Order

In Germany, the establishment of the totalitarian state and its propaganda forged the image of a perfectly monolithic party. But before the Nazis took power, the party cadre Otto Strasser (1897–1974) dreamed of rivaling Adolf Hitler. He broke away from the Nazi Party in 1930 to found the Kampfgemeinschaft Revolutionärer Nationalsozialisten (Fighting Community of Revolutionary National Socialists). In 1931 it became the Schwarze Front (Black Front) after, among other things, a hemorrhaging of its militants, who went over to the German Communist Party. Once he had established himself, Strasser made a large number of contacts: in France, with Alexandre Marc and the nonconformist review *L'Ordre nouveau*; in Spain, with Ramiro Ledesma Ramos's and Onésimo Redondo's Juntas de Ofensiva Nacional Sindicalista; in Germany, with Niekisch's Widerstand circle. The doctrine he disseminated during the interwar period played an extremely important role in later radical thought. He advocated the dismantlement of industrial and urban society, support for separatist movements in nation-states that opposed Germany (in order to provoke their dismantlement), and the creation of an economic cooperation zone to exploit the resources of eastern Europe, Africa, and Asia.[54] Beyond that, the Europe he championed was closely akin to medieval Christendom, the ideal of that revolutionary conservatism.[55] After the war, Strasser participated in the effort to launch an international organization—the European Popular Movement, proponent of Europe's neutrality—of which he was the honorary president. In the name of German reunification, Strasser cooperated with Stalinist Communists in the German Congress of Neutralists in 1958. In addition, he advocated the creation of a Eurafrican economic zone and, in the name of Arab-European unity, opposed the Suez and Algerian conflicts and supported the Palestinian cause.[56]

Nazism was elaborated via a confluence of various elements from the far-right field, combining radical Fascism, völkisch ideology, and conservative-revolutionary concepts to forge its representation of the world. The Italian and German models were widely imitated, often through the grafting of some of their elements onto homegrown nationalist movements. The diffusion of Nazism was facilitated in every country by the fear of Communist subversion, which resulted in the push for a counterrevolution, even if it had to be preventive. The Hungarian Republic of Councils was crushed by Romanian troops, who in 1920 brought to power Admiral Miklós Horthy de Nagybánya, former commander in chief of the Austro-Hungarian navy. The conservative authoritarian regime he installed did not prevent radical groups, often inspired by Nazism, from thriving (the regime itself became more hard-line between 1932 and 1936). Of these groups, the Arrow Cross Party, founded by Ferenc Szálazi, stands out. When Hitler could no longer count on Horthy, he turned to the Arrow Cross radicals, whom he had saved for that occasion. They were able to reconcile collaborationism and national imperialism through the theme of the European brotherhood of revolutionaries. In France, Marcel Bucard, leader of the Parti Franciste, declared virtually the same thing: "The Union of Fascist movements will bring peace to the world."[57] Beginning in 1941, Hungary, Bulgaria, Romania, Slovakia, and Croatia all joined the Tripartite Pact that united Berlin, Rome, and Tokyo. At the same time, the main French collaborationist groups together launched the Légion des Volontaires Français contre le Bolchevisme (LVF; Legion of French Volunteers against Bolshevism), which formed the 638th regiment of the 7th Division of the Wehrmacht (6,000 men).

The Iberian authoritarian regimes, at a remove from the question of the eastern front[58] and the desire for racial supremacy, worked to rid themselves of their radicals. The Francoist state constituted itself and consolidated itself by opposing the "leftist" Falangism of Onésimo Redondo and Ramiro Ledesma Ramos and also the appreciably more "rightist" form of Falangism embraced by its founder, José Antonio Primo de Rivera. Likewise, António Salazar's Estado Novo in Portugal rapidly brought to heel Francisco Rolão Preto's national syndicalism. In that regime, the party had less weight than the administrations. The corporatist system was inspired by the Italian Fascist model, but it added a strong dose of Catholic Socialism, the church being an essential element in Iberian authoritarian regimes. Salazarism and Francoism were certainly far-right dictatorships—like all far-right movements, they sought to regenerate society through a nonegalitarian organicism—but within that perspective they opposed the radical far right.

That type of authoritarian regime, distrustful of radicalism, arose in other countries as well: Dollfuss's Austria, Päts's Estonia, Ulmanis's Latvia, Smetona's Lithuania, Pétain's France, Horthy's Hungary, Piłsudski's Poland, and King Carol II's Romania. The authoritarian Latvian regime of Kālis Ulmanis, leader of the Peasant Union, held power from 1934 to 1940. The regime was a reaction to the rise of a strong local far right, embodied by Gustavs Celmiņš's Pērkonkrusts (Thunder Cross) and Colonel Voldemārs Ozols's Freedom Fighters Legion. Thunder Cross, composed of corporatists who sometimes made use of the swastika, affirmed their neopaganism through the resurgence of a reconstructed version of the ancient pagan Dievturība, the majority religion until the thirteenth century. In Estonia, Konstantin Päts headed the Farmers and Small Landowners Union and in 1934 established an authoritarian regime that defused the rising power of the Vaps, the local Fascist movement run by Andres Larka and Artur Sirk. But Romania would have a greater influence on the radical far right in Western Europe, when, in the 1960s–1970s, Italy and France became familiar with the Fascist movement in that country.

In 1927 Corneliu Zelea Codreanu (1899–1938) had founded Romania's Legion of the Archangel Michael, to which a mass organization, the Iron Guard, was added in 1930. In 1933 the Iron Guard took the name "Everything for the Fatherland." Leaders in the movement volunteered to fight in the nationalist ranks during the Spanish Civil War. The Iron Guard, wishing to reestablish Romania on the foundations of the peasantry, combined Christian mysticism and ethnonationalism. Its legionnaires considered themselves akin to Crusaders: Christianity served as an ideological axis, and it was the rural and nonindustrial world that constructed the ideological framework. That did not prevent the group from recruiting a number of students, which explains the presence of such intellectuals as Mircea Eliade and Emil Cioran. With the founding of the Iron Guard, the movement also took an anticapitalist turn, the final mark of that specifically Romanian Fascism. The unrest led King Carol II to stage a preventive coup d'état in 1938. Codreanu was arrested and killed, and an authoritarian Christian dictatorship, which banned all the political parties, was set in place. The Iron Guard, headed by Horia Sima, took its revenge in 1940, with the establishment of a nationalist state headed by General Ion Antonescu and dominated by the Iron Guard legionnaires. It set out to rule Romanian society by means of terror, which prompted Antonescu to ask Hitler to bring the Romanian Fascists to heel. In that case, the collaborators (who sought to work within the framework of bipartite relations between their national state and Germany) relied on the Reich to remove from power the collaborationists (who wanted to bring their country into the Third Reich's battle to build a New European Order), using the argument that the Reich would more easily wage its war if its "allied" countries were enjoying civil peace. Sima was exiled to Germany. Antonescu was therefore free to collaborate, but the Reich held over him the threat of the collaborationists, who could be called in to replace him as head of the regime. When the show of strength did not materialize, the radicals were able lead the country toward Fascism and collaborationism. The same thing occurred in France in 1943, with the advent of the Milice, the paramilitary organization formed by the Vichy government to fight the Resistance.

In countries in the Third Reich's orbit, Hitler was able to take advantage of the split within the far right: he installed "nationals" to head the regimes, incarnations of a traditional authority in the population's eyes, while keeping the radicals at hand as an alternative elite. The nationals were collaborators, generally from the traditional elites, and were motivated by anti-Communism. The collaborationists, conversely, generally emerged from the Fascist minorities. Hitler did not play the collaborationist card until he no longer had any others—in 1942, for example, when he returned Vidkun Quisling to power in Norway. Maurice Bardèche, the key theorist of European neo-Fascism, summed up the dream entertained by the collaborationists at the time: "Those who have not experienced this European spring do not know what we mean when we speak of Europe."[59] That ideological feature cannot fail to raise questions about the continued unity of the far-right field, as collaborationism became more radicalized. In 1943 the Third Reich granted French volunteers the right to join the Waffen-SS within the Frankreich Division (2,500 men). Of those in that division, the LVF and some members of the Milice were ultimately incorporated into the Charlemagne Division of the Waffen-SS, in November 1944 (fewer than 8,000 men). According to the historian James Gregor, there was a great deal of antagonism between former LVF members, marked by a metropolitan French and Catholic nationalism, and the Europeanist, Nazi, and neopagan French SS.[60] That hardly mattered for the New European Order that the Third Reich said it was now building, so great was its need for combatants. Of the 900,000 members listed as being in the Waffen-SS in 1944, more than half were non-Germans.[61]

The Charlemagne Division was not supposed to include ideological training in National Socialism as part of its instruction.[62] The legitimate ideological offering was thus provided by the SS media. The interpenetration that resulted from the Military Administration in Belgium and northern France allowed vocabulary and themes to circulate between the two countries. For example, Léon Degrelle, a Rexist leader who became a member of the Waffen-SS, came to Paris to praise the "European revolution" as being "Socialist," because it had no intellectuals or Jews. Pierre Quesnoy de Douai, associated with the Flemish nationalists and the Sicherheitsdienst (SD, the SS "security service")—and soon to be the founder of the Ligue des Droits du Nord (League of Northern Rights)—gave a class in Antwerp on the subject of the races (citing Günther and Rosenberg in particular). His students were recruits from the "Allgemein-SS du Nord de la France," to use the expression of the domestic intelligence services, which may have been referring to the former Algemeene-SS Vlaanderen.[63] A number of postwar *passeurs* wrote for *Devenir,* whose subtitle was already a red flag ("Combat Journal of the European Community"); this newspaper of the French-speaking SS is particularly worthy of note because of the authors it attracted. The themes it puts forward are very remote from French nationalism but also from the "Crusade against Bolshevism" in 1941. One article focuses on the linguistic and mythological unity of the Indo-Europeans. Another declares the death of the European nations, with the advent of "Nordic man, now being reborn," both "deeply rooted" and free of Christian "Orientalism." A third waxes enthusiastic about the god Thor and compares the SS to the Vikings. In the same newspaper, Jean-Marie Balestre flatters "the Aryan men of Normandy, Brittany, and Burgundy [who] join their racial brothers." Lucien Rebatet hails the Nazi Germans, the Romanians of the Iron Guard, the anti-Semites in the United States, the Argentine nationalists, and all who had "the European spirit, the Aryan spirit, the revolutionary spirit." And he concludes that those fighting on the eastern front are "the elite of the Aryan International, which tomorrow will remake the world, without Jews, without democrats, without trusts. SS comrades of 18 nations, I hail you, arm raised, with our salute, the Aryan salute. Death to the Jews!"[64]

With its paganism and its rejection of a narrow nationalism in favor of a European union of "carnal fatherlands," *Devenir* captures the image of an esotericist SS. Revisited, that image became the key to the success of the novels of Saint-Loup (pen name of Marc Augier, 1908–1990). Beyond that, it entered pop culture in the 1960s to 1970s in, for example, cheap paperbacks that portray alternate realities or a ufology that sees the SS as a keeper of mysteries. In emphasizing his past as a volunteer on the eastern front, the racialist writer Saint-Loup intentionally maintained the confusion between the propagandist imaginary and the reality of the New European Order. The trajectory he followed has its logic. In 1936 Augier was assigned to a mission beside Léo Lagrange, minister of youth in the Blum government. In 1941 he participated in the creation of "Collaboration, a group harnessing French energy for the sake of continental unity," which fought for the construction of a "Eurafrican economic bloc, in view of the establishment of a unified global economy."[65] Saint-Loup promoted a geopolitical reinterpretation of the conflict: "How can you not yet have understood that little national concepts were now outdated? How can you not yet have understood that it was no longer a matter of waging war for territories or dynasties but of European civil war? . . . What is truly at stake in the present conflict [is] the construction of Socialism in a unified Europe."[66] He concerned himself more particularly with Jeunes de l'Europe Nouvelle (JEN; Young People of the New Europe), then joined the Légion des Volontaires Français contre le Bolchevisme.

For the most part, JEN devoted itself to promoting the LVF and became part of Marcel Déat's Front Révolutionnaire National. Most of its militants then joined the Milice or the SS Frankreich Division.[67] They were in charge of distributing in France *La Jeune Europe,* a review intended to attract young intellectuals to collaborationism. It was launched in twelve languages in 1942, to represent the continental concord coming into existence through the European SS. This geopolitical publication developed an ideology and propaganda advocating the Europeanization of the eastern front. In it Déat said that the French presence in Africa was that of Europe as a whole. The German Matthias Schmitt insisted that Germany was unifying Europe and that Italy was unifying Africa, in order, ultimately, to create a community "from Hammerfest to Cape Town."[68] Bruno Francolini explained in the same newspaper that, after the war, the colonization of Africa would have to be grounded in an absolute prohibition on miscegenation and on intellectual labor by blacks, because "trying to impose on the natives an entirely European lifestyle and forcibly inculcating our culture could only do them harm." His Italian compatriot Julius Evola argued that "the Reich space" to come would be greater than small, narrow-minded nationalisms and would allow communities to embrace a transcendental idea, though one devoid of universalism.[69] This is far from the classic image of Fascism. We therefore run the risk of contributing to the historical reconstructions undertaken by radical circles, which portray a Fascism much more Europeanist than it actually was, disengaging it from its actual brutality and drawing it into the ether of its fringe elements. Let us be empirical, therefore: What do we see?

The Fascists of the interwar period legitimized themselves by producing a set of signs in which imported extranational elements mingled with the affirmation of a specific national tradition. That process of cobbling together models, propaganda, and ideas on the international market has been a permanent feature of the Fascist "phenomenon," whatever the time and space chosen to define it. But from the moment in 1942 that the Third Reich decided to reorient its propaganda along a Europeanist axis, Europe became both the myth and the utopia of the Fascists. After World War II, all the groups established international connections and shared that ideological Europeanist goal (the neo-Nazis even abandoned every form of racism internal to the white world). A Fascist spectrum can therefore be delineated, based on international chronology: an ideological gestation before 1919; the Fascism of 1919 to 1942, which, to be sure, unfolded in several phases; and then a neo-Fascism from 1942 on.

New Waves

Neo-Fascism, which came into existence in 1942, did not make a complete break from Fascism. In contrast to its precursor, however, it privileged society over the state, Europe over the existing nations. That aspect cannot be separated from the evolution of the social, political, and economic context, in short, from globalization and postmodernity. Nor can it be dissociated from the supernationalist fringe elements involved in the internal dialectic of Fascism during its first historical period (1919–1941)—including, among others, Ernst Niekisch and Otto Strasser. After World War II, however, Fascism confined itself to transmitting its "worldview"—a modern revolt "against the modern world," a "conservative revolution," whose ideal / type was a communitarian palingenesis. Fascism survived as an ideological substratum, but it lost all its overt signs, which in the end were only adjacent concepts, a form specific to the industrial era. It has maintained its decorum only within micro-sects that embrace folklore and which, precisely, belong no longer to the political order but to the cultural order.

French Fascism represents an extreme case of that form. It corresponds neither to the classic morphology of Fascism (a party that mobilizes the masses) nor to the totality of its signs (it entails no aggressive imperialism), but has a general form peculiar to itself. On the foundations of the "nationalism of nationalists" forged during the 1870–1914 phase, French Fascism came into being in the aftermath of World War I through a hybridization of (generally extranational) signs. It spread like a cultural rhizome, which corresponded to the rhizome structure of its organizations: located within the far-right field, it had few members and no real leader. That type of organization became more common in France during the postwar period, because of the repercussions of the purge, the grassroots struggle of the Organisation de l'Armée Secrète, followed by its defeat, and the revolution of globalization. Fascism, a reaction to the end of "the century of nations" in 1919, thus continued on its path, inquiring into the organization of organicist societies.

It is clear why all the far-right movements rejected the existing geopolitical order. Innovations on the far right are closely correlated to changes in that order. Consider the fact that the years 1870, 1918,

1941, 1962, 1973, and 2001 all marked a shift both in geopolitics and in the far right. The far right, then, is a hostile reaction to the transformation of state-society relations within the context of globalization, in both its first and second incarnations.

In present-day Europe, the radical far right as a whole is less a political family than a marginal counterculture or "subculture"—in the nonpejorative sense sociologists give that term, which is to say, a minority cultural expression. This is a significant phenomenon in France. As the voter base sympathetic to Le Pen's National Front has grown, the political space of radical groups has contracted accordingly. The FN, in fact, has become what Swiss political scientists designate by the lovely term *organisation faîtière,*[70] an umbrella organization that absorbs all existing groups, either through dual membership or through the migration of militants from the smaller groups to the larger one. French "radicals" distinguish themselves by their strategic choice of the nonelectoral path, often to the point of explicitly rejecting democracy. They also differentiate themselves from the parties seeking election by their noneuphemistic discussion of the ethnic question, their Europeanism (they oppose the "narrow," strictly French, nationalism of the FN), and their recruitment, primarily among the young. That movement, scattered among local groups and limited-circulation national reviews (with print runs of a few dozen to a few thousand) is as much a sociological phenomenon, a marginal counterculture—even an "urban tribe"—as it is a strictly political object. Nevertheless, the FN's normalization strategy, its effort to move from a fringe party into the political mainstream, has also served to strengthen the most consolidated groups.

Although not Fascist, some movements now active can be traced back to the radical far right of the twentieth century. The Flemish nationalism of Belgium's Vlaams Belang Party is heir to Joris Van Severen's Verdinaso Party of the 1930s. The Românaia Mare Party in Romania—expansionist, fiercely anti-Magyar, anti-Semitic, and anti-Roma—owes a great deal to the Iron Guard. The Iron Guard itself, however, was indebted to Professor A. C. Cuza and his Democratic National Party, which made anti-Semitism its credo from 1919 onward. Contemporary Hungarian nationalism is almost incomprehensible without reference to the reactionary regime of Regent Horthy and Ferenc Szálasi's Arrow Cross, just as Croatian nationalism must be understood in terms of its relation to Ante Pavelić's Ustaše state and the ideology of the Party of Rights, as it was formulated by its theorist Milan Šufflay during the interwar period.

Contemporary political groups often appeal to a "leftist" or "authentic" tradition of Fascism or National Socialism, in opposition to their reactionary degeneration. The Nationaldemokratische Partei Deutschlands (NPD; German National Democratic Party), for example, invokes the Strasser brothers and the revolutionary nationalists of the Conservative Revolution. In Italy, Luca Romagnoli, leader of the Movimento Sociale–Fiamma Tricolore (Social Movement–Tricolor Flame), and Alessandra Mussolini were elected to the European Parliament on a platform that referenced the Republic of Salò, the Waffen-SS's puppet state in Italy, in opposition to Gianfranco Fino's "betrayal" of Fascism. Spain has various "Falanges," each claiming to be more authentic and subversive than the others, and each also disparages the contemporary phenomenon of Francoist power. The detour by way of the left often begins with a confusion between propaganda and ideology. But it also attests to the will to restore a certain nonconformism, to overcome inertia, to recover the subversive and social spirit of the first Fascist manifesto of 1919.

The radical far right has been unable to recover from the shock of 1945. The far right of the "nationals" was in recovery for a long time. Both camps have continually sought to clear themselves of the other's crimes and betrayals. Nevertheless, ordinary language refuses to distinguish among those who bear the burden of such a past. It was after 1945 that the term "far right" became fully a part of everyday language, designating nationalist, authoritarian, and xenophobic political organizations: in France, Jeune Nation (1949–1958), then the Poujade movement (1953–1958), and, by extension, the partisans of French Algeria who, within the OAS, opted for violence.

But in spatial terms, the militancy of the phenomenon has puzzled commentators: How could anyone dare situate "far" to the "right" people who were sometimes battling "right-wing" governments by means of terrorism? In fact, it is important to situate the object of study—the far right—as a field of its own and not as an endpoint on the left-right axis. The same imperative applies when responding to critics of the concept. Some claim, in fact, that the term is not appropriate for groups as diverse as democrats and Nazis, or is valid only if the far right lies to the right of the right (though many nationalist economic programs would belie that claim). Others argue that the category neutralizes the very challenge being made to the left-right axis—by the "new right," for example, whose most prominent intellectual figure in France is Alain de Benoist. These are all mere quibbles, however.

On the far right, the economic system is never anything but a means placed in the service of a worldview and present needs. That is why Mussolini was able to move from the "laissez-faire laissez-aller" system advocated in 1921 to the totalitarian state. In the French far right of recent years, neoliberal conceptions have been incorporated into the social Darwinism of ethnic nationalism within the Club de l'Horloge (Clock Club, part of the new right) and also, later on, within the National Front, before that party came to defend an "intelligent protectionism" overseen by a "strategist state." Vichy was more economically interventionist than the Front Populaire, and it was Richard Nixon who said, "We are all Keynesians now." It is an oversimplification to evaluate political positions by the criterion of state intervention. Beyond the diversity of the far-right movements, there is a persistent desire on their part to build an "organic," holistic society, where inequalities are a function of a hierarchy considered to be legitimate.

Hence, even if one considers the left-right axis relevant, one must not think that the far right lies to the right of the conservative and liberal parties. The political is multidimensional, and every political field intersects somewhat those adjoining it—but less along a single line than in interconnected spheres, each of them autonomous. Even so, there is still a rationale for classifying the "far right" on the "right." For the record, let us cite the definition of the "right" given by a contemporary academic close to the traditionalist and royalist wing of legitimist Catholicism. According to Alain Néry, the term *droite* (right), from the Latin *directus,* indicates "the direction one must go" toward a goal, in view of "superior, disinterested values." Conversely, the term *gauche* (left), derived from "a Frankish verb meaning to yield, to bend," is linked to the French *sinistre*, from the Latin *sinister,* which translates as both "left" and "disastrous."[71] On one side lies the natural order, on the other, the disorder of revolution, to which any kind of constructivism supposedly leads. Most components of the far right come close to concurring with that characterization. The radicalized right movements that converged at La Manif pour Tous (The Protest for Everyone) in 2013 would more or less agree.[72] Even the left, in presenting itself as "progress" and "movement," in opposition to "conservatism" and "the neoreactionaries," affirms that dichotomy more or less, while at the same time inverting the moral judgment. The same idea can be read between the lines in the "new right," which made its appearance in the French media in the mid-1970s, though the association responsible for disseminating its views, GRECE (Groupement de Recherche et d'Études pour la Civilisation Européenne; Research and Study Group for European Civilization), had been founded in 1968. GRECE preferred to situate itself beyond the right-left cleavage, which it declared obsolete and reductive. In the new edition of his *Vu de droite* (Seen from the right), Alain de Benoist summed up its positions: "What I here call the 'right,' purely by convention, is the attitude that considers the diversity of the world and, as a consequence, the related inequalities necessarily produced by it, to be a good, and the gradual homogenization of the world, advocated and realized by the two-thousand-year-old discourse of egalitarian ideology, to be an evil."[73] The "new right" is in fact plural, varying from country to country, part of the specific landscape of homegrown right-wing movements.

It is somewhat "deutschnational" in the German weekly *Junge Frei-heit* and its Viennese equivalent, *Zur Zeit.* In Italy, according to the political scientist Marco Tarchi, it is very critical of the Berlusconian right and the Americanism of the Alleanza Nationale. In the far right of the Spanish review *Hesperides,* Catholicism plays a greater role and seeks to attach itself to the Partido Popular. And finally, for Synergies Européennes in Belgium, under the leadership of Robert Steuckers, it disseminates the "neo-Eurasianist" views of the Russian Aleksandr Dugin and expresses strong opposition to Islam.

The European far right, in fact, has experienced four different waves of extremist parties since 1945. The first, between 1945 and 1955, was characterized by its proximity to the totalitarian ideologies of the 1930s; it is often called "neo-Fascist." The second wave, which arose in the mid-1950s, corresponded to a movement of the radicalized middle classes. The "third wave," which a number of authors have called "national populist," arrived between the 1980s and 2001. And since September 11, 2001, the fourth wave has unfurled, a populist expression of the "clash of civilizations." Several attempts have been made to isolate transnational subgroups within that far-right family. Piero Ignzai, for example, distinguishes between "old" parties, clearly descended from Fascism, and "postindustrial" parties.[74] Hans-Georg Betz prefers to contrast the radical populism of the neoliberal or even libertarian type to authoritarian national populism.[75]

The Present Time

With respect to all the existing models of classification, founded on what the political scientist Cas Mudde calls, ironically but accurately, veritable "shopping lists" of criteria, the National Front appears to be a limit case. According to Mudde, organizations belonging to the far right combine the following traits: nationalism (state or ethnic); exclusivism (for example, racism, anti-Semitism, ethnocentrism, or ethnopluralism); xenophobia; antidemocratic traits (cult of personality, elitism, monism, an organicist view of the state); populism; an antiparty spirit; the defense of "law and order"; environmentalism; a value system that regrets the loss of traditional frames of reference (family, community, religion); and a socioeconomic plan that combines corporatism, state control of certain sectors, and a strong belief in the free play of market forces. The list of parties corresponding to that description includes all the groups in western Europe that, having had major electoral success from the 1980s to the 2000s, were spontaneously classified by observers as being on the far right (e.g., the National Front, FPÖ, Vlaams Blok, Ligue du Nord, Alleanza Nationale, the Danish People's Party, and the Progress Party in Norway). Mudde then proposes to subdivide the far-right family into moderate and radical parties. According to him, radical parties profess a xenophobic nationalism that denies certain government benefits to all those who, by virtue of their nationality or place of origin, do not belong to the dominant ethnic group, which, ideally, is the only one to possess the right of abode on national soil.[76]

The powerful National Front in France raises a methodological problem. In the 1990s, the FN clearly put forward an ethnic conception of the nation, under the influence of its neorightist framework, but it also had success in the 2010s with a normalization strategy. By that very fact, the FN raises anew the question of the validity of the thesis of the "revolutionary right"—to which, without great difficulty, some observers sought to link it, thereby connecting it to Fascism. Clearly, Jean-Marie Le Pen's National Front combined antiparliamentarianism and the populist vein, favored an upheaval and regeneration of society and of social hierarchies, and came close to a "palingenetic form of populist ultranationalism," which for Roger Griffin is the definition of Fascism,[77] the same Fascism that Roger Eatwell describes as "an ideology that strives to forge social rebirth based on a holistic-national radical Third Way."[78] Nevertheless, arguments based on ideological models cause unnecessary confusion. The FN is a national populist party. It is also a party of the "postindustrial" type, which acts within the framework of representative democracy, seeking to come to power through elections. It has no direct relationship to the Fascist-leaning parties of the prewar period or to the collaborationist organizations of 1939–1945.[79] Granted, it exhibits certain characteristics of Fascism, as the Italian historian Emilio Gentile describes it with reference to Mussolini's regime (Gentile, precisely, advocates considering Fascism a series of actions rather than a set of ideas).[80]

If we confine ourselves to Gentile's definition, however, the FN has only a few Fascist characteristics: it is not a "mass movement," its organization is not that of a "militia-party," it does not use "terror" as a means to take power, and it explicitly rejects the idea of constructing the "new man" because it is anticonstructivist, both in the ultraliberal manner of Friedrich Hayek and in the traditional way of counterrevolutionaries. Also, it does not advocate "the absolute subordination of the citizen to the state." At first, in the era of Jean-Marie Le Pen, the FN placed at the center of its program the reduction of the state's role to its regalian powers and the development of entrepreneurship and the free play of market forces. Later, in the era of Marine Le Pen, it has augmented the role to be granted to the executive branch and its intervention in the economy, but with no significant control of production units. Nevertheless, the FN does display certain aesthetic traits of Fascism: it believes it has "a mission of social regeneration"; it "considers itself in a state of war against political adversaries," even while sometimes seeking tactical compromises with them; its leader and cadres often have "a culture founded on mythic thought and on a tragic and activist sense of life." Other particularities of Fascism as defined by Gentile can also be found in the FN's ideology: "an ideology that is anti-ideological and pragmatic in character"; antimaterialism and anti-individualism (in the sense of a permanent call to mobilize "national energies"); anti-Marxism; opposition to political liberalism, which is seen as an equivalent of Socialism; populism and certain anticapitalist claims. Once that comparison has been made, however, what then? The FN is not a Fascist-leaning movement; rather, the traits it shares with Fascism are common to the far right. What a comparison between the FN and Fascism can reasonably validate is that Fascism, whatever the temptations of ideological oscillation on its fringes, is a phenomenon that participates in the far-right field—not that the FN belongs to the radical far right.

One of the most original traits of the National Front is that, over a long period of time (1972–1999), it succeeded in federating—albeit with tensions and schisms—the different components of the French far right, which sometimes have diametrically opposed frames of reference. All the while, it was able to safeguard its own existence. It thus assembles authoritarian republicans and monarchists, traditionalist Catholics and neopagans, former collaborators and former resistance fighters, militants belonging to all the nationalist groups from the time of Charles de Gaulle's "wandering in the desert" (1946–1958), and radicalized defectors from the neo-Gaullist and liberal parties, gathered together in the spirit of "nationalist compromise." That tactic, already practiced by Maurras, attests to the FN's antisystem dimension. In fact, that constant (unity beyond divisions) demonstrates that all the subfamilies of the French far right have a sense that they belong to the same camp, that of the losing side in all the major breaks that have marked the history of France: the Revolution of 1789, the Dreyfus Affair, the Liberation, the loss of the colonial empire. What unites these various components is greater than what separates them from their adversary, designated by the expression "the parties of the System," or quite simply reduced to "them" versus "us."

At present, the question of Islamism's partisan identity regularly arises within that political landscape. A portion of the Islamist movement, whether seeking to acquire political visibility by participating in the electoral process (the Parti des Musulmans de France) or, out of pietism or quietism, restricting its expression to the religious sphere—all the while totally rejecting the institutions of the "infidel" countries—defends a worldview that is in many ways close to that of the far right. For example, it has a dualist vision of society, based on the distinction between friend and enemy. Above all, it places the emphasis on the individual's place within the community, at the expense of the concepts of citizenship, individual rights, and universalism, all of which it rejects. It is theocratic and, as such, defends a model of society and of the state directly derived from religious texts, which certain of its decision makers believe can be read as a formal condemnation of democracy. It wishes to exclude and punish those who oppose religious morality, and it proposes an authoritarian and hierarchized model of social organization. Some radical Islamists incorporate into their discourse two structural components of far-right thought, especially that of integral Catholicism: millenarianism (which gives an eschatological dimension to Jihadist-Salafism) and conspiracy theories. For some Salafists in particular, such theories, constructed in the first place on the model of the "Jewish conspiracy" (renamed the "Zionist conspiracy" to avoid the stigma surrounding anti-Semitism), include a denunciation of Freemasonry, globalization, Communism, and the United States, whose collusion would explain the West's domination of the Muslim world. These ideas are accompanied by occasional convergences—either interindividual or organizational—between Islamism and the far right, which find expression in anti-Zionism / anti-Semitism in particular. That does not mean, of course, that radical Islamism can be called a "Green [i.e., Islamic] Fascism": the analogous features generally have less to do with Fascism than with the conservative revolution. But it shows that Islamism, in becoming integrated into European reality and implanted there, tends to assimilate some of the patterns of thought of the radicalism already present, in this case a far right that is now overwhelmingly Islamophobic.

It is fair to say that a hard line toward Islam is at the heart of the fourth wave of far-right parties, but that does not mean that every wave cancels out the previous one. The European elections of 2014 revealed three standard models that are being presented to the masses in their respective countries. In the Netherlands, Geert Wilders and his Party for Freedom (PVV) are indicators of the neopopulist dynamic. The PVV, Islamophobic first and foremost, denounces the elites and lauds the virtues of the people, aspiring to be the champion of freedoms for minorities (gays, Jews, women) against the Arab-Muslim masses. Geert Wilders, in the face of an erosion of success at the polls, wagered on a harder line against immigration and also in relation to the European Union. That ideological rapprochement with the FN was solidified by a partisan alliance, even though, until that time, Geert Wilders had accused the FN of being an extremist and anti-Semitic party, to emphasize that he himself was neither. His campaign did not bear the desired fruit, and the PVV, which was expecting a victory, received a disappointing 13.3 percent of the vote. At the other end of the far-right field, the results of the Greek movement Golden Dawn (Chrissi Avgi), resolutely part of the radical far right, were as expected. Golden Dawn borrows from Fascism the form of a militia-party, navigating between urban violence and electoral activity. Like Fascism, it has sought to construct a counterstate, positioning itself as a popular agent of law enforcement involved in social action and, at the same time, possessing a mandate for the legitimate use of physical violence. It took from Nazism the connection between Greek antiquity and Aryanism (it claims that Nazism may have drawn more inspiration from Hellenism than vice versa).[81] It borrows from neo-Nazism the transcendence of divisions internal to the white race, to the advantage of an esotericist and paganistic white affirmationism. At a time when, on average, wages have dropped by a third, and a quarter of all Greeks have slipped below the poverty line, racism serves as an instrument for the reallocation of social resources. Golden Dawn further increased its standing, winning 9.3 percent of the vote.

In these elections, the greatest success was registered in France, based on a third model: that of Marine Le Pen's National Front. Her party came in first, with 24.3 percent of the vote. Her electorate is more interclassist than the examples just considered. The line promoted by Jean-Marie Le Pen, perfect national populist that he is, called for a savior to rise up from the common people to put an end to the nation's destruction, which was caused by the endogenous elites and the exogenous masses. At first, Marine Le Pen incorporated the neopopulist shift into that program. Since 2012, however, the party has evolved toward the line it promoted in the European election and which can be called "full sovereignism." Until then, the FN had always been a "party of demand": sociological factors, rather than what the party had to offer, governed who voted for the FN. The party now seems capable of proposing complete protection. Its discourse is that of a political, economic, and cultural sovereignism that promises voters of every social class that they will be shielded from economic, demographic, and cultural globalization and will enjoy both the benefits of entrepreneurial capitalism (the theme of "intelligent protectionism") and the protections of the welfare state (the theme of "national preference").

When we examine these three cases, it becomes obvious that there is no ideological uniformity. Election results remain a function of national problematics and cultures. The common element is not a Europhobia without substance, but a critique of the institutions of the European Union. Their lack of democratic legitimacy is said to be a trap, intentionally set up as a way of installing liberalism, both economic and cultural. These institutions supposedly produce the fissures in postindustrial society (social atomization, mass unemployment), which on the far right are portrayed as the fissures in multicultural society. These elections also give us a glimpse of the simultaneous reactions of territories that are divided between different nations. Such is the case for Catalonia, which was split up by the Treaty of the Pyrenees (1659). A deep-seated independence movement exists in Spanish Catalonia, whereas the Catalanism of the zone that remained in France is superficial, stemming in great part from a revival dating to the last few decades. The major nationalist movement south of the Pyrenees is not propelled by the far right. It is not fueled by resentment of globalization, but rather by the desire to participate optimally in it. Even though many völkisch-leaning groups have been created in Catalonia since the 1960s, the Movimiento Social

Republicano (MSR), nationalist-revolutionary in its orientation (it received only 0.05 percent of the vote in the European election), considers separatism a bourgeois demand and advocates the formation of a federation of Spains within a European federation that would include Russia.

Since the brief quasi-success of Fuerza Nueva,[82] the Spanish far right has been marked by a compulsive factionalism and an incapacity for reform except by imitation of European experiments, primarily French and Italian. Yet the election results in Spain are entirely different from those in France. The five far-right slates in Spain divided up 0.38 percent of the vote. In Barcelona, their success was negligible: 0.05 percent for the Falange Española Auténtica de la Juntas de Ofensiva Nacional Sindicalista, 0.03 percent for the MSR and for the Islamophobic Democracia Nacional, and so on. Although the plurality of candidacies might make it possible to at least detect what line has the most weight, all forms of the far right are at an impasse there. Across the border in Perpignan, the political offerings of the far right were also multiple, given the interest in proportional representation. Whereas the small far-right organizations had results equivalent to those in Barcelona, in France, the National Front slate came in first, with 35.89 percent of the vote.

These results underscore the fact that "the crisis of 2008" is not the cause of a "rise of extremes in Europe." The severity of the crisis in Spain is beyond doubt, and in Catalonia, the number of unemployed receiving no benefits has tripled since 2010. Roussillon, moreover, is one of the most fragile French territories: 32 percent of the population of Perpignan lives under the poverty line. In view of the disparity in the far-right election results in adjoining territories that face similar financial difficulties, the economic explanation is not sufficient. The far-right vote depends on an intersection between a coherent political offering and a social demand for authoritarianism, reinforced by a sense that a community of common destiny is falling apart. In the face of the acceleration of the welfare state's decline as a result of Euro-liberalism, a new portion of the European electorate is ready to listen.

This is not, however, a return to the 1930s or a reaction to an economic situation supposedly set in motion in 2008. For the last forty years and on both sides of the Atlantic, a process has been under way that can be called, in the French context, *droitisation,* a swing to the right. In conjunction with an ethnicization of social questions and representations, the welfare state and egalitarian humanism are being dismantled, to the advantage of the penal state. That process entails a social demand for authoritarianism, a reaction to the transformation and atomization of modes of life and representations, within a globalized, financialized economic universe where the West no longer occupies the center. That is why socioeconomic indicators alone are not sufficient. France is certainly having difficulties, but it is more than that: its culture was for five centuries built on unitary values. For France, therefore, the crisis is both political and cultural, and full sovereignism comes as a response to the fissures. The swing to the right is an ongoing process, and it offers the far right in every country the possibility of adapting its political offerings to fit its own national society.

1

What to Do after Fascism?

After World War II, far-right movements faced the necessity of rein-venting their radicalism. This was especially true of those that laid claim to the Fascist and Nazi political experiments. They immedi-ately undertook a "revision" of recent history, or rather, a denial of the extermination of the European Jews. The Swiss Gaston-Armand Amaudruz took on the task in 1946, the Frenchman Maurice Bardèche in 1948.[1] The very term "revision" made its appearance in that con-text, as the name of the newspaper launched in Denmark by the Landsforeningen af 6. maj 1945 (May 6, 1945, Foundation) and pub-lished until 1972. The organization, founded in August 1945, based its name on the date that the Danish Nazi party, the Danmarks Nationalsocialistiske Arbejderparti, was banned: May 5, 1945.[2] Clearly, both the facts of history and past doctrine had to be revised to ensure a future for neo-Fascism.

Henceforth, laws often banned the expression of Nazi or Fascist views, particularly in Germany, Austria, and Italy. As a matter of fact, most of the movements now called "neo-Nazi" by the militants who oppose them or by the press emerged from homegrown authoritarian nationalism, though they certainly accommodated Italian Fascism and/or German National Socialism in the 1930s and 1940s. The Narodowe Odrodzenie Polski (National Rebirth of Poland), for example, ought to be linked first and foremost to the Obóz Narodowo Radykalny (National Radical Camp), founded in 1934. In Hungary, Jobbick embraces the legacy of the Arrow Cross Party. Other groups with roots in autochthonous Fascism can be found in Croatia, Lithuania, and Romania.

The label "neo-Nazi" should be attached only to those movements that defend racialism,[3] biological and eugenicist racism, the superiority of the white race (a heterodox idea if ever there was one, given that Nazism considered the Slavs among the inferior races), and racial anti-Semitism, all basic tenets of the *Social Racist Manifesto,* which was drafted by the New European Order (NEO) in 1971 and is one of that group's key texts. These groups embrace conspiracy theories as their worldview and deny the material reality of the genocide of the Jews. They worship National Socialism and the person of Adolf Hitler and in this respect often resemble sectarian movements.

Reevaluating Nazism

In countries whose laws allow neo-Nazis to take part in elections, neo-Nazi groups have sometimes chosen to express themselves without pretense, wishing to demonstrate publicly their existence and their way of thinking. In such cases, their success has been quite limited. The Nederlandse Volks-Unie has played a role in legislative elections in the Netherlands since 1977, but the party has never received more than 0.4 percent of the vote. In 2005, during the regional elections on the island of Zealand in Denmark, the Danmarks Nationalsocialistiske Bevaegelse (DNSB) received only 0.1 percent. In the 2010 municipal elections, the Swedish party Svenskarnas, the successor to Folkfronten, won 2.8 percent of the vote in Grästorp. And in a city in West Yorkshire, England, in May 2010, the British People's Party received 4.95 percent—only 283 votes.

The Greek Golden Dawn Party is a special case. It received the largest proportion of neo-Nazi votes in Europe in recent decades. Its sudden change of fortune is clearly correlated to the national and social humiliation of Greece in the wake of the financial crisis. Golden Dawn received 0.75 percent of the vote in 1999 and 0.46 percent in 2009. That jumped to 9.32 percent in 2014, stabilizing at 7 percent in the legislative elections of September 2015. The party knew enough to make concessions, evolving from a half-Hellenistic, half-Nordic paganism to a defense of Greek Orthodox identity. It benefited from the normalization of the Laikós Orthódoxos Synagermós (LAOS; Popular Orthodox Rally), which lost its populist appeal when it participated in a government coalition in 2011, even though it defended a dissident position (pro–national security, antiglobalist, xenophobic, and Islamophobic). Having won 7.13 percent of the vote in the elections to the European Parliament in 2009, the LAOS attracted only 2.69 percent in 2014. Golden Dawn, for its part, not only promotes an imperialist ethnonationalism, it also clearly constitutes a militia-party: between January 2012 and April 2013, it was involved in 281 racist attacks, killing 4 and injuring 400.[4]

Germanic neo-Nazi organizations enjoy a special status, since they supposedly benefit from a direct connection to the Nationalsozialistische Deutsche Arbeiterpartei (NSDAP, the National Socialist German Workers' Party), though they cannot adopt either its program or its norms without becoming illegal. The movement mobilized internationally when Michaël Kühnen and Friedhelm Busse (of the Freiheitliche Deutsche Arbeiterpartei), as well as Christian Worch (of the Aktionsfront Nationaler Sozialisten), all three Germans, and some leaders of the Austrian Volkstreue Außerparlamentarische Opposition were prosecuted in their own countries. Nevertheless, German organizations cannot play a leading international role because they are so closely watched by the Bundesamt für Verfassungsschutz (Federal Office for the Protection of the Constitution). The five to six thousand neo-Nazis in Germany, who constitute the second-largest such group in Europe (after Russia), therefore have no strategic potential. Since the post–World War II period, the political experiments they have attempted have demonstrated the difficulty they have maneuvering.

Most of the former mid-level cadres from the NSDAP who continued to have a political life after 1945 worked within democratic parties that were not on the far right, or they served in the state apparatus. Nevertheless, from 1946 to 1953 the Deutsche Konservative Partei-Deutsche Rechtspartei (German Conservative Party-German Right Party), the Sozialistische Reichspartei (Socialist Reich Party), and the Deutsche Reichspartei (German Reich Party) did have an impact on German political life. In the Bundestag they represented the portion of the population that had lost its standing as a result of the economic collapse following the defeat, as well as a number of ethnic Germans displaced from Eastern Europe and some of Hitler's former militants affected by denazification. In Austria, likewise, the Verband der Unabhängigen (VdU; Federation of Independents, founded in 1949) and, as of 1956, the Freiheitliche Partei Österreichs (FPÖ), brought about the political reintegration of the former National Socialists and incorporated into their program the idea of a Greater German community of common destiny, as well as a certain historical revisionism. These parties participated in the democratic process, like the present-day Nationaldemokratische Partei Deutschlands (NPD), which exhibits certain traits beholden to Nazism, but has toned them down to remain within the legal framework.

The NPD, founded in 1964, comprised all the neo-Fascist movements until 1970, and two-thirds of its political bureau came directly from the NSDAP. It entered electoral politics in 1965 with the slogan "Germany for the Germans, Europe for the Europeans," introducing a large dialectical gap between its rehabilitation of the Nazi historical experiment and its conservative and populist platform, intended to respond to voter discontent of all kinds.[5] It was weakened by its change of focus and its respect for democratic institutions, and by 1976 it faced competition from many new organizations. After 1997, it called for Germany to return to its 1938 borders, but the appeal did not resonate with the masses. Conversely, it reaped the benefits of its grassroots efforts in the eastern Länder, where it reached out to the networks of small groups that developed after the fall of the Berlin Wall. Striving to gain a foothold in Saxony beginning in 1989, it was able to win 9.2 percent of the vote there in 2004, earning twelve seats in Parliament.[6] But sociological factors do not seem to favor the NPD's success at the national level: in 2014, having received 1 percent of the vote, it earned a seat in the European Parliament only because German law requires it.

Given the political forces currently at work, neo-Nazism cannot possibly make inroads in electoral politics in Europe, where the violence of neo-Nazi groups represents a threat to public order more than a political risk. That is particularly the case in Russia, where, despite the increase in state repression since 2011, such groups are proliferating: for example, the Russkoe Natsionalnoe Yedinstvo (Russian National Unity) and the Slavianski Soyuz (Slavic Union), whose initials refer explicitly to the Nazi SS. These organizations combine National Socialism, Orthodox fundamentalism, and hatred of the West, a mix hardly consistent with canonical Hitlerism but with a mobilizing capacity that has resulted in a large number of homicides of non-Russians, especially those from the republics of the Caucasus and Asia. The violence itself should not be considered incidental. It corresponds to a reality both cultural (the expansion of the representation of Orthodoxy as an ethnic Russian religion)[7] and sociological (58 percent of Russians surveyed in 2002 believed that the skinheads were doing the state's "dirty work").[8]

Although all the neo-Nazi groups are negationists (Holocaust deniers), negationism is not confined to neo-Nazism. The negationists are a cult, both because they are completely out of touch with reality and because, to function as a group, they depend on a quasi-theological affirmation of their credo and the absolute delegitimation of their adversary. They are an informal network of individual believers more than an organized movement. The negationist phenomenon developed first in France, with Paul Rassinier and Maurice Bardèche, then spread throughout the world, beginning in the 1950s. As of 1978, it picked up speed, fueled by support from ultraleft militants, who

broke the political quarantine on the subject, and by Robert Faurisson's agitpro.[9] The best-known authors of European negationism
come from various countries in addition to France: Germany, where
the minimization or denial of the Holocaust has been punishable
by law since 1985 (Wilhelm Stäglich, Thies Christophersen, Udo
Walendy, Horst Mahler); Austria (Gerd Honsik and Walter Ochens-
berger, both of whom emigrated to Spain in 1992, fleeing prosecution); Belgium (the Verbeke brothers and their organization, Vrij
Historisch Onderzoek, or VHO); Great Britain (David Irving); Italy
(Carlo Mattogno); Sweden (Ditlieb Felberer and the Moroccan-born
former Islamist officer and Hitler lover Ahmed Rami); and Switzerland (Gaston-Armand Amaudruz, René-Louis Berclaz, and Jürgen
Graf, who, fleeing prosecution, sought refuge in Iran in 2000).
Germany and Austria, though possessing a great deal of influence
in the negationist network, do not have preeminence. Noteworthy
in those countries is the continuity of the ideological engagement of
some National Socialists who became negationists, for example, Major
General Otto-Ernst Remer, one of the architects of the repression of
the failed putsch of July 20, 1944, as well as the publisher Herbert
Grabert and the former SS-Sonderführer Christophersen.

The most famous European Holocaust denier at present is no doubt
David Irving, a best-selling author of books with historical preten-
tions. At first, Irving attempted to relativize Nazi crimes by over-
stating the number of people killed in the Allied air attacks on Germany (*The Destruction of Dresden,* 1962). Then he placed in doubt the
deliberate nature of the genocide and Hitler's personal involvement
(*Hitler's War,* 1977), before arriving at negationism pure and simple
in about 1988. Irving acquired global notoriety through the lawsuit
he filed in 1998, and lost in 2000, against the American historian
Deborah Lipstadt, who had accused him of being a falsifier. Irving's
reputation as a historian was destroyed by the legal proceedings, and
he was bankrupted by the verdict, which required that he pay court
costs. At that time, he moved closer to the fringe neo-Nazi movements. He was barred from several countries, including Austria. When

he entered that country nonetheless, he was arrested, and he served a prison sentence there in 2005–2006.[10] The vast majority of European negationists now operate through the Internet, which allows them to make their writings available to a large audience while circumventing antiracist laws, given the legal gray area surrounding the question of criminal accountability for authors of online articles. Rulings issued in France in 2005 established the responsibility of Web hosts and ordered them to install filters to make negationist sites inaccessible in practice. Some of the most commonly consulted sites are now unavailable, as the large search engines no longer reference them. But the legal situation prevailing in the United States, by virtue of the freedom of expression guaranteed by the First Amendment, still gives Holocaust deniers a great deal of latitude. They often make use of American Web hosts or those located in Eastern Europe (Russia in particular); as a result, the filters can be easily circumvented.[11] In any case, neo-Fascism has played a substantial role in restructuring European far-right movements. The Italian model has had sweeping effects.

The Italian Laboratory

Founded in 1946, the Movimento Sociale Italiano (MSI) claims to perpetuate the spirit of the Republic of Salò, which the neo-Fascists imagine to have been a purified and revolutionary Fascism. For initiates, the group's initials signify "Mussolini Sei Immortale" (Mussolini, you are immortal). For a long time, that party served as the flagship of European far-right movements. It is true that the geostrategic position of Italy allows the neo-Fascists to shift back and forth between subversion (in the hope of bringing down the republic) and countersubversion (support for the repressive state apparatus). For example, the Gruppi d'Azione Rivoluzionaria was a subversive organization of Fascist partisans active in 1945–1947. But, under the aegis of a former member of the Sicherheitsdienst (SD), they took part in the "Los Angeles" network set in place by the CIA to spy on Italian

Communists.[12] A number of their members then joined Stefano Delle Chiaie's Avanguardia Nazionale (founded in 1959, dissolved in 1966, and reactivated in 1970), which was very involved in the "strategy of tension" conducted on the peninsula between the attack on the Piazza Fontana in Milan (1969; 16 dead and 88 wounded) and the assault on the Bologna train station (1980; 85 dead, 177 wounded).

The MSI was at the center of activist ferment, producing innovative ideas and practices for the radical far right, including the revival of populism. The terrorist path was taken by those who believed the MSI was too bourgeois. In 1956 Pino Rauti founded the Centro Studi Ordine Nuovo, commonly known as the Ordine Nuovo (New Order). The Italian radicals reconfigured Fascism based on their readings of the philosopher Julius Evola and his aristocratic and esotericist conceptions of Fascism. That often brought them closer to the Third Reich than to Fascist Italy, particularly in the virulence of their anti-Semitism (Ordine Nuovo is also anti-Zionist, negationist, racialist, and Europeanist),[13] and also influenced their political strategy. In 1953 Evola published *Gli uomini e le rovine* (Men among the ruins), with a preface by the Fascist navy commander Julio Valerio Borghese, nicknamed "The Black Prince."[14] In it Evola advocates unifying the "true" right, spurred on by "combat groups" that, in cooperation with the police and army, would be duty-bound to defend the state against subversion. From the first, the book had a considerable influence on Ordine Nuovo, so much so that one of the cadres of the Italian radical far right, Clemente Graziani, rightly considered it "the gospel of [Italian] nationalist revolutionary youth." According to Graziani (1925–1996), a neo-Fascist leader who had in the past supplied arms to the OAS, the book led Ordine Nuovo to seize on the strategy of alliances with the forces of oppression, within the perspective of "the inevitable final confrontation" with Marxists and democracy.[15]

The group, linked both to the Organisation de l'Armée Secrète (OAS) and to the neo-Nazi New European Order, sought above all to establish ties with Italian military circles, in order to stage a coup d'état—consistent with a strategy that appears to have been developed at meetings under the Greek dictatorship in 1965 and 1968. Ordine Nuovo knew that democracy had to be destabilized through both physical violence and ideas. The name it chose for itself was a reference to the Marxist theorist Antonio Gramsci, proponent of a cultural and activist destabilization of the bourgeois state. In 1963 Pino Rauti set four priorities: redefine the social agenda; reshape the fight against Communism through new types of propaganda, calibrated to different socioeconomic milieus; develop a more complete doctrine; and train and educate militants.[16] But in 1969, after the former Fascist dignitary Giorgio Almirante was named head of the MSI, Rauti and his friends decided to bring the organization back into the mainstream. The militants who rejected that return to partisan politics founded the Movimento Politico Ordine Nuovo. The symbol chosen did not equivocate: a Nazi flag, its swastika replaced by the "labrys," a black double-bitted ax that was the symbol of the "Fourth of August Regime" in Greece (1936–1941). The time had come for violence: of the 4,290 acts of political violence that struck Italy between 1969 and 1980, 67.55 percent could be attributed to the neo-Fascists of Ordine Nuovo and its satellites.[17] It was then that Borghese founded a putschist organization, the Fronte Nazionale; only about two hundred members from Ordine Nuovo remained in it. The military officer had long been under surveillance because of his putschist inclinations and the contacts he had made in that aim with industrialists or political staff members from the MSI and the Italian Socialist Party. In 1971 he and his men (from Avanguardia Nazionale especially) occupied the Ministry of the Interior, but the operation was unsuccessful because Borghese had no sense of the realities on the ground.[18]

After Borghese fled to Spain, other military personnel, technocrats, members of the intelligence services, and neo-Fascist activists were also tempted by the putsch strategy. The Italian state took its distance from Ordine Nuovo and in 1973 dissolved it (it had 2,500 members at the time), for having reconstituted the National Fascist Party. The ban led to the creation of new terrorist groups, particularly Ordine Nero (Black Order). That organization adopted the logo of Ordine Nuovo and published a bulletin, *Anno Zero,* under the directorship of Clemente Graziani. A specialist in antisubversive warfare, he received training in that field from the OAS veterans who founded Aginter Press, a Portuguese pseudo press agency in charge of anti-Communist destabilization operations in Western Europe, and which also played a role in the strategy of tension. Graziani fled to Spain to escape the Italian justice system, which was pursuing him for his involvement in terrorism. That did not prevent him from working actively with the Frenchman François Duprat to launch his own periodical, *Année Zéro,* which bore the black double-bitted ax on its cover.[19] That sequence of events played such a large role in the European neo-Fascist imaginary that, twenty years later, the Spanish group Vanguardia (to cite only one example) was still using the bipennis.

In that specific context, the MSI quickly understood the imperative not to position itself within a quaint neo-Fascism. Almirante declared to the group's young members in 1970: "We must be very careful . . . not to portray Fascism in a grotesque way, and especially not in an old-fashioned, anachronistic, and stupidly nostalgic way."[20] During Italy's long, drawn-out version of "May 1968" (the name for the widespread student protests, civil unrest, and general strikes in France during that month and, more generally, for the revolutionary leftist ferment of the late 1960s), the MSI was able to rally hard-line anti-Communist forces, which gave it standing in electoral politics; it became the "Destra nazionale" MSI in the 1972 elections. It thus served as an example for the French neo-Fascist movement Ordre Nouveau (ON; established in 1969), which in 1972 founded the National Front based on the Italian model. But the MSI was unable to join the government until after its congress of 1995, when Gianfranco Fini proclaimed it was shedding its Fascist past. The reform was symbolized by the adoption of the name "Alleanza Nazionale." The AN was part of the right-wing bloc within the government, but it lost its voter base by virtue of its very normalization. The change in orientation also had an effect on partisan European relations. For decades, the MSI played a leading role in setting up neo-Fascist international organizations. In 2002, Fini co-founded the Union for Europe of the Nations in the European Parliament, with Pia Kjaersgaard's Danish Fremskridtspartiet, Charles Pasqua's Rassemblement pour la France, Israel's Likud Party (admitted as an observer with full right of participation), and the Irish Fianna Fail (Republican Party).

Italy was the main driving force in attempts to transcend nationalism in favor of internationalism, and it produced a large number of strategical innovations, whether in partisan politics or the cultural battle. It was therefore an important nation in international neo-Fascism, which Roger Griffin judiciously sums up as an internationalized cultural battle in the form of a leaderless polycratic network.[21] Overall, the neo-Fascists were often in the forefront when it came to imagining and questioning the forms a united Europe would take. Some of these projects were disorganized, mere odds and ends. For example, the activist and Evolian Europa Civiltà movement in Italy formed a Central Council for European Solidarism with the Front de Libération de l'Europe de l'Est (Eastern European Liberation Front), launched in 1969 by the French members of the Mouvement Jeune Révolution (Young Revolution Movement)—an offshoot of the OAS-Jeunes-Métro (Metro Youth OAS)—and by the White Russians of Narodno Trudovoi Soyuz. They then participated in a congress "for a global Solidarism" (1971) and together published a *Bulletin of European Solidarists* (1972–1974).[22] This was not, however, a coherent international organization. Each group understood differently the meaning of the word "solidarism," and the real leader (as opposed to the official one) of the Italian movement appears to have been a French-speaking Belgian journalist posted to Rome.[23] The notion that an internationalist framework that encompassed three national languages had been constructed is therefore subject to a large number of qualifications.

European Nationalism

A Europe-wide organization of the far-right movements has been an elusive creature for the militants concerned, often a chimera for those trying to track down a mythical Fascist international. The theory that a secret organization was preparing for the advent of a Fourth Reich has long haunted the popular imagination and pop culture. In part, it stemmed from the realization that Fascism had undergone an international transformation, both in its organizations and in its ideas. Immediately after the collapse of the Axis powers, Fascist militants saw a united Europe as the justification for their previous positions and as the horizon of expectation that could legitimize their continued political struggle. In particular, the pro-Russian leanings declared by some of these militants allowed them to claim that their plans for Europe could be a solution to the Cold War. Pierre Clémenti (the pseudonym of François-Antoine Clémenti) was one of these neo-Fascists. The founder of the Parti Français National-Communiste (French National-Communist Party) in 1934 , he renamed it the Parti Français National-Collectiviste (French National-Collectivist Party) at the request of the German Occupier and declared war on England "in a private capacity." With the beginning of the Occupation, Clémenti rejected the idea of collaboration in favor of an alliance between the Reich and France, but he also supported Pierre Laval and participated in the founding of the Légion des Volontaires Français contre le Bolchevisme (LVF). He himself went to the eastern front. Clémenti was sentenced to death in absentia in 1948. He sought refuge in Switzerland, publishing *La troisième paix* (The third peace) in 1949, while on the run. Significantly, his short book was published by "Éditions de la Jeune Europe," a name that referenced the collaborationist newspaper *Jeune Europe*. Clémenti said he was convinced that the new imperatives of the anti-Communist struggle would quickly lead to the rehabilitation of the SS. He emphasized that he and his companions had never wanted the victory of Nazi Germany but rather that of Socialist Europe. He saw the confluence of former Nazis and Fascists from Germany, Italy, and France, as well as former anti-Communist resistance fighters, as the base for a possible European third way, leading to the creation of a single state that would unite the three nations. He thought that, in their opposition to Communist and capitalist materialism, they might in the future garner the support of the Soviet Union, which would take its distance from Marxism in favor of a national Socialism. That change in his view of the USSR, he explained, could be attributed to the time he had spent on the eastern front, where he discovered "that magnificent [Russian] people, healthy and friendly and good."[24] That same notion of a third way was espoused by other "veterans" and ultimately played a role in the reorganization of nationalist structures.

The history of what would be called "European nationalism" (Europe embraced as a single nation) is in the first place the history of various individuals, unevenly distributed across the continent. In 1956, a CIA report listed the 134 leading personalities of what it termed "the Fascist international": 31 Germans, 30 Frenchmen, 17 Swedes, 11 Belgians, 10 Italians, 9 Danes, 6 Austrians, 5 Spaniards, 5 Norwegians, 4 Englishmen, 4 Dutchmen, 4 Swiss, and 1 Finn.[25]

In France, two men were at the helm, both of them convinced of the need for European unity. Maurice Bardèche (1907–1998) was an academic, a specialist in Balzac and Stendhal, who was proscribed during the purge because his brother-in-law was the Fascist writer Robert Brasillach, though Bardèche himself had published only a few literary articles in the collaborationist newspaper *Je suis partout*. René Binet (1913–1957) was an indefatigable organizer of small groups and international organizations. By turns a Stalinist militant, a Doriotist, and a leading Trotskyist cadre who ultimately joined the Waffen-SS, he became the champion of reforming National Socialist doctrine, after spending half a year in a French prison for serving in the German military.[26] He maintained ties with the Arab League, as several other French nationalist leaders would do, François Duprat, for example.[27] Binet wanted to federate the nationalists of Europe, from former members of the Waffen-SS to former resistance fighters, in order to put an end to the supposed Russo-American "occupation" of the continent, which, in his view, was an occupation by "niggers," "Mongols," and "Jews." He also sought to establish a federation of National Socialist states based on a racist policy that, beginning in 1950, he called "biological realism."[28] Bardèche and Binet were led to reestablish contact with Francis Parker Yockey—considered after the fact one of the fathers of European nationalism—in order to set up an anti-American European organization.

Yockey, however, was a U.S. citizen. Initially, he was a militant in Father Coughlin's American right-wing movement, which combined Catholic Socialism and an anti-Semitism that trafficked in conspiracy theories. The tone of the movement, though quasi-Fascist, was reactionary more than anything else. Yockey served in the U.S. army, and the time he spent in Germany made him a believer in the Europeanist cause. Under the pseudonym "Ulrick Varange," he published *Imperium* in 1948. This book was inspired by the German conservative revolutionaries and saw Europe as a community of common destiny, based more on culture than on race. For the author, however, the fundamental issue was that white culture would be destroyed by the Jewish conspiracy, which supposedly controlled both the United States and the USSR (one of the major arguments of Nazi propaganda). The following year, shortly before becoming a member of the German neo-Nazi Sozialistiche Reichpartei, Yockey founded the European Liberation Front (ELF). The red cover of its manifesto adopted the Nazi flag, replacing the swastika with a sword. In its conclusion, the manifesto changed the Nazi slogan "Germany, Wake Up" to "Europe, Wake Up." The goal was to liberate the soil and spirit of Europe from Jewry, in order to build an organic society based on an equivalence between race, culture, and state. That united Europe would supposedly cover a territory stretching from North Cape to Gibraltar and from Ireland to Lithuania. The creation of the state of Israel radicalized Yockey, who believed that the neo-Fascists had an ally in the Soviet Union, which alone could break the Jewish-

Israeli grip on the West. That representation spread quickly to American neo-Nazi circles, particularly the National Renaissance Party,[29] founded in 1948 by James Madole, its leader until his death in 1979.

The neo-Nazis jointly developed the idea of a global apartheid. Those who were U.S. citizens proposed that their own state was a "Zionist Occupation Government" (ZOG). The Germanic people no longer had a specific role, and Aryanism was confined to the proclamation of the supremacy of the white race, which therefore included the Slavs—the question of imperialism directed against white peoples was thus settled. The anti-Zionism of the USSR led the neo-Nazis to believe that, after the Third Reich, the Soviet Union would be the last figure of the organic state.[30] In France, the Parti Prolétarien National-Socialiste (National Socialist Proletarian Party) supported "the Algerian revolution," pan-Arabism, and the "Russo-Aryan" USSR. Its aim was to see European ethnic groups ultimately form a "global Aryan state." By contrast, it said, "Catholicism = Latinicism = democracy = capitalism = jews = marxism = chineses = niggers" [*sic*].[31]

These ideas and these men played an important role in what followed. But the individuals involved were little known in their own time. Much more prominent was the Englishman Sir Oswald Mosley (1896–1980), former minister without portfolio in the Labour government and leader of the British Union of Fascists. Winston Churchill ordered him interned during World War II.[32] In 1948 Mosley founded the Union Movement; Yockey was part of it for a time. The movement proclaimed that Europe was a unitary nation and the Third Force in the making, and that it ought to possess the northern third of Africa. Mosley thus adopted and amplified a debate from the interwar period regarding the possibility of building a "Eurafrica."[33] This is a tricky issue, since many different meanings lie behind that word.

The idea of Eurafrica had arisen in French political debates in 1921 and had endured ever since. It initially entailed bringing about a

Franco-German rapprochement and contributing to the construction of a unified Europe, by making the colonies a joint possession of the European nations. That project became entangled with planism and was envisioned within the perspective of an autarky to be built within the vast Eurafrican space. The idea also had real success in Belgium; there too it was supported by personalities on both the left and the right, and then within collaborationism. The concept was also backed by the Austrian Richard van Coudenhove-Kalergi's Paneuropean Union. In 1930 Mussolini's Italy was impelled to hurriedly co-opt the idea, stripping it of its pacifism, in its desire for a Fascist Eurafrica.[34] That receptiveness to the idea on Italy's part was of great import. In fact, the Italian theorist of Eurafrica was Ernesto Massi, a professor in Pavia and at the Università Cattolica del Sacro Cuore in Milan, co-director of the review *Geopolitica* (1939–1943) and author of *L'Africa per l'Europa, l'Europa per l'Africa* (1934; Africa via Europe, Europe via Africa). A renowned geographer, Massi was a leading ideologue of the Fascist state and later of the MSI. In Italy, he disseminated the writings of the father of geopolitics, Karl Haushofer, a German conservative-revolutionary academic who theorized the notion of large political zones that would provide a people with *Lebensraum*. Eurafrica gave a new luster to imperialism and thus became a possible horizon after the Fascist invasion of Ethiopia. Within the Third Reich, the theme of Eurafrica was promoted by the Ministry of Foreign Affairs (which conceived it as a system of exploitation ultimately in the service of the Germans), and by the Ministry of the Economy (which wanted to set up a free trade zone, with each nation possessing a specialized economy). In 1941 Hitler himself mentioned the creation of a "unified Europe within an economic zone that includes the African colonies." In Vichy France, the Eurafrican theme for the most part combined the technocratic aspirations of the French State's staff with those of the new European order.[35]

Mosley's proposals, then, were not some personal reverie, and they were not taken as such. Oswald Pirow (1890–1959), a South African former state minister with pro-Nazi sympathies, made contact with Mosley. In 1948, the year apartheid was established, they proposed jointly a new Eurafrican plan: set aside a third of the continent for the white nations, the other two-thirds for black nations. Their plan brought together a new legal reality (apartheid) and an already-established geopolitical proposal (the construction of *Lebensraum*). It is significant, in fact, that the Eurafrican problem was addressed by the negotiators of the Treaty of Brussels of March 1948, when Belgium, France, Great Britain, Holland, and Luxembourg created a defensive alliance. On the question of decolonization, the French ministers on the left envisioned the construction of the Common Market in Europe as a means for sharing among Europeans the costs of developing Africa and of attaching it to Europe. In 1954 François Mitterrand took up the theme of Eurafrica, following in the footsteps of Coudenhove-Kalergi. In 1956 the French Socialist politician Gaston Defferre conceptualized the status of the overseas territories from the standpoint of building a "Eurafrican market." The same year, a note from the State Secretariat for Economic Affairs modestly observed that "there seems to be a link between the Eurotom [the treaty establishing the European Atomic Energy Community] and common market plan and the conception of Eurafrica already developed before the war." In fact, the reason that Eurafrica was a theme debated within the framework of negotiations for the Treaty of Rome, which laid the foundations for the European Union, was in great part that France wished to mutualize its overseas costs.[36]

With the theme of Eurafrica, therefore, the radical far right could believe it possessed a plausible and inspiring utopian dream. That theme allowed them to redefine a large number of ideological schemes in a more acceptable manner. According to Mosley, Eurafrica could not be allowed to foster miscegenation but had to be based on a strong apartheid, so that the African and European souls would not be destroyed. Like Yockey and Bardèche, he believed that the United States and the USSR were converging toward a materialist civilization that

would destroy European culture. That was his justification for oblit-
erating the geopolitical order and starting over again from scratch.
His Eurafrica would be constituted as an autarky but would share
with the United States influence over South America, while the
Arab countries would constitute a buffer zone between Eurafrica and
the USSR. (In that regard, his positions were close to those of Otto
Strasser when he split off from the NSDAP and then, after the war,
when he advocated a neutral Europe lying between the blocs and
possessing "an Afro-American economic zone.")[37] The groups that
aspired to be radical and at the same time to form a coherent philosophy were well aware of the interest of that ideological offering: Ordine Nuovo drew from it its conception of geopolitical and interracial
relations.[38]

Indeed, the practical impetus that these views acquired came not
from France or Great Britain but from Italy and Sweden (a neutral
state during World War II). One man proposed that the European
nationalists cooperate: Carl Ernfrid Carlberg, publisher in Swedish
of the SS newspaper *Signal*. And one organization thought it necessary to coordinate the reconstruction of the far-right movements:
the MSI. In 1950 it held two meetings that brought together the
top nationalists and those who had been the object of the purge in
France, England, Spain, Italy, Sweden, Denmark, Norway, Germany, Belgium, and Switzerland, as well as Albanian and Romanian
émigrés. The militants made official the idea of creating a European-
national movement and set in place a European committee, with two
delegates from each nation. A second meeting, organized by Per
Engdahl—who in 1941 had launched a pro-Axis movement—took
place in Malmö, Sweden, in May 1951. In addition to Mosley and
Bardèche, sixty delegates, from Germany, Denmark, Spain, France,
Italy, Sweden, Switzerland, and Norway, were in attendance, as well
as Baltic émigrés. An international study commission was established,
with Engdahl, Bardèche, Karl Heinz Priester (a former cadre in Hitler
Youth who headed the German Social Movement), and Ernesto Massi
(MSI). An international organization was founded: the European

Social Movement (ESM). According to U.S. intelligence services, a Euro-Arab economic organization was added to it, charged with covering up and financing the activities of the ESM. This European-Arabian Study Commission implicitly proscribed all French, English, or "Jewish" businesses.[39] U.S. intelligence services also specified that the representative of the Hungarian refugees was none other than a minister who had outlived the Arrow Cross government: Árpád Henney (1895–1980). Having fled to Austria, he had the good fortune to reach the French occupation zone, given that the Americans considered him a war criminal. The French army is said to have provided him with its protection, because Henney offered to place a Hungarian intelligence network in its service.[40] This case indicates perfectly how, beyond Europe's proclamations of independence within the context of the Cold War, anti-Communism and what remained of collaborationism tended to tilt the far-right movements toward the Western bloc.

According to the French intelligence services, the ESM, the first serious attempt to organize the far right, received funds from the Portuguese government, the Banque Worms, and Christian Wolf (a French industrialist who sponsored the post-1945 Pétainist press).[41] The financial support of the Banque Worms is explained by the importance of the French delegation, which included Victor Barthélemy, Georges Albertini, and Guy Lemonnier. That bank had also provided financing for Jacques Doriot's Parti Populaire Français. Under the Vichy regime, Marcel Déat and those close to him, in competition with Doriot, had denounced the enterprise as an essential instrument in the "synarchic" conspiracy to take over the new regime, a conspiracy theory that has been revived in the last few years on the French far left. Georges Albertini, Déat's second-in-command during the collaboration, joined the Banque Worms after his release from prison. He became one of the key men behind the scenes of the Fifth Republic; his influence was particularly strong during Georges Pompidou's presidential term. Guy Lemonnier (also a former militant in Déat's ranks), under the name "Claude Harmel," ran the Institut d'Histoire Social (Institute of Social History), the flagship of the "Maison Albertini," which after 1968 funneled militants from the Occident movement into the liberal right.[42] Barthélemy was not part of the Déat clan: a former member of the Komintern, he had become Doriot's right-hand man and was a member of the LVF's central committee. In Germany, where he had sought refuge in 1944, he received the order to organize from Italy the infiltration of far-right partisans. He thus had many international contacts and continued to make his organizational skills available to the French movements (Jean-Marie Le Pen made him administrative secretary of the National Front in 1973, when it came time to finalize the separation from ON).[43]

The ESM set out to rehabilitate Fascism, but not slavishly, despite the strong presence of former members of the Waffen-SS in its midst: it also felt the need to improve the movement. It advocated the construction of an anti-Communist, corporatist European empire, under the leadership of a man chosen by plebiscite. The empire would set common rules regarding defense and the economy for all its member nations, including, under certain conditions, some colonies. The desire of the ESM to modernize Fascism did not entail any rupture, either in its mode of being or in its way of presenting itself. For example, the Nationaal Europese Sociale Beweging (NESB) constituted the Dutch and Flemish branch of the ESM, under the aegis of a former member of the Waffen-SS, Paul Van Tienen (who had participated in the Malmö congress and was in exile in Spain). Granted, in its various slogans, the NESB emphasized the social and Europeanist dimension of its doctrine ("For a Europe free from Russia and America"; "For national recovery, European collaboration, and social justice"; "We want social interventionism, not economic interventionism"). But Van Tienen (1921–1995) chose the organization's name as an allusion to the collaborator Anton Mussert's Nationaal-Socialistische Beweging in Nederland (NSB).[44] Because the NESB included former militants from the NSB and from the other banned Dutch Fascist movement, the Zwart Front, as well as people who had belonged to the Stichting Oud Politiek Delinquenten and had been proscribed during the purge, it was outlawed in 1955.[45] In addition, the ESM faced a crisis from the start, with the meeting convened in Zurich by René Binet and the Swiss Gaston-Armand Amaudruz. In 1941 Amaudruz had founded the Mouvement Eurafrique (Eurafrican Movement) in Lausanne, and he was the first negationist author. He had been invited to Malmö but refused to go, judging that the attendees' conception of Europe did not rest solidly enough on a racial foundation.[46]

From Nazism to Neo-Racism

The attendees of the Zurich congress launched a new organization, which did not declare itself a splinter group: the European Liaison Bureau. It became the New European Order (NEO)—a provocative name, given its explicit reference to Nazi slogans. The declaration it adopted affirms the equality of all ethnic groups within the white race, the Slavs being explicitly included, and the need for a European confederation of neo-Fascist states. But here racism introduced a rupture from both Eurafrica and the accepted image of the far right. The organization defended what it called a "neoracism": it supported the independence of the colonies, to foster racial empires that would be homogeneous because continental (the question of miscegenation had preoccupied the Italian authorities since the invasion of Ethiopia in 1935). According to the NEO,

the hierarchy of the races can be based only on their confrontation and subsequently on the respect for the distinctive characteristics and traditions of each one. The reestablishment of a certain world equilibrium is possible only if a radical break is made with colonialism based solely on the exploitation of the colored races. It is our responsibility: 1) to assert our will to return the races of the countries colonized by Europe to their own traditions; 2) to substitute, for the current colonialist regime, a regime of association that shows respect for the traditions proper to each race, accompanied by a strict racial segregation in the interest of each of the contracting parties; 3) to call for and realize the return of the nonnative groups to their traditional space.[47]

Overt racism paved the way for anticolonialist differentialism as well as anti-immigration. That discourse would have many incarnations and transmutations, given the centrality of its theme (the right to "identity" via the rejection of globalization).

Amaudruz became involved in the NEO, taking charge of *Courrier du continent,* a newspaper still active today,[48] but, rejecting schism, he did not withdraw from the ESM. The situation was more delicate in France. Bardèche had accepted the mission of federating the small groups. Thanks to MSI funding, in 1952 he launched *Défense de l'Occident,* a doctrinal review of debates among all the far-right factions. He had others officially launch the Comité National Français (CNF), which brought together many small groups, including the Phalange Française (French Phalanx) and the Mouvement Populaire Européen (MPE; European People's Movement), which supported Europe's neutrality. The honorary president of the MPE was Otto Strasser, who, in the name of German reunification, cooperated with the Stalinist Communists at the German neutralist congress in 1958. Strasser supported the Palestinian cause, but he did not manage to reach an agreement with any international organization because of the presence in the MPE of Italian Fascists, who rejected the Germanic claims on South Tyrol (Alto Adige for the Italians). The MPE's contact in France was the Phalange Française—renamed the Mouvement Populaire Français after it was dissolved by the state in 1958—under the leadership of Charles Luca, Déat's nephew and a founding member of the ESM.[49] The newspaper of his movement clearly affirmed a conspiratorial view of immigration, denouncing globalist miscegenation manipulated by the Jews.[50] Neopaganism began to be part of the culture of that fringe group, providing a common foundation for an internationalized insularity. In 1958, for

example, the Phalange Française organized its winter solstice celebration with a delegate from Wiking-Jugend (Viking Youth). Established in the Federal Republic of Germany in 1952, Wiking-Jugend
had branches in the Netherlands, Belgium, Italy, and France in the
1970s; it was dissolved in 1994, having become the largest German
neo-Nazi activist organization, with nearly 500 members, organized
on the model of Hitlerjugend.[51]

Order would not reign in the ranks. Binet clashed with Bardèche
on the theoretical level, advocating a revolutionary line, and on the
political level, by taking control of the committee. Bardèche was
forced to found a new unitary entity: the Comité de Coordination
des Forces Nationales (Coordinating Committee for National Forces).
The result was that, when a new ESM congress in Paris was being
planned, the CNF sent out invitations but spurned Priester, who was
linked to Bardèche, and invited in his place Karl Meissner, leader of
the Deutsche Block, even as some outside France challenged the CNF's
right to represent that country. Only a few groups, such as the Falange
Española, remained in contact with the two rival internationals. Despite an abortive attempt in 1953 to unify the NEO and the ESM in
a European People's Movement—which, ideologically, would have
taken a middle way and a moderate line, even while designating
Jewry, Communism, and Freemasonry as its adversaries—neither of
the two groups escaped the destructive effect of the rivalry. The NEO
did manage to unite a certain number of groups. For example, in
January 1956, it counted among its members one organization
each in Austria, Belgium, Finland, the Netherlands, Norway, and
Switzerland, two organizations in Denmark, and thirteen in Sweden.[52]
In 1968, according to the domestic intelligence services, the NEO
had acquired a hegemonic position in French neo-Nazism.[53] Attempts were made in the direction of reconciliation. With additional
help from a former Belgian member of the Waffen-SS, Jean-Robert
Debbaudt, from the very Fascist Italian Stefano Delle Chiaie, from
the Portuguese Zarco Moniz Ferreira, and from a former German
member of the Waffen-SS, Jean Baumann, Per Engdahl maneuvered

to establish the Young European Legion in Milan in April 1958, with the proclaimed goal of forming the sole organization of European youth.[54]

In retrospect, the brouhaha seems insignificant. But that race among radicals produced ideas. It led to the creation of the principal French doctrinal review to unify the nationalist base. The ESM's defeat also resulted in the creation, by former member of the Waffen-SS Arthur Ehrhardt, of *Nation Europa,* a West German review that performed the same function as its French counterpart, with financial aid from Georges Albertini, Bardèche, Mosley, and Goebbels's former state secretary, Werner Naumann. That was not a negligible legacy: the review managed to find a place for itself in the debate, with 6,500 subscribers in 1953 and 18,000 in 2004.[55] In short, the failure to form an international organization led a certain number of cadres, beginning in the 1950s, to move toward what twenty years later would be called "metapolitics": the "cultural battle," the will to impose a change in representations, in order, ultimately, to achieve a political transformation. Moreover, that metapolitics targeted the masses as much as the elites. Consider the case of the Austrian Wilhelm Landig (1909–1997). He represented the Österreichische Soziale Bewegung within the ESM. In the 1920s, he had belonged to a *Freikorps* (a German volunteer military unit), then joined the Deutsche Wehrmacht and, finally, the Austrian Nazi Party. He later joined the SD and then the SS Florian-Geyer Division. Landig sought to remake Fascism not only as a political offering but also as a "worldview." He was an important countercultural author, and his "mysterious history" novels were published in Spanish, French, and English. In them he revisited Nazism, fusing it with a number of mythemes (Cathars, UFOs, the Holy Grail, and so on). His pop culture writings allowed him to disseminate a clearly anti-Semitic and negationist discourse to segments of the population that probably would not have purchased a neo-Nazi political brochure.[56] Other authors have traveled the same path: esoteric neo-Nazism is represented, notably, by the theories of Miguel Serrano (1917–2009)[57] on the use of UFOs by German Nazis who had taken refuge in South America; by those of Savitri Devi, née Maximiani Portas (Lyon, 1905–Essex, 1982), who associated Hitlerism with the Hindu tradition; and by the Nazi-Satanism of the Briton David Myatt. Esoteric Nazism, which has the enormous advantage (in terms of winning acceptance) of portraying Nazism in a manner less overtly focused on a vindication of the Reich and its racial policy, has found an audience, albeit small, among believers in "alternative" spiritualities and conspiracy theories. Neo-Nazism, the absolute incarnation of evil in democratic societies after 1945, is thus above all a fringe culture. That aspect shows the postmodern dimension of the phenomenon, its ability to mix together heterogeneous elements. A number of neo-Nazi militants take at face value—and hence as the underpinnings of their ideology—the relation between esotericism and Nazism, even though Hitler despised Odinism and the various neopagan constructs.[58] The runic insignia of the European SS divisions are currently being mixed and matched by the most radical groups, who use them in their brochures and logos, particularly the insignia of the Das Reich, Nord, and Prinz-Eugen divisions and, to a lesser measure, the Nederland, Langemark, and Landstorm Nederland divisions.[59] That amalgam of signs allows these groups to assert both their radicalism and their possession of a cultural capital of their own (knowledge of what the SS "really" was: an esoteric black order). The Greek militants of Golden Dawn sometimes use a Nazi flag with the swastika replaced by the runic insignia formerly used by the Landstorm Nederland Division, while the Ukrainians in the Svoboda (Freedom) Party use its variant from Das Reich Division.

Nazis new and old cooperated. The NEO established ties with the Hilfsgemeinschaft auf Gegenseitigkeit der Angehörigen der ehemaligen Waffen-SS (HIAG, mutual aid association of former members of the Waffen-SS), founded in 1951, which received state approval from the Federal Republic of Germany in 1959. Its French branch was under the patronage of Bardèche. The HIAG's newspaper even invited the former members of the Waffen-SS from the Wallonien

Division to work with Debbaudt (who ran the newspaper *L'Europe réelle*).[60] Within the framework of the NEO, Pierre Clémenti launched the newspaper *L'Action européenne* and the European action committees. The development of NEO offshoots demonstrates that its conception of Europe coincides with white affirmationism: there is both a Canadian and a Turkish section. The Turkish Fascists claimed that their ethnic group was a branch of the Aryan race, an idea still embraced by Aleksandr Dugin, the neorightist doctrinaire of Russian imperialism.[61] The international organization maintained strong enough ties to the Francoist regime that it was able to hold its congresses of 1969, 1979, and 1981 in Barcelona.[62] The first of these brought together delegates from Germany, France, Great Britain, Italy, Sweden, and Switzerland, as well as representatives of the Croatian, Hungarian, Polish, and Romanian refugees. The Belgian, Canadian, Danish, and South African sections sent their regrets.[63] According to some sources, representatives of the Palestinian Fatah also attended. Debbaudt, who wished to place the NEO "in the service of the Palestinian resistance," supposedly sought to set up a network to recruit mercenaries on behalf of the Popular Front for the Liberation of Palestine, seeking support from the World Union of National Socialists.[64] In any case, the decision was made to reorient the NEO's efforts, first, to focus on the fight against immigration, perceived as the result of a Jewish conspiracy to mix the races, and second, to promote a eugenics that would improve the white race. To do so, Amaudruz and Jacques de Mahieu (1915–1990) co-founded the Institut Supérieur des Sciences Psychosomatiques, Biologiques, et Raciales (Higher Institute for the Psychosomatic, Biological, and Racial Sciences). The institute's mission was to continue "the magnificent work" of the 1936 Congress of the New German Science of Medicine.[65] Mahieu, claiming he had belonged to the Charlemagne Division,[66] went to Argentina, where he became a major ideologue of the national-syndicalist tendency of Peronism, then of Fascist Catholicism in the Tacuara movement during the 1960s. Having become an academic, he published studies claiming that the Vikings had founded pre-Columbian civilizations, thus repeating themes of the Nazi raciologist Hans F. K. Günther and of the Ahnenerbe, the SS's cultural institute. Many of Mahieu's ideas were adopted by the Groupement de Recherche et d'Études pour la Civilisation Européenne (GRECE), with which the institute was associated, and he was published by Copernic (the Nouvelle Droite publishing house) and by more mainstream presses, such as Robert Laffont and J'ai Lu.[67]

The Jeune Europe Moment

One experiment, though part of these European-nationalist dynamics, would prove to be particularly innovative: Jeune Europe (JE). Its name cannot be separated from the person of the Walloon Jean Thiriart. Since the 1990s, the revolutionary nationalists have portrayed him as coming out of a far-left German organization of European dimensions: the Fichte Bund.[68] In reality, the Fichte Bund, far from being on the far left, was a nationalist-völkisch movement founded in 1914. During the French occupation of the Ruhr, the group spearheaded the anti-French campaign targeting the role of black colonial soldiers. Even before 1933, it became a sort of clearing-house, known as the "Union for World Truth," for National Socialist propaganda directed at foreign countries. In France, the Fichte Bund's propaganda was picked up by fringe pro-Nazis of the rabid anti-Semitic variety, such as Roger Cazy, who headed the Front Franc (Frankish Front) with Jean Boissel, a man who had "the honor" of speaking at a Nazi meeting in Nuremberg in 1935.[69] Thiriart then spent time in the Association des Amis du Grand Reich Allemand (Association of Friends of the Greater German Reich), an organization overseen by the SD of Liège.[70] So much for Thiriart's "anti-Nazism" and "far-left orientation."

For the most part, JE grew out of the opposition to decolonization. In July 1960, in the face of the decolonization of the Congo, Jean Thiriart and Paul Teichmann founded the Comité d'Action et

de Défense des Belges d'Afrique (Committee of Action and Defense
of the Belgians of Africa). The group evolved from a pro-Belgium colonialist nationalism faithful to the crown to white supremacism,
advocating support of the OAS and the integration of Algeria into
France. It adopted the Celtic cross as its logo. It later became the
Mouvement d'Action Civique (MAC; Civil Action Movement),
which recruited about 350 active militants, by means of a circular to
veterans of the Légion Nationale (National Legion). It appealed to
"a community from Narvik to Cape Town, from Brest to Bucharest,"
published coded communiqués for the use of terrorist groups located
in Algeria, printed the OAS-Métro's newspaper, and organized the
withdrawal of its members to Belgian territory. Its aim was to use
the tensions associated with decolonization to foment discontent
and then to direct it toward a partisan organization that it would
discreetly control through infiltration.[71] Thiriart got in touch with
French neo-Fascist organizations.[72] In August 1961, moreover, he participated in a meeting with Peter Kelist, leader of the Deutsche
Reichspartei; Ion Emilian, former cadre of the Iron Guard, editor of
the newspaper *Svastica de foc* (Swastika of Fire), and president of the
Anti-Bolshevik Bloc of Nations; "and with white 'colonizers' from
South Africa, Angola, Congo, and Algeria."[73] On March 4, 1961,
he attended the international neo-Fascist meeting held in Venice at
the instigation of Oswald Mosley and with the support of the MSI.
The declaration it adopted laid out two initial phases: first, the creation of a liaison bureau uniting the Reichspartei, the MAC, the
Union Movement, and the MSI; and second, the transformation of
all their names, in their respective languages, into a single name in
French, "le Parti National-Européen" (the European-National Party).
The party was to work toward the construction of a unified Europe,
rejecting "Western Europe's satellization by the United States" and
demanding "the recovery of our eastern territories."[74]

Upon his return to Venice, Thiriart was arrested in conjunction
with the repression of OAS supporters. Imprisoned for a month, he
began to write what would be his magnum opus, which he self-

published in 1964: *Un empire de 400 millions d'hommes: L'Europe* (An empire of 400 million men: Europe).[75] The European Party he defended in the book was no longer a union of European national-ists; rather, it saw itself as Leninist, "imbued with the faith of a reli-gious order and with the discipline of a military order." It would lead the struggle, "clandestine" in the east and "underground" in the west. The MAC appropriated the goal of the Venice Protocol: the formation of the European Party. *Jeune Europe* became the name of the group's newspaper, and the MAC decreed itself the Belgian branch of the JE. The movement was centralized, and it opened branches in many countries (always with a modest number of members): Spain, Austria, Germany, Italy, England, the Netherlands, South Africa (where it adopted the name Eurafrika), Portugal, Switzerland, and, for a time, the Americas.

The first ideologue of JE was not Thiriart but Émile Lecerf (1921–1990), an author formerly published by the collaborationist La Toison d'Or, who also contributed in 1944 to the *Cahiers de la roue solaire,* published by the SS's cultural institute. For JE, Lecerf wrote his first official manifesto, *La Révolution national-européenne* (The European-National revolution). In it he forcefully argued that Europe had to retake Africa and set up a single government, but that the continent had to be organized regionally on "ethnic, cultural, and economic foundations." He thereby placed himself fully within the völkisch perspective of the Waffen-SS, disseminated in France by Saint-Loup.[76] Thiriart, however, challenged nationalism based on language or heritage, in favor of a revolutionary nationalism emerging from a vanguard that would force the merger of all states into a single continental Jacobin entity (this analysis was greatly influenced by Machiavelli's thinking).

JE's unity of action was ensured by the creation of national lead-ership staffs overseen by a European staff and subdivided into spe-cialized bureaus (everything was foreseen, from social assistance for militants to the collection of information about adversaries), which organized the activities of six-member "cells." Several national staffs, however, had no one in charge of one of their bureaus, thus indicating the perpetual difficulty of making "right-wing Leninism" a viable reality. In 1963 JE had leadership staffs for Austria, Belgium, Italy, France, Portugal, and Switzerland.[77] Some national leaders, moreover, personally exercised centralized control over their branch. The leader of Jovem Portugal, for example, was Zarco Moniz Ferreira from the NEO; disregarding Thiriart's subversive tendencies, he guided his men toward the ultra faction of the Salazarist regime after JE went downhill.[78] Among the groups worthy of note were the Italians of Giovane Nazione, who represented the bulk of the troops but were equally influenced by Julius Evola's views. Their discourse was very sharp-edged.[79] The Austrian branch, Junges Europa, also distinguished itself: it split off from JE over the South Tyrol question and became the Legion Europa. Headed by former member of the Waffen-SS Fred Borth, the movement perpetrated attacks in Italy and Austria. It also organized a dissident international organization, Europafront, with a Flemish-speaking splinter group from Jong Europa, which Thiriart had relegated to the "neo-Nazi ghetto." (In 1963, the splinter group retaliated, claiming that Thiriart had boasted in front of the militants that he had murdered "kikes" during the war.) Borth also restored the ties that the MAC and then JE had had with the New European Order. Europafront reorganized the Germanic elements of JE and contributed to the tensions within the Nationaldemokratische Partei Deutschlands. It also participated in the creation of the German revolutionary nationalist movement and the introduction of neo-rightist theories to Germany, by conducting a policy of infiltrating the Greens.[80]

As for the French, they struggled to put a group together, particularly after the JE was banned in 1961 and its newspaper in 1963. The ties established with Pierre Sergent had led them to imagine entrusting the leadership of the French branch to the OAS-Métro officer, but in 1963 it broke all ties with Thiriart and maintained friendly relations solely with JE Suisse. In reality, JE was well established only in Paris and Lille. In those cities, it was supported by two mainstays: Jean-Claude Jacquard (future president of GRECE), who later left to join Lecerf's völkisch splinter group; and Gérard Bordes, from the Jeunes de l'Esprit Public (Public-Spirited Youth), an organization that popularized the views of Jean Mabire, also a believer in an ethnically based Europe. For a time, they published *L'Europe combattante,* which was an exact replica of *Jeune Europe* but for its title; the subterfuge lasted only from September 1964 to April 1965. The group first infiltrated the Fédération des Étudiants Nationalistes (FEN; Federation of Nationalist Students).[81] Those who were members of both organizations are said to have considered assassinating Maurice Thorez, head of the French Communist Party. They were thwarted in their aims, because their attempts at manipulation attracted hostility, to which the central bureau proved unable to respond. For example, the FEN suspected that one of the principal French cadres of JE was behind a break-in at its offices, having intended to steal its files. He is said to have been kidnapped, taken to a wine cellar, and subjected to the bath and electrode tortures by eight members of the FEN, including some of its chief cadres. All the members of JE were ousted from the FEN, yet the central bureau of JE could assure the poor man only that, if "something serious" were to happen, a commando would set out from Belgium.[82] That undermining activity, intended to produce a split in the FEN to wrest it away from Europe-Action and make it a JE spy, was a failure. When the split did finally occur, therefore, the Front Universitaire Européen (European University Front) that emerged from it immediately escaped JE and became the Occident movement (1964).[83]

JE had vast ambitions, however. In July 1964 a meeting in Madrid brought together the JE leadership, Pierre Lagaillarde of the OAS (1931–2014), and various European movements. The next month, a meeting took place in Nice, organized by JE. Attending were cadres from both Latin American and European movements (France, Spain, Holland, Portugal, West Germany, Sweden, and Italy were represented). The decision was made to create a Légion Internationale (International Legion) that would take action in the countries concerned

"as soon as the domestic situation called for it." The legion's leadership was entrusted to Otto Skorzeny (1908–1975).[84] That former SS
officer had become a far-right legend when he led the airborne commando that liberated Mussolini in 1943, after Il Duce was imprisoned by order of the Italian king and the Grand Council of Fascism.
After the war, Skorzeny was head of the secret Odessa network, which
was in charge of exfiltrating former members of the SS from the countries where they were subject to prosecution. Having sought refuge
in Spain, Skorzeny organized an operation to smuggle weapons into
Egypt. He was suspected by the CIA of having links to Tehran and
of having arranged for Russia to finance his network of former SS
members. Supposedly, he chose Moscow over Washington because
he was persuaded that only the USSR could bring about the reunification of Germany.[85] What the documents seem to show, in fact, is
that these groups and men had dreams of playing their own game
(installing Fascist-leaning regimes) within the Western camp, hoping
to take advantage of the contradictions arising from the Cold War.
In the last instance, however, it was the Cold War that dictated the
course of events. After the fall of the Berlin Wall, for example, when
the Stasi archives were opened, it was discovered that, beginning in
the 1950s, the East Germans had financed neo-Nazi activism in West
Germany to damage the image of the Federal Republic of Germany
in the eyes of the French public and to sabotage the plan for the European Defense Community.[86]

The manner in which the Francoist regime offered safe harbor to
Jeune Europe, then withdrew its support, is also significant: to be
accepted, the radical fringe had to submit to the Western order. In
1966 Jeune Europe's summer camp was held in Spain. Sports activities were combined with debates, and a wreath was laid on the grave
of José-Antonio Primo de Rivera, founder of the Falange Española.
At campfires, efforts were made to produce a transnational and transpar-
tisan political folklore, by singing in unison the songs of the Falange,
of Afrika Korps, of the French Resistance, and of the Italian Partisans. But in March 1967, at the last minute, the authorities banned a

conference that was supposed to bring members of JE from nine countries together in Madrid. Thiriart saw that as a sign of American influence over the Francoist state. Ernesto Milá, a Spanish European nationalist who knew Thiriart, has suggested more prosaically that, despite JE's good contacts within the Francoist regime, Thiriart had no understanding of Spain's pro-American geopolitical positioning and had made the blunder of using inflammatory anti-American language when speaking with the authorities.[87] Spain was a rather special case, however.

The Círculo Español de Amigos de Europa (CEDADE, Spanish Circle of Friends of Europe) emerged in 1962 from a split in Jeune Europe de Madrid, then became a "cultural association" in Barcelona in 1966. According to those in this splinter group, Thiriart's essential error was his materialism. The CEDADE rapidly underwent an ideological evolution. Beginning in 1969, it adopted a neo-Nazi position that promoted a racialism and anti-Semitism of a virulence previously unknown on the Spanish far right (only 0.05 percent of the population was Jewish; opposition to Israel was common, however).[88] The group benefited from protection, and perhaps financial contributions, from Nazi figures who had taken refuge in Spain, such as Skorzeny and the Belgian Léon Degrelle (he died there in 1994), as well as the generosity of Arab countries and dignitaries, including Saudi Arabia and the Grand Mufti of Jerusalem, Haj Amin al Husseini.[89] The CEDADE also maintained relations with the NEO, particularly the French neo-Nazis of the Fédération d'Action Nationale et Européenne (FANE; National and European Action Federation). That led to the creation of a French branch of the CEDADE in the late 1970s.[90] Iberian neo-Nazi groups proliferated, therefore, especially in Catalonia. This was not, however, a völkisch conception of Catalan nationalism; on the contrary, Catalanists were the target of organized attacks.[91] These neo-Nazi groups were often influenced by Italian neo-Fascist ultras.

In 1979 the CEDADE formed its own party (the Partido Europeo Nacional Revolucionario), but it put most of its energies into publishing anti-Semitic and negationist texts. The existence of that relatively important forum made possible the translation of the American Francis Parker Yockey's *Imperium* in 1977, a key racialo-Europeanist text for the CEDADE.[92] The organization was also marked by a pronounced Wagnerian aesthetic and a keen interest in environmentalism and regionalism, as evidenced in the bulletin of its French branch, *Projets et Références* (Plans and references), which reported the first attempts toward a political unification of environmentalists. Based in southeastern France, it retained the acronym CEDADE, which now stood for Cercle Écologique des Amis de l'Europe (Environmental Circle of the Friends of Europe). It also disseminated the Aryanist, racialist brochures of the NEO, the Iron Guard, and other organizations.[93] Even as the German revolutionary nationalists joined the environmentalist movement in the late 1970s, the Spanish radical far right made a specialty of setting up environmental and anti-speciesist associations. These experiments inspired various efforts. The magazine *Nationalisme & République,* launched in 1991 to organize Jean-Marie Le Pen's opponents within the French far right, called for a convergence of the sovereignist left, environmentalists, and the far right, and promoted a virulent anti-American and "anti-Zionist" line. It participated in a new European Liberation Front, which laid claim to Niekisch, Yockey, and Thiriart. In a coordinated effort, the ELF groups attempted to infiltrate the environmentalist parties in Spain, France, Germany, Poland, Great Britain, and Italy.[94] The CEDADE, having won back the leadership of the NEO in 1987, opted to dissolve itself in 1993. Some of its militants put their energies into the cultural battle, others into the Democracia Nacional (an Islamophobic, populist, and Spanish nationalist group established in 1993).[95]

The problem with Jeune Europe was that, though its project attracted the neo-Nazis, they rejected Thiriart's anti-völkisch Jacobinism. In Belgium itself, JE was composed of Walloonian and Netherlands-Flanders branches directly attached to the European leadership staff, but the ideologue Thiriart advocated not an ethnically based Europe but a single European state, Jacobin and secular, with all citizens—whether from Marrakesh or Bucharest—equal before the law. The resulting crisis prompted Lecerf to leave JE in August 1964, because he had rejected the directives that Thiriart had dispensed: a more moderate racist discourse (until then, Thiriart's own racialism had been very pronounced) and support for de Gaulle, whom Thiriart now described as a leader opposed to the Russo-American continuum. De Gaulle could be the "Victor Emmanuel II" of a France that would become the "Piedmont of Europe." Lecerf, conversely, advocated a radicalization of the propaganda, as evidenced by the distribution of a tract that proposed a twenty-five-point program, like that of the Nazi Party. Within a short time, 172 members resigned or were ousted from the organization. Two hundred Belgian members remained in late 1964, according to the historian Francis Balace. JE claimed to have 5,000 in all of Europe in 1965; according to an estimate of the domestic intelligence services of the prefecture of police, only 66 Belgians and 300 in all of Europe would remain in 1966.[96]

The student branch of JE, called the Fédération Générale des Étudiants Européens (General Federation of European Students), joined with Lecerf, who founded the Front National-Européen (FNE; European-National Front, initially called the Front National-Européen du Travail, the European-National Labor Front), and the newspaper *Révolution Européenne.* His group was joined by the French students from JE, who in April 1964 had founded the Fédération Générale des Étudiants (FGE; General Federation of Students), headed by Jean-Claude Jacquard. The FNE was thus clearly a joint Belgian-French movement. Lecerf's writings were resolutely in the tradition of post-1941 Nazism: American capitalism was run by the Jews, and the Jews also controlled the USSR, their final goal being to install a world Jewish dictatorship whose political order would be a brutal Communism and whose economic order would be an extreme monopolistic capitalism. The white race was said to be the sole master of creative genius, which constituted its only capacity for resistance against the imposition of a "1984 world." That resistance would give rise to every sort of propaganda promoting miscegenation, even though only racial segregation and the buildup of Europe could in reality save the European people.[97] The French FGE collaborated with other far-right organizations in a tactical effort to infiltrate them. It became deeply implanted in the Comités Tixier-Vignancour (CTV) in the run-up to the 1965 presidential election in France and established solid contacts with the Fédération des Étudiants Nationalistes.[98] Dominique Venner agreed to the idea of jointly producing propaganda documents on the racial question.[99]

The FGE appears to have been an organization, neo-Nazi in its ideology, that became part of European nationalism in the interest of modernizing its discourse and in the hope of being better received. On one hand, it sought to preserve the worldview of collaborationism and, on the other, to engage in politics within the context of the 1960s, at the cost of making ideological sacrifices in its propaganda. The group struggled, never reaching the threshold of forty members. For a time, it moved closer to the neo-Nazis of the Fédération d'Action Nationale et Européenne and became associated with the "European-Socialist" wreckage caused by the dissolution of the Occident movement and the breakup of the Europe-Action network (1968). All these groups together went on to form the Rassemblement Socialiste Européen (European Socialist Union).[100] From that point on, the trajectory of Lecerf's group was inseparable from the history of the new right.

In 1964 the French members of JE who had not split off from the group formed the Centre d'Études Politiques et Sociales Européennes (CEPSE; Center for European Political and Social Studies). Their leader was Gérard Bordes, but they were in fact overseen by the Belgian Jean Van den Broeck, and their treasurer was a cadre from Colonel Trinquier's Association pour l'Étude de la Réforme des Structures de l'État (Association for the Study of the Reform of State Structures). The CEPSE specialized in switching back and forth between subversion, countersubversion, and antisubversion. It founded a new newspaper, *La Nation européenne,* which replaced all the other far-right titles being printed up to that time and aspired to be resolutely European. It counted among its managers the Italian Claudio Mutti, who would become a central figure in the radical right. The only identifying initials appearing in the newspaper were "CEPSE," but, in about the summer of 1965, JE was transformed into a new entity, the Parti Communautaire Européen (PCE; European Communitarian Party). That new incarnation aspired resolutely to be a "historic party," that is, one that would found a nation, of which it was the prefiguration. It accepted only European militants assembled in language-based sections (French-speaking, German-speaking, and so on). The PCE was organized entirely by and around its leader, Jean Thiriart. Van den Broeck was the last cadre to abdicate in protest against Thiriart's leadership: he resigned in October 1965 to found the Union des Syndicats Communautaires Européens (USCE; Union of European Communitarian Syndicates), taking with him the bulk of the French members who had remained faithful until then.[101] The USCE advocated an ethnically based Europe and nationalization, managed across Europe by extra-continental businesses. The newspapers of the USCE and the Rassemblement Socialiste Européen merged in 1969 to create a new title, *L'Europe combat,* which denounced the right, participated in strikes, and embraced Peronism. In its issue of December 1969, it said that it refused to fight the leftists "even if we, European Socialists, do not approve of their internationalism. Until the end of the regime, they are tactically our allies."[102]

The American question quickly became the focus of Thiriart's preoccupations. He believed that the United States constituted Western Europe's economic, political, and strategic enemy. He therefore rejected any solidarity with the white West.[103] That meant committing himself to "a global front against U.S. imperialism." The movement no longer hesitated to quote Che Guevara, and its newspaper published an article from the Havana press agency. For Thiriart, the matter at hand was to build "the national-communitarianist," "*that is, non-Marxist,*" Europe, thanks to the bases Maoist China could offer the European nationalists leading the offensive against the United States. Contrary to what has often been written, that new position was not a move to the left or a conversion to Maoism. It is perfectly summed up in an image that appeared on the front page of Thiriart's newspaper under the headline "European-National Communism?": a Celtic cross behind a Communist flag that is being pulled down.[104]

The former supporter of the OAS did not hesitate to establish numerous contacts with the Arab-Muslim world. He wanted to create international brigades that would come fight Israel and would acquire a base from which to organize anti-American guerilla warfare in Europe. By turns, the ambassadors of Syria and Iraq, as well as Palestinian and Algerian leaders, wrote for *La Nation européenne*,[105] which specialized in advocating the assimilation of Zionism to Nazism (*Jeune Europe,* by contrast, had supported Zionism).[106] The Jews were accused of controlling the West and of wanting to extend their domination to the world via Israel. The newspaper was distributed in Algeria by a state-owned enterprise. Thiriart also met with the new head of the Iraqi state, Ahmed el-Bakr, after his coup d'état in July 1968. And after Iraq, the Walloon militant was received in Lebanon and Egypt, where he participated in the congress of the Arab Socialist Union. *La Nation européenne* accepted advertising from the League of Arab States and the Palestine Liberation Organization. It appears that it was the PLO's support that allowed it to survive financially. When Ahmed Shukeiri was replaced by Yasser Arafat as head of the PLO, the newspaper and the organization went under.[107]

The connections with the Arab world were considered so extensive that the secret services of the Portuguese dictatorship accused Thiriart's group "of being linked to the intelligence services of certain Arab countries."[108] It is difficult to say at present whether that was a well-founded point of view or the brainwashing of the self-promoting Thiriart. He boasted of many meetings, claiming he was able to see Chinese premier Zhou Enlai in Bucharest, and prided himself on having trained militants destined for notoriety in the

Red Brigades, a Third Worldist Marxist-Leninist Italian terrorist organization—including its leader, Renato Curcio.[109] In the absence of evidence apart from his statements long after the fact, there is reason for doubt. The end of the PCE in 1969 occurred under murky circumstances. According to one of Thiriart's disciples, it may have resulted from "a meeting of the leadership at the Imperia in Italy, where Thiriart was outvoted on the question of entryism by the militants of our organization in the mass organizations coming out of the student movement." The militant Franco Freda (b. 1941, still the director of Edizioni di Ar) had visited the Greek Regime of the Colonels and had without question been introduced to such methods there. He therefore published a speech that, beginning with a critique of Thiriart's experiment, launched what the Italian press nicknamed "Nazi-Maoism," but which, above all, provided ideological ammunition for the "strategy of tension."[110]

A Long, Dragged-Out Anti–May 1968

Franco Freda called for terrorism and the union of all anti-American and anti-Zionist forces until the fall of the "System," that is, capitalist dictatorship in its liberal or Socialist form. His goal was the installation of the "organic state" and "the hierarchical order," which would clean up what remained of liberalism in the Fascist states and would become the ally of all the anticapitalist states.[111] Lotta di Popolo, established on his precepts, was founded by former members of Giovane Nazione, Ordine Nuovo, MSI, and the Movimento Studentesco Operaio d'Avanguardia, formerly the Movimento di Giurisprudenza—founded by Serafino di Luia as a splinter group of Avanguardia Nazionale, after he had returned from training in Greece in countersubversive techniques. The political tone of the far right was changing because, with the Italian "May 1968," an oscillation in its ideological positions was set in motion, sending mixed signals about its ideological offerings. For example, the PLO's most famous slogans were: "Long live the Fascist dictatorship of the

proletariat!" and "Hitler and Mao united in struggle."[112] Lotta di
Popolo was soon imitated in France by the Organisation Lutte
du Peuple (Struggling People's Organization), founded by Yves Bataille after he was ousted from the neo-Fascist ON. All the groups
were trying to scramble the ideological lexicons to adapt to the
leftism of their respective countries: Lotta di Popolo borrowed from
the Maoists, the PLO from the Trotskyists (it explained to its militants:
"Don't be afraid to use so-called leftist terminology, provided, of course,
you specify or modify its meaning").[113] The PLO denounced the West
and "a Europe mentally and politically colonized" by cultural imperialism, the only solution to which was "a class struggle between ruling
nations and ruled nations," that is, a "fight for liberation from imperialism (USA-USSR-ZIONISM)," which was the work of the Jews.
That liberation was supposed to eliminate the "pro-Russian or pro-
American Kollabos," and "it will build a new cultural order founded
on a virile Socialism: European Socialism."[114]

Franco Freda used his position as a publisher to familiarize Italians with the ideas of Codreanu and Duprat, for example. When he
was incarcerated for his role in the Piazza Fontana bombing, the
European radical far right was prompted to mobilize on his behalf
and to disseminate his writings.[115] The beginnings of an international
organization were set in place with the Comité de Liaison Européen
Révolutionnaire (CLER; European Revolutionary Liaison Committee).
The French announced that, with their impending arrival on the
Iberian Peninsula, the committee would give rise, "under cover,"
to a Lucha del Pueblo branch, built by members of the Partido Español
Nacional Socialista and the Movimiento Social Español. The operation foundered, because the Spanish preferred to come to an agreement with the Italian "Nazifascist" militants (as the Italians called
them) of Avanguardia Nazionale.[116] The CLER nevertheless received
extra assistance from a German branch, after the founding in 1974
of the Nationalrevolutionäre Aufbauorganisation-Sache des Volkes
(NARO-SdV; National Revolutionary Organizational Structure–
People's Cause). The NARO-SdV brought together about 450 mili-

tants on the doctrinal foundations of Henning Eichberg's *Manifesto of the People's Cause* (Eichberg began as an activist in Otto Strasser's Deutsche Soziale Union in 1956, adopting Europeanist and neutralist positions, while at the same time discovering the Conservative Revolution). The organization attempted to reach out to both the far right and the far left, declared an anti-Christian orientation, and then, from 1979 on, moved in the direction of the environmentalist movement. Ernst Niekisch was promoted to chief opponent of Hitlerism; the NARO-SdV also revived the nationalist proclamation of the German Communist Party regarding the "national and social liberation of the German people" (which dates from 1930), as well as a line from Lenin: "Make the people's cause the nation's cause, and the nation's cause will be the people's cause." This slogan was already very common in the National Bolshevik movement during the Weimar Republic, and it became a mantra for the revolutionary nationalist groups in Europe. Several Belgian groups, though not linked to that network, were greatly inspired by these experiments until the late 1970s. They included the Association Politique pour un Ordre Nouveau (Political Association for a New Order), which became the Mouvement Socialiste Populaire (Popular Socialist Movement).[117]

The acculturation of leftism to neo-Nazism was attempted in particular by the most notorious French group in the NEO. The Fédération d'Action Nationaliste-Européenne was founded in 1966 via the merger of three groups: Action-Occident, established in 1966; the Comité de Soutien (Support Committee) at Debbaudt's newspaper, *L'Europe réelle;* and the Cercle Charlemagne (its name was an allusion to the eponymous SS Division), a European Socialist group that broke away from Jeune Europe, preferring Lecerf to Thiriart, and was headed by Jean-Claude Jacquard. They had made the pseudo-leftist turn in 1968, even claiming that some of their militants had been arrested on the barricades—which law enforcement officials by no means confirm. But they now claimed that the heirs of René Binet could make common cause with those of Che Guevara.[118] For the most part, the French groups in the NEO followed François Duprat when he left—and then returned to—that organization. Duprat, an ON doctrinaire and a key figure in the creation of the National Front in 1972, was ousted from both movements in 1973. He then spent a brief period back in the NEO. He left it again in early 1974, with a portion of Jeunesses d'Action Européenne (JAE), in order to support Jean-Marie Le Pen's presidential candidacy that year. Duprat subsequently rejoined the National Front, becoming its second-in-command, while the militants from JAE organized the FN's youth branch. The FANE offered Duprat the joint commission journal bequeathed to it by a Hungarian refugee, thus making possible the production of the first and last revolutionary nationalist weekly in France: *Les Cahiers européens*. Duprat, in fact, had adopted concepts from Arrow Cross to establish ON's geopolitical doctrine. Around this newspaper, which was also distributed in Belgium, he organized the Groupes Nationalistes-Révolutionnaires de Base (GNR; Rank-and-File Revolutionary Nationalist Groups), in which the FANE participated. At the same time, the radical militants became FN cadres and candidates. After the GNR's leader was murdered in 1978, the groups broke apart. Because of the financing the FANE received from the British National Front, its propaganda capacities grew exponentially. But, because of its activism, combined in 1980 with its plausible but false claim of responsibility for the bombing of a synagogue on Rue Copernic in Paris (four dead and ten wounded), perpetrated by a Zionist militant who had infiltrated the movement, the state outlawed the FANE, renewing the ban twice on a legal technicality.[119]

That does not mean that French neo-Nazis stood apart from the European terrorist unrest occurring at the time (it was in fact very intense in France). Contacts between the FANE and the authors of the Bologna massacre have been alleged, and their concealment of German neo-Nazi terrorists has been proven, as have close ties to the Hoffman group, a neo-Nazi terrorist organization in Germany linked for a time to the Fatah. One of the members of the FANE even participated in the Hoffman group.[120] The FANE's attempt to organize, on a continental scale (its "first European Fascist council" in 1980 brought together Walloon, Flemish, Austrian, German, and Swiss neo-Nazi militants in Paris), a form of neo-Nazism with both activist and political ambitions met with failure.[121]

That raises the question, painful for the parties concerned, of what nationalist internationalism ultimately accomplished. European conferences, but without any real inclination to build an organic framework, were also attempted. The first major neo-Fascist meeting of the post–World War II period took place in Munich in 1972. Twelve hundred attended, representing, for Germany, the NPD and various newspapers, including *Nation Europa*; for Austria, the Nationaldemokratische Partei (NDP) and various small groups; for Italy, Ordine Nuovo and Avanguardia Nazionale; for Belgium, the Vlaamse Militanten Organisatie (VMO) and Were Di; for Great Britain, the Union Movement; and, for France, ON. The World Union of National Socialists was the only international organization in attendance. A meeting in Antwerp in 1973 included the VMO, Aktion Neue Rechte (essentially) for Germany, the MSI, the Austrian NDP, and members of the newly dissolved ON, the FANE, and *Combat européen* for France.[122] International relations often amounted to what Thiriart mocked under the nickname "mailbox internationals." Such was the case for the revolutionary nationalist international established in the 1980s. On April 3, 1987, the French Troisième Voie (Third Way) movement assembled in Paris an international group called the Coordination Européenne Nationaliste (European Nationalist Coordination) that comprised the British National Front, the Basas Autonomas and Falange Española de las JONS from Spain, the Parti des Forces Nouvelles (Party of New Forces) from Belgium, and the Movimiento de Accao Nacional from Portugal. The ideological charter that united them was drawn up by Troisième Voie. In early 1986 it published its *Manifesto of the Nation Europe*, which was later approved organization by organization (with the Spanish Falange in the lead). After the meeting, the Italians of Terza Posizione and the Swiss of Troisième Voie also joined the Coordination

Européenne Nationaliste.[123] Clearly, the weak link was Germany, where Troisième Voie considered establishing ties with the NPD, but that group did not really fit the ideological brand, and no real contact was made.[124]

That fluid form of international cooperation is not without interest, however, as evidenced by the propaganda campaign that took place with the founding of Troisième Voie. In view of the context, opposition to immigration was the chosen theme, the desire being to establish a better niche market in that area than the French National Front had.[125] A poster proclaimed "Bon voyage mon pote!" (So long, pal!) with a graphic of an Arab in a djellaba, a bundle of clothes on his shoulder. The humorous tone reconciled an ethnodifferentialist posture with racist political consumer appeal. The document so pleased militants that supplies quickly ran out. It was then perpetually reprinted in France, Unité Radicale having made it a hot item. That French success led correspondents across Europe to co-opt it. Furthermore, when a suit was filed against the Belgian Parti des Forces Nouvelles (Party of New Forces) on the grounds of racism, after it produced a poster and sign with the slogan "Nous nous les rapatrierons" (We will repatriate them), inspired by the French poster, a Belgian cadre wrote to the Troisième Voie leadership to ask "what decision is expected on your lawsuits on the same grounds, so that [you] may aid in our defense."[126]

An overhaul of Fascism had certainly taken place. But, despite the desire of Fascist movements, a supernational and social reorientation has not really taken hold. Their efforts have not been fruitless, however, because their innovations were useful to both populist and neorightist factions. The neo-Fascists, in their organizations, their human capital, and their ideas, tend to wander from one camp to another. The acute shortage of capable cadres in every nation has given their "pooling" of resources and their interconnections a great deal of importance. The internationalization of the neo-Fascists lies in their *doxa* and in their praxis, which means that everything normally considered constitutive of the political has now become nothing but exchangeable signs: their doctrinal designation, their logos, and their slogans are available within a market of political semiotics that has realized the utopian dream of a free global supply of information and communication. Just as Fascism, with its mass movements and hierarchization, revealed something about industrial society, so too neo-Fascism has come to fit the mold of postmodernity. The persistent failure to constitute international organizations can therefore be viewed from a completely different angle: for if the model of the international was politically relevant during the industrial era (consider Stalin's use of it), its efficacy beyond that era has not been demonstrated. The relational networks for the transfer of signs, methods, vocabulary, and ideas acquired a completely different efficacy in the last decades of the twentieth century. That has tended, however, to push the neo-Fascists toward intellectual products much less elaborate than what they wished for, and in particular, toward white affirmationism.

2

White Power

The constitution of an international union of white people is the guiding principle behind certain movements, for example, the World Union of National Socialists (WUNS), which best represents what Roger Griffin calls "Universal Nazism." It came into existence in England in the summer of 1962, thanks to the rapprochement between George Lincoln Rockwell (American Nazi Party) and the Briton Colin Jordan (National Socialist Movement). Its foundation charter reads like a declaration of religious faith and embraces seven principles: "the struggle for race," the organic character of every society, the respect for the eternal laws of nature, the struggle for life, the denial of the supremacy of money, the individual's right to personal development, and the belief "that Adolf Hitler was the gift of an inscrutable Providence to a world on the brink of Zionist-Bolshevik catastrophe."[1]

A Transatlantic Sectarianism

One of the cadres of the WUNS is Yves Jeanne. He was a monarchist militant, a member of the Parti Populaire Français (PPF), a recruiting sergeant for the Waffen-SS, the Algiers president of the Friends of *Rivarol,* the leader of the Friends of *Défense de l'Occident,* and the head of the European Social Movement (ESM). One indication of the atmosphere of the WUNS is that Jeanne swore an oath to Colin Jordan with his hand on a Sturmabteilung (SA) dagger.[2] The organization has remained an oddball cult in Europe, but it flourished in Latin America, particularly in Argentina and Chile. Colin Jordan's marriage to the niece of the fashion designer Christian Dior attracted media attention, especially since Françoise Dior was not afraid to wear a gold swastika around her neck. But in May 1964, when the police broke up the West European Federation of the WUNS, established in September 1963, the group had only about fifty members, most of them social misfits.[3] The ambience was hardly political: at the time, Jean-Claude Monnet was trying to achieve recognition as the French leader of the WUNS, turning his Organisation des Vikings de France (Organization of the Vikings of France) into a Parti Prolétarien National-Socialiste (PPNS; National Socialist Proletarian Party), whose newspaper, *Le Viking,* praised the "Russo-Aryan" USSR and affirmed that it wanted a "federation of the ethnic nations" in Europe, leading to an "Aryan world state." Ultimately, in 1969, the PPNS was replaced by a Grande Loge Du Vril (Grand Lodge of the Vril), whose name is a reference to theories about the occult foundations of Nazism.[4] The French remnants of the WUNS would become part of the New European Order (NEO).

After Rockwell's murder in 1967, committed by a member of the American Nazi Party, the WUNS leadership was transferred to Matt Koehl. Koehl, who looked like someone doing a bad impression of Hitler, was a believer in a religious conception of Nazism (inspired by the esoteric Nazi views of the Frenchwoman Savitri Devi, the Chilean Miguel Serrano, and the Dutchwoman Florentine Rost van Tonningen), which created tensions in the organization: its secretary general, Poul Heinrich Riis-Knudsen, head of the Danmarks Nationalsocialistiske Bevaegelse, did not share that mysticism. The difference between the two men is in fact transatlantic. A myriad of neo-Nazi "religious cults" had developed in the United States but were transplanted to European organizations only with great difficulty. For example, the World Church of the Creator, founded in the United States in 1973 by the Ukrainian-born Bernhardt Klassen, did not gain a foothold in Sweden until 1989, followed by France in 2001. Its "chapters" combined practices imported from the Adventist churches with a parodic neo-Nazism (the formation of a "Security Legion," the Nazi salute accompanied by the shout "RaHoWa," a contraction of "racial holy war").[5] These cult forms of Nazism appear inassimilable to secularized European societies. In fact, the tensions raised within the WUNS around that question led to its takeover by Colin Jordan, who managed to span the difference between the two shores of the Atlantic.

At that stage, however, "Universal Nazism" had primarily become the concern of Gary Rex Lauck (b. 1953), founder of the National-sozialistische Deutsche Arbeiterpartei—Auslands-Organisation (NSDAP-AO, that is, the Nazi Party "in exile"). Lauck epitomizes the sectarian cult leader with solid entrepreneurial abilities. The NSDAP-AO is a company that exports propaganda in twelve languages (books, posters, military souvenirs, the reviews *NS-Kampfruf* and *The New Order*) and whose specialty, within the context of the American system of freedom of expression, is the distribution of the most extreme examples of Nazi literature, which are generally banned in Europe. The Web has become central to that type of neo-Nazism.

After Jordan's death in 2009, the WUNS was relaunched by Jeff Schoepp (American National Socialist Movement), who adapted it for a young skinhead audience, offering video games and clothing via the White Power music Web site. The WUNS is now primarily a network of Web sites, sometimes providing a wealth of background information and theoretical documents (such is the case in Spain and France), but the group lacks a militant base. The largest affiliated organizations are the Russian National Union, the former British People's Party (which dissolved in 2013 in favor of the British National Front), and the Italian Fascismo e Libertà (Fascism and Freedom), founded in 1991 by Movimento Sociale Italiano senator Giorgio Pisano, on a platform that referenced the Republic of Salò.

The phenomenon of "exotic Nazism" is very much in vogue in certain media outlets, and the WUNS has not avoided it any more than the NSDAP-AO and its various branches. These outlets showcase small groups throughout the world, generally with only a handful of members. The element of surprise lies in the contrast between the ethnonational group concerned and the ideology it embraces. For example, the WUNS will introduce among its affiliated members an Iranian or a Japanese, or perhaps a Brazilian Nazi Party. They are symptomatic of a recurrent phenomenon: neo-Nazism is more cultural than political in nature. It is often a mode of expression for the young, a rejection of the generally accepted codes, a mimicking of what is judged to be the most transgressive ideology.[6] That approach has many weaknesses but also a few advantages. In terms of militancy, the Universal Nazism framework allows for joint propaganda actions and for the establishment of contacts via networks. In early 1983, in the absence of any official international organization, "many tracts appeared (especially in London, Cologne, Bern, Madrid, Milan, and Poitiers), taking as their pretext the Nigerian government's measures to require immigrants to leave the country."[7] Although completely unstructured, this was practical militant action extending beyond mere personal relations between militants and groups.

This type of neo-Nazism, because it is in part a segment of youth culture, is also well adapted to a Western society where youth "movements" have been able to flourish since the 1960s, provided they are "cultural" and not "partisan." The influence of the English-speaking world on European neo-Nazism is significant in that respect. White affirmationism has truly supplanted the hierarchizing racialism of Hitlerism. Its vehicle is less a written doctrine than a slogan: "White Power," which George Lincoln Rockwell launched in response to the Black Power movement. The principal demand is the territorial separation of whites from the other races. White people, though considered genetically and culturally superior, would be in need of a politics of race consciousness. For the most part, as in the doctrine of apartheid in South Africa, the Jews are not included in the white race. American Renaissance, created by Jared Taylor, is one of the few movements that embraces the opposite view. It holds annual conferences, whose speakers have included Bruno Gollnisch (French National Front), Nick Griffin (British National Party, or BNP), and the Canadian negationist Frederick Paul Fromm. Taylor expressed his agreement with the French Nouvelle Droite essayist Guillaume Faye, after one of his books launched a controversy in far-right circles. For Faye and Taylor, the Jews must be considered tactical allies in the impending race war against Islam.[8] The theme of White Power provided a rallying point for both the skinhead sociocultural phenomenon and the activist groups proper.

The Far-Right Skinheads

The skinhead movement emerged in English working-class neighborhoods in the late 1960s. In the postindustrial era, it is the only real far-right proletarian movement and one of the very few on the international scene to have organized the political through both business concerns (record companies, distribution networks) and the noncommercial sector ("skinzines," that is, skin fanzines). In that respect, it is a prototypical case of postindustrial society's modes of life and of violence. It is one of the rare places where the far right has managed to create a discourse of social protest without having to borrow its rhetoric from the left. In addition, the skinhead "uniform" has become a widespread symbol of self-marginalization, even on the ultraleft, and—a particularly significant phenomenon—has ended up being co-opted and depoliticized by consumer society. The first skinheads came out of the Mods youth movement, a product of the 1960s: apolitical, enthralled with rhythm and blues, soul music, and Vespa scooters equipped with rearview mirrors. These first skinheads asserted their working-class pride, in opposition to leisure society. They sometimes beat up groups of Pakistanis, but this was gang violence, not political action, just as their rioting outside soccer stadiums was a tradition of the English lumpenproletariat, one that had taken a more radical turn in the 1950s but that dated back to the early part of the century. The skinhead movement, inactive for a few years, was rediscovered by a new generation in 1977, in reaction to the punk movement, some of whose members radicalized it as "street punk" and accentuated the aggressive character of certain aspects of the skinhead uniform they had adopted.[9]

This was also a time when radicals were becoming receptive to pop culture. The Italian neo-Fascists in the Janus group produced a militant strain of hard rock music in the 1970s. Rock can be assimilated to a white culture and can become an element of revolutionary nationalist culture. One of the essential markers of that fringe culture is the cartoon character Black Rat, invented by the artist Jack Marchal in 1970 as a mascot for the Groupe Union Droit (GUD), and which was adopted by young neo-Fascists in various European nations. After designing the Janus album cover, Marchal tried his own luck as a musician. With friends, he recorded an album of French hard rock, *Science & Violence* (1979). German students in the Nationaldemokratische Partei Deutschlands (NPD) formed the first German nationalist rock group in 1977. At this early stage, the British National Front, losing ground in electoral politics, turned toward that movement, even as it began to scout out the hooligan movement.

The skinhead music scene became more organized with its new music, a variant of punk called "Oi!" a contraction of "Hey, you!" pronounced with a Cockney accent. Rock against Communism (RAC) made its appearance in England in 1982 in reaction to the Rock against Fascism movement. A British National Front channel of communication within the skinhead youth movement, it was launched by Ian Stuart Donaldson (1957–1993), leader of the group Oi! Skrewdriver, which achieved mythical status among European skinheads. The movement took shape in 1985, with a split within White Noise Club, which had been launched by the British National Front. That led in 1987 to the creation of Blood and Honour, whose name was taken from a Nazi slogan. Blood and Honour "divisions" manifest an uninhibited racism and embrace neo-Nazism, but they are clearly more interested in concert reviews than in partisan political action. They have attracted attention from time to time, for example, when they attacked two journalists at the end of the Fête de l'Identité (Identity Festival) held in Versailles in 2003. In 2007, when the French National Front, under Alain Soral's influence, exhibited on one of its posters a young Frenchwoman of North African descent with a navel piercing, the French members of Blood and Honour clearly stated their absolute distrust of electoral nationalism of any kind.[10] The group called for the unity of skinheads and was close to Combat 18, the "international" that truly represents the world of skins. Its logo is the Totenkopf SS, the infamous skull of the SS in charge of the concentration camps; "18" refers to the first and eighth letters of the alphabet, A and H, for "Adolf Hitler." Blood and Honour is not an internationally organized movement but a sort of franchise chain; each cell forms autonomously.[11] Another international organization, the Hammerskins Nation, was founded in Dallas, Texas, in 1986, and has sought to federate the skinhead movement globally.[12]

The skinhead sociopolitical construction occurred at a time when the proletariat was deconstructing. Because this deconstruction occurred simultaneously with that of international borders, the phenomenon was easily exported. The skinhead movement became polarized on the radical far right between 1983 and 1986 in most European countries (France, Greece, Hungary) and shortly after 1989 in some Eastern European countries (the Czech Republic, Romania).[13] Since the transition to capitalism, the movement has become particularly strong in the eastern part of the continent. In Slovakia, the Nové Slobodné Slovensko and Slovenská Pospolitost' political movements are closely linked to that scene. At times, the skinhead movement portrays itself as a defense group against the Roma: in the Czech Republic after 1993, the Bohemia Hammerskins dedicated themselves to anti-Gypsy violence.[14] In the Baltic countries, the movement appeared in the 1980s as an expression of patriotic pride, in protest against Russia. And in Russia, skinhead groups emerged in about 1996: some were autonomous, while others were homegrown branches of Blood and Honour or the Hammerskins. Their violence attracted the attention of the Russian nationalist network and of the German nationalists and the Americans. The change of scale was enormous: the number of Russian skinheads can be estimated at about 50,000, and in 2006 an anti-Chechen pogrom may have attracted 2,000 rioters (both government authorities and the general public took some satisfaction in these "outbursts").[15]

The apolitical or leftist skinheads reject the use of the word "skinhead" for right-wing extremists, believing they themselves hold the monopoly on that designation and that the others ought to be called "boneheads." But that notion is mocked by the far-right skinheads. Ian Stuart spelled it out when he declared that "to be a skinhead is to be a National Socialist"; and the Italians of Verde Bianco Rosso say that "Il Duce was the first skinhead."[16] The assertion of autonomy by young skinheads on the far right has been accompanied by attempts at self-organization. In 1986 Gaël Bodilis, a worker at the Brest Arsenal, founded the music label RAC Rebelles Européens, which has an allegiance to neo-Nazism. It rapidly became the second-largest far-right skinhead label in Europe. It was active in the Front National de la Jeunesse and in the neo-Fascist group Troisième Voie, and later became associated with the neo-Nazi Parti Nationaliste Français et Européen (it adopted the Totenkopf logo at that time). This is an indication of the difficulty the skinhead scene has had in acquiring a stable political structure.[17] Its commercial organization is also fairly weak: for the most part, it was only in Sweden that White Power rock briefly penetrated the mainstream market, when the group Ultima Thule reached the top of the charts in 1993. The only structured skinhead organization in France was Jeunesses Nationalistes-Révolutionnaires (JNR; Revolutionary Nationalist Youth), under the leadership of Serge Ayoub, alias "Batskin," who did not himself come from the proletariat. Founded in 1987, the group was linked to the Rebelles Européens label and to the RAC Evilskins, but also to the revolutionary nationalist movement Troisième Voie, then to the Parti Nationaliste Français, launched in 1983 by two former members of the Waffen-SS, Pierre Bousquet and Jean Castrillo, after they split off from the FN in 1980 (on the grounds that Jean-Marie Le Pen was a puppet of the Jews).[18]

Serge Ayoub, in addition to being comfortable with managing unruly troops, knows how to express himself to a vast audience, and was for some time a regular in the mass media. He succeeded in situating the unrest within a historical and political perspective, proposing parallels between skinheads and the Nazi Party's SA, but also claiming that his revolutionary nationalism had its origins in Gracchus Babeuf's Société des Égaux (Society of Equals), the same organization that Karl Marx judged to be the first draft, historically speaking, of a Communist party. The JNR also performed policing functions for the French National Front, which even proposed placing Serge Ayoub at the top of the ticket in the municipal elections. He refused, protesting that the FN's law enforcement arm had collaborated with the police in the arrest of the skinheads who had killed Brahim Bouarram on the sidelines of a May Day parade.[19] Nevertheless, violence is no longer an instrument for constructing the political, as it was during the interwar period. After mass attacks on immigrants by skinheads in Rouen and Brest, the skinheads were isolated politically; even radical far-right groups feared their excesses. Isolation and police repression (which became intense after racist murders committed in 1988 and 1995) led a number of skinheads to abandon their fringe status, while others preferred to switch over to hooliganism. Serge Ayoub returned to politics in 2010, (re)launching Troisième Voie and the JNR, and succeeded in distributing a newspaper on the newsstands (its name, *Salut public,* was borrowed from the theoretical review of Duprat's Groupes Nationalistes-Révolutionnaires). These ventures have been well received and seem to have filled the void left by the dissolution of Unité Radicale (UR) in 2002. The Nord-Pas-de-Calais branch of Troisième Voie, launched on August 27, 2011, had thirty-two members by late September, while the Hérault branch had twenty-two.[20] Troisième Voie and JNR, though they remained discreet during the protests against marriage equality, were dissolved by the government in 2013 after the murder by skinheads of Clément Méric, a young "antifa" (anti-Fascist) militant. That death was in fact one of several violent racist attacks committed by skinheads.[21]

The question of violence also played an important role in the fate of the Parti Nationaliste Français et Européen (PNFE). The birth announcement of that splinter group of the Italian Partito Nazionale Fascista (National Fascist Party) was issued in 1987, at Euroring, a conference of Belgian, English, French, and German neo-Nazi organizations. It had no political ambitions but confined itself to building group solidarity.[22] The white supremacy of the PNFE led to a backward-looking utopianism with respect to European nationalist advances. In fact, its slogan was "France first, white always," even though the Maurrassian expression "France first" had already been mocked by Robert Brasillach for being too narrow. That did not prevent the PNFE from serving as a model, as attested by the 1991 creation of a sister party, the Parti Nationaliste Suisse et Européen, composed primarily of skinheads and later replaced by a Hammerskins branch. The PNFE did not adopt a more moderate tone as a result: the characterization of blacks as animals and hatred of the "kikes" are omnipresent in its writings. Nor did it modulate its methods: the PNFE welcomed the skinheads with open arms and was involved in a series of attacks against immigrant housing (leading to a wave of repression, with 399 arrests of PNFE members in 1987–1989). It was also members of that group who profaned the Jewish cemetery of Carpentras in 1991. The PNFE had about a thousand sympathizers and militants, but it was compelled to dissolve in 1999. The main leader of the group, Erik Sausset from Normandy, later participated in the activities of Terre et Peuple (Land and People), the new right völkisch movement of Pierre Vial, who regularly invited cadres from the NPD to his conferences. Another PNFE cadre, the skinhead Didier Magnien, followed a remarkable trajectory: leader of the movement in

Île-de-France, he was a militant in Unité Radicale beginning in 1999. He appeared in that movement's press in conjunction with the NPD's activities. He in fact migrated to Germany and was a major presence in the most activist circles. That led to his arrest in 2004, during a police operation to prevent a neo-Nazi attack on a Jewish community center in Munich. But it was also revealed that he was a member of the Federal Office for the Protection of the Constitution and was in charge of surveillance and repression of neo-Nazi activities.

What ideological foundations can unite such diverse individuals? The central ideological themes that have appeared in the skinhead movement are the ethnic war to be waged and the denunciation of a global Jewish conspiracy promoting miscegenation. In a surge typical of cultural globalization, and despite the weight of esoteric neo-Nazism, what is developing is a new youth culture, with rituals and an antidogmatism that are by no means a carbon copy of the Fascist youth organizations of the first half of the twentieth century. Whatever their references to totalitarian regimes, it is obvious that the skinheads ascribe much more value to disorder than to order. These sociological elements emerged from a movement of defiant young proletarians (except in Russia, where the skinheads in the big cities have come from the educated middle classes), where the Nazi reference was at first largely provocative; they crystallized thanks largely to the contribution of American neo-Nazism.

In the end, the far-right skinhead can be distinguished by a few general characteristics: racism; proletarian consciousness; an aversion to organization, dismissed in favor of gang behavior; an ideological training that began with or is based on music. A skinhead need not be neo-Nazi, but neo-Nazism is hegemonic in the far-right skinhead groups. He is not necessarily physically violent, but he participates in a group that extols and practices violence. His involvement is emotional first and foremost, which explains why he may occasionally move from the neo-Nazis to anti-Fascist skinhead groups, depending on the circumstances. These young proletarians turn neither to the left, which according to them is more inclined to defend the "immigrant delinquent" than "the hard-working white guy," nor to the right, whose conservatism is alien to their own mind-set and mode of life. For them, "the system" has abandoned the little guy, and gangs constitute a countersociety of pleasure and solidarity. Their Nazifying provocations are also a way of responding to the sacralization of the memory of World War II. In fact, their violence and their belligerent discourse raise real questions, not the least of which concern the hypocrisy with which their activities are sometimes met. In Rostock, Germany, racist violence occurred in late August 1992, to the applause of neighbors, while the law obligingly looked the other way. Alongside the skinheads, ordinary citizens lynched immigrant workers, as passersby cheered. In every country, the White Power movement shows what happens when entire swathes of marginal populations are abandoned to economic violence. In the absence of a social movement on the left capable of producing "class consciousness" (that is, a collective identity) or of an ideological movement on the right able to legitimize social hierarchization, racialism takes the upper hand and divides up the social body based on its own criteria. The anomie of the proletariat and of the pauperized middle classes provides fertile ground for an ideological product manufactured through hybridization and taking different forms each time. And that very plasticity allows for new dynamics, whether political or cultural.

The Norwegian Kristian "Varg" Vikernes launched the musical trend for National Socialist Black Metal (NSBM) on the European continent (he was arrested in France in 2013), but few skinheads in Western Europe have taken any interest in it. NSBM is primarily a phenomenon of northern and eastern Europe. All the hottest bands on the Europagan scene since the 1990s have played industrial music and dark folk (the English groups Death in June, Current 93, and Sol Invictus, and the Slovenian Laibach, among others), which involve the full range of provocations: SS runic insignia, antimonotheism, references to Julius Evola, and so on.[23] Musical diversification has occurred, however, and corresponds to political patterns, but that dynamic is the mark of America's influence on the European environment. These new musical forms have as much to do with the cultural battlefield as with violence.

Violence, Radicalism, Populism

In 1969 the American neo-Nazis Joseph Tommasi and William Pierce founded the National Socialist Liberation Front in the hope of fusing a mystical neo-Nazism with the counterculture and of forming a link with leftist revolutionaries (a perspective altogether similar to that of their European counterparts during the same period). In 1974 Tommasi (who was murdered the next year) invented the "lone wolf" method, which was supposed to allow for action despite the power of the "Zionist Occupation Government" (ZOG), supposedly capable of infiltrating any group. That methodology of individual action should not be confused (as it often is) with the question of self-radicalization: the lone wolf belongs to a milieu. In 1971 Pierce became leader of the National Alliance. He maintained ties with English neo-Nazi groups, which would later work their way into the skinhead milieu. He was aware of the need to present politics in a different way. In 1978 he published what would become the global best seller of the neo-Nazi movement: *The Turner Diaries*. The book tells of the final race struggle, the uprising of white supremacists against Zionist power. It provides many details on the art of bomb making (it influenced both Timothy McVeigh, the far-right militant who committed the 1995 Oklahoma City attack that left 168 dead, and the Norwegian terrorist Anders Behring Breivik) and many fantasies about nuclear, chemical, and biological warfare against non-Aryan populations. The book fired the imaginations of skinheads internationally, providing a perspective that went far beyond mere racist brawls. Young militants in the National Alliance, fans of the book, turned to terrorism, creating The Order in 1983. One of their members, David Lane, invented the Fourteen Words, destined to be translated and adopted by various European skinheads: "We must

secure the existence of our people and a future for white children."
(David Lane is currently serving a 150-year prison sentence for
murder.) And finally, these elements were complemented by the the-
orization in 1983 of the "Leaderless Resistance" by the American
white supremacist Louis Beam (Aryan Nation). He said he was inspired by a model developed by a U.S. intelligence officer to fend off
a potential Communist takeover in the 1960s. It consisted of setting
up terrorist cells bound together by an objective and a strategy, but
which maintained no relation to one another, either horizontal or ver-
tical.[24] His theory spread in American neo-Nazi circles in the 1990s,
in tandem with the "lone wolf" theory and *The Turner Diaries*. The
two theories reached Europe together, thanks to the rise of the
Internet.

The new methods, in addition to evoking somewhat the practices
of antisubversive struggle developed in Europe, particularly in France
and Italy, beginning in the 1960s, are closely linked to Islamist
terrorism in the twenty-first century. They are also at work in the
attacks committed by the European radical far right: the bombs set
off in London by the white supremacist David Copeland in 1999;
the attacks perpetrated by Anders Behring Breivik in Norway in 2011;
and the xenophobic murders committed in Germany since 1997 by
the Nationalsozialistischer Untergrund (NSU), which spent fourteen
years underground without ever being identified, and whose actions
came to light in 2011. These attacks demonstrate the validity of the
hypothesis that radical militants disappointed by the few political
outlets provided by the legal parties turn to armed struggle.

The adjective "neo-Nazi" cannot be applied to Anders Behring
Breivik, though the notion of the hybridization of factions across
countries and continents sheds light on his actions. Breivik transferred to Europe the American far right's hatred of the state: he
destroyed a government building and attacked the members of Ar-
beidernes Ungdomsfylking, a social democratic youth movement to
which Jens Stoltenberg, Norway's prime minister at the time, had
once belonged. A number of the European revolutionary nationalist

movements of the 1980s–1990s had already taken to combining Fascist references with a permanent denunciation of the state and its repressive functions, praise of the nation with the defense of a regional and productive federalism that sometimes verges on councilism. The Norwegian terrorist imported the American distrust of the federal government, a distrust rooted in the conviction that the only legitimate power is one exercised at the county or state level. That attitude dates back to the Antifederalists of 1788 and remains part of the democratic consensus, as the Tea Party movement demonstrates. Nevertheless, it is the notion of a Zionist Occupation Government that Breivik both used and inverted: on one hand, he considers the legitimate government of Norway to be complicitous in a veritable ethnic and cultural occupation; on the other, the force that is supposedly bringing about the disintegration of national identity and civilization is no longer the Jews but Islam. Breivik, like his European predecessors in the twentieth century, believes that the "System" and its "cultural socialism" liquidate the ethnic community, but he conceives of them within the framework of an Islamophobic Occidentalism. What is most notable about the cobbled-together ideology that motivated his recourse to violence is that the central idea of his manifesto, titled *2083: A European Declaration of Independence,* is now the basis of the new political program of European neopopulism. The terrorist Breivik is not a neo-Nazi but an Occidentalist, even more than a Norwegian nationalist. It is significant, in fact, that he wrote in English and not in his native language. Central to his worldview is the concept of Eurabia, developed by the British essayist Bat Ye'or (the pen name of Gisèle Littman-Orebi).

The fantasy of Eurabia rests, first, on the belief in a voluntary cultural and political submission on the part of Europe (France in the first place) to multiculturalism, for which globalized elites are responsible; and second, on the obsession with "dhimmitude" (which also means "submission"), supposedly being imposed on Europeans by an Islam that by its very nature is totalitarian and seeks to conquer. (In fact, the belief is that Europeans consent to dhimmitude, either out of weakness or because of an atavistic anti-Semitism.) In this view, Islam is in the process of becoming the majority religion, by means of the immigration and settlement of Muslim populations. That radical simplification of the theory of the clash of civilizations is also found in the discourse of the fourth wave of the European far-right parties, represented primarily by the Dutchman Geert Wilders and the Swiss Oskar Freysinger. The fundamental difference is that they (like Bat Ye'or) absolutely reject political violence. Breivik, however, shares with them several ideas that are at odds with the traditional far right, which explains why, for ten years, he was a militant in the Parti du Progrès, one of the first xenophobic populist organizations to win votes (in 1973) without being part of the neo-Fascist family. The first similarity is support for the culture defined as "Judeo-Christian" and for Israel, which distinguishes neopopulists from far-right anti-Semites. The second is a cultural, and no longer dogmatic, Christianity: Breivik, neither a Protestant fundamentalist nor an integrist Catholic, values Christianity as a historical component of European culture and of its landscape. In the same way, the Swiss centralist Union Démocratique opposes the construction of minarets in a country dotted with church steeples. As is fitting in the post-Communist world, Breivik's anti-Marxism is clearly secondary to his vilification of the mingling of peoples and cultures. Finally, he blithely mixes together the components of several fringe cultures that proliferate in cyberspace, in particular, those that embrace conspiracy theories, a fascination with the occult, and a completely antitraditional and almost counterinitiatory pseudo-Templarist Freemasonry.[25]

Like the new generation advocating cultural war against Islam in Europe, Breivik is in fact a cybermilitant whose references are drawn from the Islamophobic texts, most of them in English, that abound on the Internet: he is representative of the "far right 2.0," which primarily uses forums, Web sites, and social networks. He is also, like a number of radical Islamists unaffiliated with a terrorist network, an isolated individual radicalized by the escalation of verbal violence on the Web. At the same time, the organized far-right parties, including the French National Front, have had a tendency, by virtue of their electoral success, to lead their most radical sympathizers in the direction of mass violence. The Breivik case, along with that of David Copeland and of the Germans in the NSU, demonstrates that the "lone wolf" and "leaderless resistance" cannot be reduced to self-radicalization. Breivik's life was marked by militantism in the Fremskrittspartiet, Copelands's by the meetings of the British National Party he attended; and the Germans in the NSU spent time in the NPD. The importance of the Breivik case for the future development of the European far right is clear: the fourth-generation neopopulist parties, obliged to inscribe their discourse and practices within the democratic consensus if they want to break out of their isolation and participate in the exercise of power, generate individual aberrations of the terrorist type among their sympathizers. These individuals take at face value the slogans of the neopopulist parties, which proclaim the ineluctability of a race war and the need for a *reconquista* in the face of Islam. Clearly, the far-right field can be interpreted only in terms of the international dialectic of its tendencies (collective, ideological, and sociological). The Islamophobic theme taking hold among the general public and the spasms of the ostracized fringes are not disconnected phenomena. To quote Mao Zedong: a single spark can start a prairie fire.

The trajectories of the leaders of the Bloc Identitaire (Identity Bloc) are evidence of that. Fabrice Robert and Philippe Vardon were originally French revolutionary nationalist skinheads and members of the hardcore rock group Fraction (called Fraction Hexagone when it was founded in 1994). Robert attempted to unite the skinhead movement around his fanzine *Jeune Résistance,* first on behalf of the "Bolshevik-national" Nouvelle Résistance, then for Unité Radicale. The importance of that axis is indicated by Unité Radicale's use in its tracts of David Lane's Fourteen Words and of the expression "ZOG," claiming it is equivalent to "System." Fabrice Robert's choice of music as a means of politicization was inspired by changes in the American scene. In 1994 the American group Rahowa created a record company, Resistance Records, whose products were exported throughout Europe, and a newspaper, *Resistance,* which disseminated globally the acronym ZOG. Inspired by *The Turner Diaries,* it called for terrorist acts against that "Zionist Occupation Government." The record label was ultimately bought out by the National Alliance, which reoriented it toward black metal, but with the same aim. The originality of *Resistance* lay in its approach to the relationship between music and politics: it argued that music ought to lead people who are not racist at the outset to become politically involved in the movement, not just consolidate the convictions of listeners already won over to the cause, as RAC had done. In fact, the group Fraction participated in the launch of the Rock Identitaire Français (RIF) scene. The expression "French Identity Rock," which appeared in 1997, is misleading, in that RIF covers all musical genres, having no fear of rap or techno. RIF's declared objective is a far cry from that of RAC: it seeks to attract new people to nationalist ideas. In that sense, RIF is also a means to open the minds of the radical young to the social reality around them, to get them out of the "ghetto" where they tend to congregate. In short, the influence of the tactics of Resistance Records is obvious, but it is expressed for and by an ideology whose aim, this time, is to lead the radical movement away from provocative Nazifying references. But its base is strongly polarized: it is less interested in the themes with leftist connotations sometimes put forward by Fraction and Unité Radicale than in the ethnic and Islamophobic question. Fraction was in the forefront of that change, with its album *Reconquista* (2001). Likewise, the Unité Radicale newspaper *Resistance* and, in Spain, the Alternativa Europa-Liga Social Republicana's *Resistancia* are interested in techno on ethnic foundations, setting up an opposition between that "white" music and "black" rap. These groups thus anticipated the sociological phenomenon of the gabber-skins (fans of hardcore techno in Belgium, Holland, and northern France, who adopted the skinhead look and white affirmationism) and the *makineros* (their counterparts in Spain and Roussillon, France), but were unable to spearhead the movement.[26] Likewise, Fraction, good rock group that it was, chose a logo: that of Otto Strasser's Schwarze Front (Black Front) of 1931. Although the French revolutionary nationalists had made Strasser a historical point of reference for more than twenty years, the symbol had been adopted only by the Rebelles Européens. After Fraction, references to Strasser spread, and the symbol appeared on the posters of the political organizations Nouvelle Résistance and then on those of Unité Radicale in France; from there, it spread to Europe as a whole. In this case, the role of the skinhead scene cannot be called avant-garde. Unlike Italian futurism before the advent of Fascism, it has not sought to deconstruct the political system through its cultural structures; the work of art is not considered a sign that is supposed to subvert the bourgeois moral and legal order. But the skinhead scene did serve as a laboratory for creating forms that could make popular what was not so, just as the Bloc Identitaire continues to do through its agitprop.

Maxime Brunerie's attempted assassination of Jacques Chirac in 2002, which led to the dissolution of Unité Radicale, introduced the lone wolf strategy into the struggle against the "ZOG" in France. Moreover, the leaderless resistance tactic resurfaced in 2003 and 2004 in various attacks: for example, a man formerly close to Unité Radicale tried to blow himself up in a Paris mosque, taking as his model Palestinian suicide bombers. That tactic was also at work in the dismantlement of the armed cell of the Fédération Nationale Catholique. The group, in connection with the musical network Bleu Blanc Rock created by UR, had the originality of embracing both integrist Catholicism and skinhead ideology. The anti-Semitism of its bulletin was very pronounced: it contained articles on Édouard Drumont and Robert Brasillach and claimed responsibility for the anti-Semitic graffiti on an intermediate school in Châteauroux where a Jewish teacher was employed.

Given the state of the movement, the efforts at political reorganization by the Bloc Identitaire have been far reaching. It abandoned anti-Semitism, anti-Zionism, totalitarianism, activism, neopaganism, and other views. It subdivided into various organizations, giving the movement a horizontal structure and protection from legal prosecution. It is no longer attractive to young skinheads: in skinhead forums, they mock the "Bloch Identitaire," claiming that the movement has sold out to the Jews. Although its transformation into an electoral party was a failure, the Bloc Identitaire did manage to organize a targeted agitprop campaign and to federate a vast militant zone. It claims that, when it asked its sympathizers to choose which candidate it ought to endorse in 2012, it received votes from 2,014 Identitaires.[27]

Similar reforms have been set in place in other radical youth groups. Inroads are therefore being made by so-called autonomous groups, such as the German Freie Kameradschaften (Free Fellowships), that have a local and compartmentalized organization to avoid repressive measures and the capacity and desire to go underground or even to engage in terrorism. They also invert themes that, in the eyes of public opinion, are considered leftist: antiglobalization, radical anti-Zionism, and the will to fight the state and its symbols, including the police and the army. The autonomous German nationalists thus combine the tactic of leaderless resistance with the methods of the autonomous Italian ultraleftist movement of the late 1970s. Also gaining a following is an Italian effort to update Fascism, undertaken by the Romans in the CasaPound movement, proponents of an anticapitalist, countercultural, and communitarian Fascism of social action. It has served as a model in various places (for the Movimiento Social Republicano in Madrid, for example), but without the Italians' capacity for countercultural activity. In all cases, individuals who emerged from the skinhead movement have been able to achieve political aims, contrary to the label of imbecility often attached to them.

Greece's Golden Dawn is an important phenomenon in that regard. The group, founded in 1980, was at first an ideological clearinghouse on the model of the Círculo Español de Amigos de Europa (CEDADE), and was affiliated with the NEO. It was so closely associated with the White Power scene that it sought to organize a

Hatewave Festival in 2005. The militant library of the Greek radicals abounds in occultist neo-Nazi titles and, of course, includes *The Turner Diaries* as well as the works of Bardèche, Evola, and Mosley. The party went international, opening branches among Greek minorities living in Germany, Australia, the United States, and Canada. Since 2015, several groups have been constituted throughout Europe that take the name, forms, and slogans of the Greek neo-Nazis: Amanecer Dorado (Spain), Alba Dorata Italia (Italy), Magyar Hajnal (Hungary). For the moment, they have not found the formula that would successfully adapt the dynamic of Golden Dawn to their own national society, given that no country is in the same situation as Greece. Golden Dawn's international ties indicate the interest it has elicited, but not a general programmatic unity: in Spain, for example, Greeks have joined with the Catalanists of Plataforma per Catalunya and the Movimiento Social Republicano, which embraces a federative unity of Spain within the context of an anti–American Zionist Europe, or with the "clash of civilizations" ultras of Democracia Nacional. Golden Dawn maintains regular relations with Jobbik (Hungary), with Forza Nuova and CasaPound (Italy), with the Svenskarnas Parti (Sweden), with the NSU and NPD (Germany), and with Svobodo (Ukraine), despite the latter party's pro-Russian orientation. A quasi-symbiotic partnership exists between Golden Dawn and Ethniko Laiko Metopo (ELAM) in Cyprus. Forza Nuova and Golden Dawn federated the movements with the greatest affinities to one another to form the European National Front, headed by the Italian Roberto Fiore. In addition to these two parties, the front includes the NPD, the British BNP, the Falange Española de las JONS, the Noua Dreapta (New Right, Romania), the Renouveau Français (French Renewal), and the Narodowe Odrodzenie Polski (National Revival of Poland).[28]

In short, the White Power movement and associated groups show how the regeneration of the radical far right is strained by the race question. Although the doctrinaires and cadres of the post–World War II decades have continually sought to breathe new life into Fascism and to disengage it from the liabilities of racist politics, the ethnocultural question probably remains the best catalyst for that movement. In addition, the European national ferment has ultimately proved ineffective. The context for thought and action is clearly transatlantic. However virulent the anti-Americanism of the revolutionary nationalist leaders, Occidentalism likely endures. That is because, in the formulation of the political scientist Gaël Brustier, Occidentalism is the "ideology of the crisis" of the West after 1973. The White Power movement is and aspires to be proletarian, but these same ambiguities undergird the new right, which sees itself as aristocratic.

3

The New Right in All Its Diversity

The political nature of the new right has been the object of a large number of studies in political science. The volume of writings is not unreasonable, since many movements fall under the new right label, and some of the most important, for example, the Groupe de Recherches et d'Études pour la Civilisation Européenne (GRECE), have undergone major changes in the views they express and in how they position themselves—not without an acute tendency to rewrite their own history. The concept of the new right did not originate with the new rightists, who spoke instead of a "new culture." The expression has come to be used in the singular, but in fact it designates ideological currents that may have nothing in common but their "metapolitical" practice. Jacques Marlaud, former president of GRECE, defined that practice as "any work of reflection or analysis, any diffusion of ideas, any cultural practice liable to influence political society over the long term. It is no longer a matter of taking power but of providing those in power with ideological, philosophical, and cultural nourishment that can shape (or contradict) their decisions."[1] The idea of that "right-wing Gramscism"—that is, of the need to wage a cultural battle that imposes, first, the vocabulary of the right, then its ideas—is profoundly marked with GRECE's seal and has become an obligatory formula in the discourse of the French right. But the new right phenomenon is not limited to the intellectual sphere. The new right had not ruled out the possibility of exerting an influence on an eventual intellectual rearmament of the right, in view of recapturing the positions it had lost to the left, which was still hegemonic in the cultural field of the time. The instrument of that influence was the Club de l'Horloge, a think tank of journalists, essayists, and high officials. Founded in 1974 by Yvan Blot, Jean-Yves Le Gallou, and Henry de Lesquen, who were soon joined by Bruno Mégret, the club was for a time under the patronage of Michel Poniatowski. It produced a few books, which received a great deal of commentary on the right (e.g., *Les racines du futur*; [The roots of the future], 1977) and were inspired by a doctrine that can be called social Darwinist (neoliberalism combined with racialism, leading to an integral neo-Darwinism). The club's economic theory gradually became liberal-national. The controversy surrounding GRECE in 1979 would oblige the members of the Club de l'Horloge to distance themselves from the new right in the strict sense and would force the right wing within the government to take its distance from the club. When a number of leaders of the Club de l'Horloge joined the National Front beginning in 1985, the club became merely a bridge between the FN and the classic right. A second factor in the marginalization of the new right was its expulsion in 1981–1982 from the national mainstream press. It had acquired a position of influence there in 1977, when Robert Hersant took over *Le Figaro* and *Le Figaro-Magazine* (whose editorial staff included Louis Pauwels, Patrice de Plunkette, and Jean-Claude Valla; Alain de Benoist himself wrote a regular column for the magazine). The new right's influence had also extended to the Valmonde media group, which was headed by Raymond Bourgine.

Ultimately, the new right fell victim as well to the hegemonic position the National Front achieved on the far right and to its electoral success and media impact. Militant anti-Fascism focused on the FN, leaving the new right to evolve in an atmosphere of indifference. In France, the left, and the vast majority of intellectuals, particularly the leftists, repeatedly refused to establish a dialogue with the new right, even one based on reasoned refutation. (Such a dialogue does exists in Italy, however, and in the columns of *Junge Freiheit* in Germany.) That meant the new right could do no more than spin its wheels. It was placed in a strictly untenable position: that of addressing exclusively an audience that, though it identified with the far right, denied its own participation in that realm. All these elements taken together fostered laziness within a fairly large contingent of the new right. They believed that their solitude was sufficient proof of their value, and their large stock of quotations took the place of intellectual work.

The Plasticity of the New Right

The expression "new right" was first used in the United States after Barry Goldwater's unsuccessful presidential bid in 1964. It marked the emergence, in response to liberalism (in the American sense of the term), of an uninhibited right: ultraconservative, imbued with religious values, openly populist, antiegalitarian, and intolerant of racial desegregation. In the United States, Australia, and Great Britain, the term "New Right," popularized by the American advertising executive Richard Viguerie,[2] among others, later came to designate a broader movement, reactionary and moralistic, proponent of a state reduced to its regalian functions. Its leading figures were Ronald Reagan and Margaret Thatcher.[3] But that right, which can be identified with the right wing of the Republican Party in the United States, with the British Tories, or, in another variant, with the New Zealand First Party, has very little to do with the new right that grew out of GRECE or its friends abroad. In fact, their philosophies are diametrically opposed. The ultimate paradox is that both new right movements employ the expression "conservative revolution," but only the European new rightists use it to indicate a continuity with the thought of Moeller van den Bruck and his associates, as presented by Armin Mohler in 1948.

To add to the complexity of the problem, in French, "Nouvelle Droite" is a term invented by the press during the major controversy surrounding the ideas of GRECE, which began with the publication of an article by Thierry Pfister in *Le Monde* on June 22, 1979. GRECE then adopted the term as either a stopgap measure, a matter of convenience, or out of defiance, aware that it constituted a strong identifier but not being completely comfortable with it. The intellectual personalities and groups that laid claim to that new right did not by any means form a coherent whole, rather a network based on affinities and similarities. The preeminence of the original French nucleus seems to have declined over time. The most recent synthesis of its doctrine dates back some fifteen years and is hardly consistent with the ideas currently defended by most of the groups. That manifesto of "the new right in the year 2000," composed by Benoist and Charles Champetier, set out its main ideas:[4] a critique of liberalism and of the commodification of the world; the rejection of individualism; an attachment to an organicist and communitarian view of society; the rejection of egalitarianism and of the various forms of monotheism from which it arose; the valorization of well-rooted collective identities and of the "right to difference" (this marked an evolution from the hierarchizing racism of the early days in the direction of differentialism, that is, the idea that each culture must pursue its own development, if possible on the territory where it was formed); the rejection of the nation-state as a form and the promotion of a federalist model that applies the principle of subsidiarity; and a view of international relations based on the idea of a multipolar world in which Europe would be endowed with its own nationhood, apart from American omnipotence, which is designated the chief enemy of the European peoples.[5]

This list does not mean that GRECE, in the course of its evolution, had moved closer to the left. Even while situating itself indisputably on the right, it simply defended ideas that have sometimes migrated to the left (in the particular case of communitarianism and federalism, to what is called the "second left"), or which are largely anchored on the left—such is the case for its opposition to liberal globalization. The essential idea is a rejection of what Benoist called "the ideology of the Same," that is, the eradication of cultural identities through uniformization and the egalitarianism contained within the principle of human rights. The new right is thus a far-right movement by virtue of its organicism; it stands apart from the liberal-conservative right in that it chooses the figure of the rebel over that of the technocrat or entrepreneur.

The plasticity of the new right is exemplary. One can only be struck by the difference between the ethnobiological perspective of the early issues of *Nouvelle École* (1973) and the way that, in 1992, Benoist replied to a question from *Le Monde*. Asked what he thought of "the discriminatory use the FN makes of the right to difference, which you yourself contributed toward popularizing," he condemned the FN perspective on the grounds that it portrays "difference as an absolute, whereas, by definition, it exists only relationally."[6] Furthermore, after decades of railing against the reactionary character of sovereignism and nationhood, Benoist recently affirmed his sympathy with the line defended by Florian Philippot, vice president of the National Front and a proponent of full sovereignism (political, economic, and cultural). Guillaume Faye, another key personality in the movement, formulated the ethnodifferentialist credo, saying in 1979 that it is not immigrants who must be combated but immigration, in order to preserve cultural and biological "identity" on both sides of the Mediterranean. Thirty years later, he wrote works that flirt with the White Power movement.

The most heated controversies surrounding the new right took place in France, first in 1978–1980 and then again in 1993, upon the publication of the "Appeal to Vigilance" in *Le Monde* on July 13 of that year. Co-signed by forty intellectuals, the appeal was accompanied by an article claiming that the political scientist Pierre-André Taguieff, who at the time had taken the new right as his chief object of study, had crossed the line separating observation from complicity.

Yet the Francocentrism of the French controversies must not keep us from seeing that the new right is at the very least a European school of thought, and that its influence in Germany and Italy is at least equal to that which it has had in France. A school of thought it certainly is, with a common trunk and distribution and exchange networks. But a dogmatic, centralized, and homogeneous school the new right is not and never has been. It exhibits as many facets as there are national variations, and it has been subject to both evolutions and breaks. The new right contingent is composed largely of GRECE and the publications associated with it (*Éléments, Nouvelle École,* and, to a lesser degree, *Krisis,* which is more a personal intellectual venture on Benoist's part) as well as groups and publications outside France that are akin to GRECE. The review *Éléments* provides a list of them in its issue of February 1999: they include the Belgian review *Tekos,* published in Dutch and run by Luc Pauwels in the name of the Delta Foundation; Italian publications under the direction of Marco Tarchi (*Tragressioni, Diorama letterario*) and the review *Futuro Presente;* the Berlin weekly *Junge Freiheit;* the Viennese weekly *Zur Zeit;* the review *Disenso,* published in Argentina by the leftist Peronist Alberto Buela; the Romanian review *Maiastra,* published by Bogdan Radulescu and his Club of Accolades; and the Spanish review *Hesperides,* under the direction of José Javier Esparza. As it happens, this list, which includes a number of titles that have since disappeared, constitutes a patchwork of different ideological positions.

The review *Tekos,* for example, is strongly marked by the influence of Flemish nationalism, defended before 1940 by Joris Van Severen and his Vlaams Nationaal Verbond. *Tekos* arose in reaction to Catholicism's hold on the political expression of postwar Flemish nationalism.[7] Nevertheless, it assumed the weight of its past more readily than did *Junge Freiheit,* a high-quality publication and one quite appropriately sold on the newsstands, but which has sometimes remained prisoner to the questions raised by the National Socialist past. In March 2005, for example, *Junge Freiheit* launched a large-scale reader survey on the subject "May 8, 1945: Liberation?"

In Austria, *Zur Zeit,* under the direction of Andreas Mölzer, a former Freiheitliche Partei Österreichs ideologue, is defined as "a true *conservative* weekly for Austria,"[8] which is enough to differentiate it both from GRECE and from the publications of Marco Tarchi. A renowned political analyst and very good specialist on the Italian right, Tarchi, having once been a central figure in the development of the Movimento Sociale Italiano's youth counterculture, has refuted any allegiance to the right. He was also highly critical of the Berlusconi system. The Spaniards at *Hesperides* could never rid themselves of the temptation to influence the ideas of the Partido Popular, even though it is the European political organization on the right most closely aligned with the positions of the American neoconservatives.

Some epigones of the new right outside France even misuse the label and are scarcely recognized as part of the family. The Romanians of Noua Dreapta (New Right) claim an allegiance to the Iron Guard and are clearly neo-Fascist, imperialist, anti-Gypsy, and anti-gay, among other things. There is no greater affinity between the "new right" as GRECE understands that term and the "nye højre," which in Denmark is used to describe the Dansk Folkeparti, an anti-European, nationalist, Islamophobic, and xenophobic movement. The Portuguese new right, launched by Jaime Nogueira Pinto to revive the metapolitical strategy, introduced Benoist's ideas into Portugal, but its "conservative revolution" refers not to Mohler or Niekisch but to Reagan and Thatcher. That seems quite incongruous when one thinks of GRECE but is no longer so when one considers the Club de l'Horloge.[9] Jaime Nogueira Pinto published a book that took its title, *Visto da direita* (Seen from the Right),[10] from an influential book by Benoist, and in 1980 he founded a review with a characteristically new right name (*Futuro Presente*). But he joined the Heritage Foundation and placed at the center of his ideological project "the importance of the spiritual rebirth of John Paul II's Catholic Rome and the importance of Reagan's America, as well as America as the power of the future." That profusion of tendencies can be better understood in light of the movement's history. The new right resulted, in the first place, from the organizational failure to build a European nationalist party in France. It is therefore no longer Benoist who must be considered at the "center" of the question but rather Dominique Venner.

The New Right and European Nationalism

A great deal of confusion about Dominique Venner arose following his suicide in the Cathedral of Notre-Dame de Paris in spring 2013. His act has frequently been portrayed as a reaction to the decision to grant homosexuals the right to marry. Over six decades of political activity, Venner had developed a line that had nothing to do with conservative Catholicism. His suicide was a political gesture, as he explained: "I believe it necessary to sacrifice myself to break through the lethargy that is overwhelming us." It would be a mistake to believe that he understood that "lethargy" solely in terms of the vote on marriage equality. Like most in his political camp, he was persuaded that that law was part of a larger context: the ongoing destruction of European civilization through "globalism." For him, the imminent end of civilization was the result, in the first place, of what he called "the crime of seeking to replace our populations," that is, the structural and definitive change—forced, according to him—of the French and European ethnic substratum through immigration and intermarriage. He had supported the anti–gay marriage network Printemps Français (French Spring), while distinguishing between two components within it: one Catholic, conservative, and bourgeois, from which he expected nothing; the other an "identity" politics, from which he was hoping for an insurgency. He thereby reactivated the infamous distinction he had made in 1962, and which he had borrowed from the radicals of the Conservative Revolution under the Weimar Republic: the far right is said to be divided between "nationals" (conservatives and bourgeois reactionaries, legalists or putschists) and "nationalists" (a revolutionary elite

seeking the overthrow of the system).[11] The place where he chose
to kill himself, a cathedral, was surprising for a man who made no
mystery of his rejection of monotheistic religions. But his choice made
sense: for him, as for a number of militants in his movement since,
Catholicism is a matter not of belief but of culture, and churches are
the expression of the European ethnocultural genius. That is what
Christine Boutin, president of the Christian Democratic Party, did
not understand when she expressed the hope that Venner had converted at the last moment.

Dominique Venner's involvement in politics began at Jeune Nation and can be explained by the colonial conflicts. In the press of
Pierre Sidos's movement, Venner had already set forth reflections that
went beyond national imperialism, orienting himself in the direction
of European nationalism. According to him, given the Arab unification accomplished by Nasser, and the power of the USSR, the United
States, and Maoist China, the time had come for ethnonational empires. The unification of the peoples of Western Europe would allow
the liberation of those in Eastern Europe, and Europe united would
be able to impose its Eurafricanism.[12] Venner was imprisoned during
the repression of the Organisation de l'Armée Secrète (OAS) networks, and, after he was released, revamped the ideological line of
the Fédération des Étudiants Nationalistes (FEN). That was the beginning of *Europe-Action,* where the young Benoist published under
the name "Fabrice Laroche." Venner had made reference to Thiriart
and the defense of the West against Communism in his *Pour une critique positive,* but he now reprinted passages from his book with significant modifications: Western nationalists are called the "militants
of a white nation," whose battle no longer belongs to the realm of
anti-Communism but to that of the race struggle.[13] The review disavowed the classic positions of French nationalism: Catholicism was
rejected in favor of neopaganism; the nation was abandoned in favor
of a spirited defense of the white world; and racialism was used as an
ideological foundation, which led to a major break with some mili-

tants, whose involvement was motivated by the defense of the colonial empire but who believed that the review was coming dangerously close to Nazism.

The metapolitical strategy began there, not, as is often claimed, with the founding of GRECE. At the time, it specifically targeted the far right, to impel it to switch directions and adopt the views defended by the editorial staff. Twenty-five hundred of the seven thousand copies of the newspaper were distributed free of charge to military personnel and in repatriated communities. According to Venner, the formation of distribution committees under the aegis of Pierre Bousquet was a minor deception that would make the cultural battle possible and, in the end, would lead far-right militants to shift over to organizations run by members of the FEN. Likewise, Bousquet was asked to infiltrate the Comités Tixier-Vignancour (TVC) and to prove himself "indispensable" there, in particular, to hijack all the financial posts in order to constitute a network of financial backers.[14] Metapolitics was thus originally not exclusive of partisan action, nor was it understood as an ideological offering external to the far right. According to a report of the intelligence services of the prefecture of police, after Jean-Louis Tixier-Vignancour was defeated in the 1965 presidential election, the cadres of Europe-Action who had insinuated themselves into the TVC leadership took advantage of the dissension between Tixier-Vignancour and Jean-Marie Le Pen. They produced an "appeal to the base" signed by 150 leaders in the TVC—all of them, in fact, entryists from Europe-Action—for the creation of a "unitary party." The Mouvement Nationaliste du Progrès was presented to the press as the union of various groups that could no longer tolerate division or the ineffectiveness of the top advisers. In fact, all the members of its leadership belonged to an underground Centre Nationaliste, composed of former members of Europe-Action, which borrowed the postwar idea of inserting cadres into various movements to achieve de facto unification. Its commission on doctrine was entrusted to four people,

three of whom (Benoist, Jean Mabire, and Jean-Claude Rivière) participated in what would become the doctrinal kernel of GRECE.[15]
That ideological work was consolidated through exchanges across
European borders.

Contacts were made with many groups across the Rhine, including the Nationaldemokratische Partei Deutschlands (NPD)—a
far cry from the traditional Maurrassian Germanophobia. Beginning in 1965, the FEN was associated with *Junges Forum,* a review
founded in 1964, which became the flagship of the German new
right. The review would be steeped in French new right theories
and would communicate them to all the German nationalist movements. In return, the innovations of German nationalism would
greatly enrich the French new right. One of the go-betweens was
Henning Eichberg (b. 1942). A contributor to *Nation Europa,* he
participated in the FEN summer camp of 1966, which other Belgian and German militants also attended. There he subscribed to
the ideological about-face advocated by Europe-Action: he abandoned the cult of the savior and embraced an ideology based on
what he called "a realist conception of race."[16] Upon his return, he
popularized the theories of Europe-Action in German nationalist
circles, and then, as a German correspondent for *Nouvelle École,* performed the same task for GRECE, particularly in *Junges Forum.*
He forged a concept that has become central to the thought of the
European new right: ethnopluralism (the notion, supposedly "antiracist," that every individual is attached to an ethnocultural group
that would protect its identity by avoiding racial mixing, a notion
close to the neoracism of the New European Order [NEO] but
with a human face).

The young German nationalists evolved in the late 1960s, opting
for a modernized formulation of their *doxa.* The tipping point was
the "Resistance" campaign launched by the NPD in late 1969, which
included most of the nationalist organizations. A common front was
founded the next year: Aktion Widerstand (Resistance Action). Although the name was a transparent reference to the Bolshevik national

theorist Ernst Niekisch, it was Adolf von Thadden, leader of the
NPD and former member of the Nationalsozialistische Deutsche
Arbeiterpartei (NSDAP), who elaborated its theory of action in
December 1969, in a document titled *The Conservative Revolution.*
In it he speaks of the need for an uprising to preserve the ethical and
biological traits of the German people, an uprising that would entail
both the organization of cadres into movements and revolutionary
violence. Toward that goal, some members of the NPD founded the
terrorist group Europäische Befreiungsfront (European Liberation
Front). A top leader of Aktion Widerstand, Jürgen Rieger, a member
of the Northern League, directed one of the largest new right bul-
letins: *Neue Anthropologie,* which was later associated with GRECE
and the NEO. For the *Neue Anthropologie* circle, Günther's and
Rosenberg's raciological views were correct, but they had been over-
zealously applied (the group did revise some of their ideas, however).
Here again we find the myth of a miscegenating globalism organized
by endogamous Jews, by means of which they would soon become
the global intellectual elite.[17]

The most ardent followers of Aktion Widerstand split off from the
NPD in 1972 to found the Aktion Neue Rechte (New Right Action)
movement. The group undertook a reflection on how to make ideological inroads, rejecting political parties in favor of using the adversary's language and constituting a transparty network through
grassroots groups. Henning Eichberg's own evolution cannot be
reduced to that strategy, however. His political views changed after
he became an academic, and he committed himself to the environmentalist movement. The German Neue Rechte was quite involved with
the German Greens beginning in 1980 and with the Italian Nuova
Destra in about 1986, believing it had found an antimodern perspective in these groups consistent with the Evolian influence on its
thinking. (GRECE did not work through Julius Evola's ideas until
about 1989, within a neopagan perspective.) Eichberg, having lived
in Denmark since 1982, is now a member of the cultural commission
of the Socialistisk Folkeparti, a Danish party on the radical left.

The upsurge in German nationalism was not limited to the periphery of the NPD, however. In 1973, its youth movement declared that nationalism stood opposed to the imperialism of both American and Soviet capitalism, a system that destroys the diversity of peoples. They argued that a "national liberation" struggle must be waged against imperialism, one that lends support, "within an international and ethnopluralist framework," to the battles of Africans, Asians, Basques, Bretons, Flemings, and other such groups.[18]

There was, then, a constant exchange of ideas among different nations. Armin Mohler had been a personal friend of Benoist since the 1960s, but it was between 1972 and 1987 that the contributions of the Conservative Revolution became central. GRECE was able to assimilate Carl Schmitt, Moeller van den Bruck, Oswald Spengler, and Ernst Jünger. At that time as well, Evola was discovered in France: in Yves Jeanne's neo-Nazi *Devenir européen,* in revolutionary nationalism, and later, in the new right, which began to make reference to him in 1977.[19] But in France, the cultural dimension would be linked to a partisan strategy. Consistent with the precepts of *Pour une critique positive* (a revolutionary elite will bring about the unification of the "nationalists" and will then unify and maneuver the "nationals"), the Mouvement Nationaliste du Progrès launched an organization to unify the entire far right, the Rassemblement Européen de la Liberté (REL; European Freedom Union). The party, billing itself as populist, adopted a few major themes from Europe-Action, such as the elimination of aid to the "underdeveloped—undercapable." Catastrophic election results led it to reorganize in late 1967, under the iron rule of Pierre Bousquet and Pierre Clémenti. That takeover by two former members of the Waffen-SS who had fought on the eastern front, the contacts maintained with the NPD, and the seminars held on apartheid and *Mein Kampf* were met with a wave of resignations.[20]

Alain de Benoist claimed that it was in the fall of 1967 that he decided "to make a permanent and complete break with political action" and to launch a review. He later explained that, in the winter of 1967–1968, he had gathered together a dozen friends from Europe-

Action who were similarly inclined. He believed it was revealing that the new right came into existence at the same time as the "new left"; he saw it as "a generational effect."[21] According to that version of history, what followed was the result of the convergence between that initiative and another, spearheaded from Nice by Jacques Bruyas, former militant of the FEN. Bruyas had set up a provisional secretariat of GRECE on January 15, 1968, and he published an embryonic review, which shortly thereafter become *Nouvelle École.* Pierre-André Taguieff says that the first general meeting of the founding group took place in Lyon on May 4 and 5, 1968. But there are other statements from participants that give a different version of events. Maurice Rollet (1933–2014), future secretary general of GRECE and a former activist imprisoned for his support of the OAS, gives a precise date for the decision of several veterans of the FEN to "change course, radically": November 1967. He then traces back the real founding of GRECE to a party to celebrate his birthday, on January 29, 1968, in Marseilles. He designates the twelve founders by their initials only, but most of them can be identified: Benoist, who wrote under the name "Fabrice Laroche" at the time; Théo Balalas; Pierre Marcenet; Jean-Claude Valla; Jean-Marcel Zagamé; Dominique Gajas; Jacques Bruyas; and Rollet himself. That list is not beyond dispute, given that both the academic Anne-Marie Duranton-Crabol and the far-right archivist Henry Coston provide a different version.[22] Jean Castrillo maintains that "Venner had envisioned a sort of division of labor: Benoist would take care of the theoretical questions in a review he planned to create—and then there would be 'The Militants' (the revolutionary nationalist tendency)."[23] *Militant* is the name of the review run by Bousquet and Castrillo since 1967; it became the bulletin of the National Front when its staff joined the FN in 1972.

GRECE emerged not so much from an engagement with the critical left as from the breakdown of the far right. According to the intelligence services, the disintegration of the REL gave rise to a new strategy: the group splintered into a whole series of publications and small groups, all supposedly independent. Dominique Venner would set out to join Mitterrand's Fédération de la Gauche Démocrate et Socialiste (FGDS; Federation of the Democratic and Socialist Left). Nevertheless, the militants were swept up in a wave of revolt in March 1968. They dismissed their leadership all the more readily in that they suspected that the existing financial problems were linked to misappropriation, even fraud.[24] Then came May 1968. The various publications that grew out of the disintegration of the REL, and which claimed to be "European Socialist," sought at the time to establish ties with the anarchist movement. The parallel with the German and Italian dynamics is obvious. For example, Pierre Vial, a militant from Jeune Nation and Clémenti's godson, was part of *Socialisme européen*. The newspaper embraced the "red flag" of "national Communism" and "the young French left within the framework of clubs with flexible structures." It made many winking references to François Mitterrand's FGDS but also to Mosley, and certified that its function was to be "a laboratory of ideas to serve as the basis for potential actions."[25] The premises of GRECE can be clearly recognized in these positions. Likewise, the Fédération Générale des Étudiants Européens tried to establish relations with the anarchists and launched the ardently revolutionary Rassemblement Socialiste Européen in the name of "historical and biological materialism," the new name for René Binet's "biological realism," which Europe-Action had integrated into its dogma. But in that group a new word became the object of critique: "globalism," a form of capitalism "that knows that peoples deprived of specific structures are unable to defend themselves against its [alienating] maneuvers." Hence the necessary proclamation of a Europe based on "linguistic, economic, and ethnic borders. . . . Unitary Europe will belong to the Europeans, and we will fight the causes of racism, which disintegrates the Nations (USA), leaving only the Europeans alive [*sic*], since we have the same culture, the same mores."[26] The title *Pour une jeune Europe* (For a young Europe) managed at once to adopt a more leftist rhetoric and to engage in Nazifying provocations. These were the ideas of the NEO, reformulated in an anti-imperialist and anti-

American language that differentiated it from a certain strain of the far right. For the leftist militants the NEO was trying to address, that far right was linked to a posture of fierce anti-Communism and not to the denunciation of international capitalism, to nationalism and not to ethnoregionalism, to a zoological racism and not to a cultural differentialism. The same dialectic can be found later on, closely linked to the anti-Western turn of GRECE, which was thus a "turn to the left" and "nonconformist" only in the sense that it omitted these far-right constructs.

The bylaws of the GRECE organization were registered with the French authorities in January 1969. There were no members from the critical left among the first leaders. Instead, there was Alain Lefevre, a veteran of the WUNS; Benoist, for his part, made a visit to Greece at the invitation of the Regime of the Colonels.[27] The European Socialist effort, then, began with European nationalism, missed May 1968 altogether, and culminated in the völkisch tendency of the new right. This tendency was spearheaded by, among others, Vial, founding member of GRECE and its secretary general from 1978 to 1984. Even though Benoist had long since taken his distance from "biological realism," Pierre-André Taguieff divides the first twenty years of GRECE into four phases: racialism of the violently anti-Marxist "biological realism" type, from 1968 to 1972; antiegalitarianism and a violently anti–Judeo-Christian Indo-European cultural racism, from 1972 to 1979; violently anti-American anti-liberalism and other "reductionisms," from 1979 to 1983; and ethnopluralism and the revolutionary "third way," from 1984 to 1987.[28]

Whatever the plasticity of GRECE, its relations with other groups situate it within the milieu of the European radical far right. They also make clear that GRECE did not wish to confine itself to metapolitics but sought to participate in the efforts of political organizations, in conjunction with the revolutionary nationalist milieu. In 1984 GRECE and Jean-Gilles Malliarkis's Mouvement Nationaliste-Révolutionnaire (MNR) held a joint meeting—Vial had in fact already been in contact with Malliarkis. The following year,

Malliarkis and Guillaume Faye conducted another meeting in Paris and, in Geneva, they attended a third meeting, organized by the Cercle Proudhon, whose theme was "The Right to Identity." It included the leading figures of the European new right (Benoist, Vial, the Belgian Robert Steuckers, the Italian Tarchi, the Englishman Michael Walker, and Pierre Krebs).[29] It was a fruitful rapprochement: in autumn 1985 the founding of Troisième Voie was announced. With the support of GRECE and the Groupe Union et Défense (GUD), this organization resulted from the rapprochement between the MNR and the remnants of the Parti des Forces Nouvelles (Party of New Forces), founded in 1974 by former members of Ordre Nouveau. Also participating was the Jeune Garde (Young Guard), which was portrayed as a third group, but was actually a branch of the MNR. At the time, the radicals all concurred that the FN's success would be fleeting. They said they could provide "the ideological backbone that those disappointed with Lepenism will be searching for."[30] Nevertheless, various tensions quickly surfaced between GRECE and Troisième Voie. The revolutionary nationalist militants were informed that GRECE had not kept its promise to pay the printing costs for a national poster.[31] Although that promise and the meetings that were held attest to actions more political than metapolitical, Guillaume Faye and Vial actually played a leading role in these contacts with the revolutionary nationalist movement. Vial's involvement in the FN and Faye's expulsion from GRECE probably explain in part why, with the FN's continuing success, the dynamic stalled. Nevertheless, the new right and revolutionary nationalism constituted a community within the framework of the European Liberation Front.

Euro-Regionalism

The völkisch strain of GRECE was the most resistant to the idea of an exclusively cultural strategy. It established ties with the revolutionary nationalists, sometimes even merging with them, and occasionally joined populist parties. It also played a leading role in making international contacts. Vial joined the leadership of the National Front, then organized the neopagan völkisch faction, both outside and within the FN, with the founding of Terre et Peuple in 1995. That association lay midway between the Wandervogel[32] in its "bündisch" phase and the völkisch racialists proper. It was in no hurry to clear up the ambiguities about its ties to Nazism and made extravagant prophesies about the advent of ethnic civil war in Europe. The creation of such an external organization might have served as a means to channel the provocations. In actuality, it exacerbated the radical insularity of GRECE and demonstrated that it was not possible to disregard its cadres. The faction was very active during Bruno Mégret's attempted takeover of the FN in 1998 and allowed Jean-Marie Le Pen to set himself apart, by denouncing the "racialists" around Mégret. As a result, Mégret found himself in a bind, given the importance of Terre et Peuple in his Mouvement National Républicain. Vial walked away from the MNR after September 11, 2001, when Mégret wanted to portray himself as the defender of the Jews against Islamists. Terre et Peuple went international with the establishment of branches in Belgium, Spain (Tierra y Pueblo), Portugal (Terra et Povo), and Italy (Terra Insubre), and since 2013 has participated in the neo-Nazi network of Action Européenne, headquartered in Switzerland, which relaunched the NEO venture in 2010.

The German group Thule-Seminar, founded by the Frenchman Pierre Krebs in 1980, is close to Terre et Peuple in both its ideology and organization. Its name is clearly provocative, a reference to the Thule Society, which "mysterious history" and esoteric neo-Nazism perceive as a vast secret society that manipulated the NSDAP. "Gramscism on the right" is fueled in this case by conspiracy theories: the idea is that a sect that spreads its ideas could turn history on its head. The Thule-Seminar publishes *Elemente* and does not hesitate to use the Black Sun, the mosaic that decorates the SS's Wewelsburg Castle, a symbol that fascinates esoteric neo-Nazism and has found a place in pop culture (through Landig's books, among others). The Cercle Thulé was founded in Switzerland on that model in 1983; and the Cercle Proudhon, founded the next year, represented the Evolian new right tendency in the same country. Until it disappeared in 1990, it strove to organize international new right or negationist conferences.[33]

A Franco-Belgian axis reinforced that tendency, given that Émile Lecerf was a member of the editorial board of *Nouvelle École* and ran a large-circulation Belgian new right newspaper, *Nouvelle Europe Magazine* (23,000 copies printed in 1973). With the founding in 1972 of the Cercle Érasme (Erasmus Circle), the Belgian equivalent of GRECE, the Belgian interest in the new right became clear.[34] Robert Steuckers (b. 1956) was the most prominent figure on the local scene. In 1983, having played a role in Debbaudt's Front Nationaliste Populaire, then at *Nouvelle École,* he co-founded Études, Recherches et Orientations Européenes (EROE; European Studies, Research, and Orientations) and took charge of the main Belgian new right publications (*Orientations, Vouloir*). In 1985, with the Belgian Pierre Freson and the Frenchman Guillaume Faye, he published a book that constitutes an ethnodifferentialist ideological synthesis. It takes the form of a glossary to "impose its own notions, its own definitions," which readers are advised to learn "by heart." In that work, the new rightists did not hesitate to maintain that Thiriart "is undoubtedly the most remarkable political theorist of our time."[35] The short book was followed by the launch of a review, *Le Partisan européen,* which provides a lexico-ideological synthesis that has often been imitated since. It claims that the "Partisan" will fight for Europe against the American Zionist order and the flood of immigrants; he "lives in the interregnum," participating in the war of "the global bourgeoisie and multinational capitalism against the Peoples [of Europe], whose defenders are the Partisans," that is, in a conflict between "the American party and the anti-American party." The "political, social, and racial tensions" produced by that American party will supposedly lead to "OPEN CIVIL WARFARE," during which the European Partisans will take up arms.[36]

Interpersonal tensions occasioned a break, however. Guillaume Faye is said to have been ousted in late 1986. But his dismissal was not clearly announced until August 1987, when Vial wrote a letter about it to *Le Monde*. He claimed that GRECE refused to recognize *Vouloir* and *Orientations* and its Belgian correspondents; that, unlike Guillaume Faye, the association did not recognize Thiriart as a model; and that it was "in the aftermath of that type of appraisal that Faye no longer belongs to GRECE."[37] In 1993, a "summer university of the Fédération des Activités Communautaires en Europe" was held in Lourmarin, in southwestern France. Although a nonexistent group, this so-called federation served to rig up a new right European university that had not been convened by GRECE and that brought together people who had fallen out with Benoist. It was organized by two new rightists: Thierry Mudry, who interfaced with the revolutionary nationalist and new right circles belonging to the völkisch faction in France (he was part of *Partisan européen, Nationalisme et République,* the Forum Provence, and Nouvelle Résistance); and his wife, Christiane Pigacé (also a member of the FN's scientific council in the 1990s).[38] The conference led to the birth of Synergies Européennes in 1994, a Europe-wide organization that had split off from GRECE under the leadership of Robert Steuckers. It promoted a neo-Eurasianism differentiated from its Russian form, conceiving of a Paris-Berlin-Moscow axis. It had first been promoted in France by the milieu that emerged from the Organisation Lutte du Peuple, in particular by the Romanian Jean Parvulesco, who perceived it at the time as a stage leading to the final utopia: a union of the white world.[39] Parvulesco henceforth became a member of Synergies Européennes and was an important inspiration for the thinking of Aleksandr Dugin. In launching *Elementy* in 1992, Dugin also began to distribute texts by Robert Steuckers, Jean Thiriart, and others in Russia, but he adorned them with illustrations of the esoteric Nazi variety, which probably explains the distance that Benoist later took from him.[40]

Steuckers was critical of GRECE. He claimed that it had withdrawn to the sterile realm of metapolitics and was elaborating a disembodied philosophy with no relation to reality (particularly on the question of immigration) and that it displayed a culpable scorn for geopolitics and jurisprudence, which were indispensable for proposing a concrete political organization of the European cultural space. In addition, Steuckers strongly opposed Benoist's acceptance of the permanent presence of immigrant communities on European soil. Steuckers saw them as only "ethnic groups passing through, not assimilated because there are too many of them, [and who] develop parallel economies in order to survive, which, unfortunately, too often lead to Mafia networks."[41] That rhetoric is hardly surprising from someone who had moved much closer to political groups such as Bruxelles Identité Sécurité (Brussels Identity Security) and later Vlaams Blok.

The Synergies Européennes movement, though it received less media exposure than GRECE, was involved in a few scandals that caused an uproar, for example, the long-term implantation of a nucleus of new right faculty at the Université Lyon III, some of whom seem to have availed themselves of the facilities provided by the academic institution to do militant work. Overall, the publications under the direction of Steuckers are not without interest. He lacks neither intellectual curiosity nor a fairly solid philosophical and political background. He has an undeniable advantage over most of his former friends, now rivals: he speaks proper German and in fact rightly reproaches the French new rightists, so fond of German references, for not being thoroughly acquainted with the language spoken across the Rhine or with the culture of Mitteleuropa. Steuckers, a totally bilingual Fleming, is also no doubt the only one of the new right leaders to be able to boast of having mastered two cultures, and even of having a composite, complex identity, European through and through. Nevertheless, the impact of the Synergies network has been strangely limited by its rightist orientation, by a marked propensity for polemics incomprehensible to outsiders, and by the effusiveness of a number of texts that emerged from it, which are opaque because of the large number of references they cite. In the end, erudition masks intuition.

Then there is the case of Guillaume Faye. He returned to the new right in 1998–2000, with several books that display his old zeal for futurism, but which focus on the question of race. He is obsessed with the ineluctability of a physical confrontation on European soil between "native-born" ethnic groups and "non-natives." The violence of the views he expresses, which earned him a criminal conviction after the publication of *La colonisation de l'Europe, discours vrai sur l'immigration et l'islam* (The colonization of Europe: True discourse on immigration and Islam),[42] has attracted an audience in radical far-right circles, especially within Terre et Peuple. He is also heeded by Synergies Européennes, whereas Benoist and Charles Champetier have definitively distanced themselves.[43]

Guillaume Faye is now through with ethnopluralism. He has adopted an ultra version of the "clash of civilizations," becoming the prophet of the impending unification of the white race, first in "Eurosiberia," then on a global scale with the advent of "Septentrion" (The North). Since September 11, 2001, Islamophobia has made Faye's theories acceptable beyond his restricted circle. They nevertheless represent a dead end for the new right subfamily: on one hand, the "niche" of xenophobia and fear of Islam is occupied by the neo-populists; on the other, the relative indulgence now shown toward Israel by the new right tendency rarely gets a hearing within the radical far right (though the support Faye enjoys from Terre et Peuple and the Thule-Seminar indicates that the radical far right is not entirely indifferent).

Subculture(s)

The image of the new right is closely associated with that of neopaganism, whose importance within Nazism is often overestimated, thus fostering a confusion between new rightists and Nazis. It is true that some of the principal figures of the new right (Jean Mabire and Vial, for example) have been in no hurry to clear up the ambiguities. But neopaganism is not limited to Nazism: its aim is to produce an antimaterialist worldview. Its successes are few, but they do exist. Take the Brussels review *Antaios,*[44] under the direction of the philologist Christopher Gérard. It is an unusual case, in that it embraces a paganism that is not aesthetic, not merely a reaction against Judeo-Christianity, as is common within the new right. Rather, it is active—a pagan religion, in other words. Generally, neopaganism is not so much a faith as a representation of the role of human beings in nature. But beginning in the 1980s, "right-leaning neopaganism [became] an essential component of the subculture of the French far right," as Christian Bouchet observes.[45]

The transmission of neopagan values is accomplished through a scout organization, Europe Jeunesse, founded by Mabire and Maurice Rollet in 1973. There is clearly an ideological perspective: the groups are made up of ethnocultural "bans" (Ban Gallia Belgica for Wallonia, Ban Liguerie for the Nice region, and so on). There are currently about ten regional bans, with about sixty people in the *maîtrise* (that is, the supervisory staff), and activities follow natural pagan rhythms: the equinox, the solstice, the gathering of mistletoe, a camp for the Celtic Festival of Samhain, and so on. The organization has adopted the symbol of Europe-Action: a hoplite helmet. Europe Jeunesse, an attempt at a synthesis between the early scouting movement, as it was defended in France by the naval officer Nicolas Benoit (1875–1914), and the German youth movement before 1933, can be seen as an abeyance structure in the sense the American sociologist Verta Taylor understands it, that is, a movement that, within a period of ideological marginalization and in an unfavorable or hostile environment, allows activism to continue.[46] In this case, the abeyance structure has revived the Wandervogel spirit, even while seeking to form a "well-rooted" youth on the model of "folk high schools," which Mabire borrowed from the Danish pedagogue Nikolai

Grundtvig (1783–1872). As in any scout organization, ethics and actions coincide. Long hikes, vigils, and camp themes are channeled toward the practice of "honor: that is, loyalty to ourselves," an honor defined as "what distinguishes from all the other ancient peoples the Hyperboreans of the mysterious Thule, who built the sun temple of Stonehenge . . . which inspired the laws of Sparta . . . and gave the Saxons the strength to perish in Verden rather than deny the faith of their fathers."[47] In the 1990s, another group sponsored by Mabire, "Les Oiseaux Migrateurs" (The Migrating Birds), would develop more starkly a filiation that is mythic (in the sense of "referring to a founding myth") and Nordicist, by evoking "two irreconcilable worldviews: on one hand, the cultures and peoples of the forest and, on the other, the cultures and peoples of the desert."[48]

Neopaganism complicated efforts to import GRECE to the Iberian Peninsula. In Spain, *Hespérides* was published only from 1993 to 2000, under the aegis of José Javier Esparza and the Proyeco Cultural Aurora. Here again, charges were made against materialist and homogenizing civilization and proposals advanced for the construction of organic societies—with the idea of an interdependent interpenetration of identities, from the local to the transatlantic Spanish American space. But José Javier Esparza vigorously criticized the anti-Christianity of GRECE and Benoist. The Spanish cultural scene, even on the left, gave a warm welcome to the relaunch of the new right via its new review: *El Manifiesto,* to which Benoist contributed. (The new right's leader had been an adviser to the State Secretariat for Culture in José Maria Aznar's government, and other, less important reviews had continued to be published.) But Esparza's desire to open a productive dialogue with the left went nowhere.[49]

The Portuguese new right combines neoliberalism and the contribution of GRECE in a very specific way. That is because, though the project of *Futuro Presente* is to reinvent the right, it also wants to hold in check American hypercapitalism, and it rejects the neopaganism of the French. Has that fusion been effective? There is no question that the writers for *Futuro Presente* became important personalities in the Portuguese press and in its culture, but their ideas were unable to achieve hegemony. When a convergence with the government right did come about, it was on the question of social values, within a reactionary perspective remote from the new right corpus as it found expression in Germany, Belgium, or France. *Futuro Presente* lost its impact, but new rightists were also among the founders of the Partido Nacional Renovador in 2000. That effort to reorient the far right was greatly inspired by the French FN (including its symbol: a flame). But the party has never received even 1 percent of the vote in the various elections, and young members associated with the Hammerskins have been involved in outbreaks of violence, two indicators that this experiment is struggling to find success and that there is little likelihood it is part of Benoist's legacy.[50]

Italy is a special case, given that the far right there is strongly marked by Julius Evola's theories on the existence of a primordial tradition, mother of the various pagan religions. As a result, the Italian new right is by no means contained within Catholicism. In particular, Claudio Mutti was one of the first in Europe to portray Colonel Gaddafi's Libya and Khomeini's Iran as examples for European nationalists, a point of view that was then disseminated by the group Terza Posizione and adopted by Benoist, who sees the Shia regime as "revolutionary traditionalism."[51] Nevertheless, the various references to Iran must be considered within an endogenous perspective. Up to that time, there had been "European Socialism," "Nazi-Maoism," "National Bolshevism," and so on. Mutti has now embraced a "European Shiism." This is a poetic usage of ideological oscillation, an appreciation for political oxymorons, where "Shiism" comes to replace "Socialism" after the modifier "European." The ideological substratum has not changed, and Mutti remains primarily an Evolian Aryanist. The subversive charge lies no longer in the reference to the left but in the Islamic reference, which amounts to saying that, for the Fascists since Mussolini, the term "revolution" has tended to be a metaphor, a poetic trope, rather than a program. A similar phenomenon is at work here: Islam allows the Fascists to reestablish a connection with the subversive charge of early Fascism, Fascism as movement; but, within its geopolitical context, the horizon is no longer marked by Russian Socialism but by Iran. By contrast, these perspectives did not take root in the Italian Nuova Destra, founded by young members of the Movimento Sociale Italiano in 1977. Marco Tarchi criticizes Christianity in a manner similar to Benoist, seeing it as the model for universalism and egalitarianism, and the Nuova Destra is receptive to both the Evolians and the Catholics. The confluence between Evola's writings and the new right dynamic is clear: Evola criticizes modernity, which he perceives as an involution; lauds the spiritual return to the earliest times, when tradition was embodied spiritually and politically; extols the aristocracy of heroism; rejects political parties in favor of a sacred Order; and defines a nonbiological racism based on the "spiritual race" (Evola's *Synthesis of the Racial Doctrine* received the backing of the Fascist regime). He wishes, finally, to replace the nations with an empire that federates plural ethnocultural spaces. A number of new rightists defend notions that allow for a hybrid version of Evola's thinking, whether these concern European roots that need to be recovered, the federation of "carnal fatherlands" (in Saint-Loup's expression), or racism.

There is an ideological and dialectical coherence to the parallel paths taken by the French and Italian European nationalists, that is, the pursuit by the French of the new right metapolitical venture and the Italians' embrace of revolutionary traditionalism and terrorism. In publishing *Cavalcare la tigre* (1960; Ride the tiger), Evola gave new impetus to nationalism, though an impetus sometimes contradictory in its expressions. In that book, he moves in the direction of political action, even as the West is said to be sinking into "Kali-Yuga" (the dark age that, in Hindu cosmology, precedes the golden age). His hypothesis is that there has been a conversion to *apoliteia:* absolute detachment focused on the "greater jihad," the internal holy war. Traditional man—also called "differentiated man," because his worldview stems from the fact that he has delivered himself from homogenizing globalism—can nevertheless partake in political and violent action as a sentinel, or because, after his own life ends, the ascendant cycle will resume its course. Evola's ideas have been put to use in conjunction with those of Armin Mohler. According to Mohler, the West is in an "interregnum": that is, it is between two cycles of a time he calls "spherical," which will lead it to the next phase, Conservative Revolution (Evola would say to the "true state"). As Roger Griffin has pointed out, these are two dialectics of a single metapolitical discourse on the Fascist intellectual, who is considered marginalized but part of an invisible elite of spiritual warriors with a shared worldview. Evola's and Mohler's influence resurfaces within the new right as a revolutionary traditionalism, whose project is to produce an ontological break, that is, to create a European revolution based on a revolution in Being. The new right's goal is a communitarian palingenesis that will give rise to an imperial Europe, grounded in its regions and its well-rooted peoples, rid of the homogenizing uniformization introduced by American cultural imperialism and brought on by immigration, which gives rise to miscegenation.[52]

The influence of that mode of thought within the Italian radical far right also explains Evola's importance in the *British* new right. In 1980 a group of presumed terrorists from Italy, including Roberto Fiore (the current head of Forza Nuova), fled to London. Steeped in Evola's philosophy and Codreanu's mysticism, they disseminated their notions among the young people in the British National Front (NF). They appealed to the British militants to forge a new type of man, the "political soldier," the enlightened warrior, who, they said, had previously been embodied in the Christian Crusaders, the legionnaires of the Iron Guard, and the Guardians of the Islamic Revolution in Iran. Michael Walker, one of these young people from the NF and a friend of Roberto Fiore, launched the magazine *National Democratic* in 1981 (it was renamed *The Scorpion* in 1983). An organ of the British new right, it was profoundly influenced by Evola and thereby allowed the English far right to discover a body of work with which it had been unfamiliar. *The Scorpion* also took a clear stand against the United States.[53]

Within GRECE itself, the Evolian positions were reached by various paths, including those of the French neo-Nazis but not limited to them. In addition to the Italian referent, a Franco-Swiss axis was imported: the Centre d'Études Doctrinales Julius Evola (Julius Evola Center of Doctrinal Studies), an offshoot of the Italian Centro Studi Evoliani. The members of that organization include the Swiss revolutionary traditionalist Daniel Cologne (from the Groupes Nationalistes-Révolutionnaires de Base and the Nouvel Ordre Social) and Philippe Baillet, a veteran of *Pour une Jeune Europe* and translator of Evola. Their group, founded in 1970, launched the review *Totalité* in 1977. In addition to Evola's works, it made texts by Claudio Mutti and Franco Freda available to the French-speaking public and introduced the pro-Libya and pro-Iran arguments to the French far right. Baillet was editor-in-chief of *Nouvelle École* in 1985–1986, having been a member of its editorial board since 1984. In 1982, the staff of *Totalité* founded Éditions Pardès, which took over the publication and distribution of the new right's writings. Evola's works played an important role, but at various times they were criticized as being incapacitating, by both Faye and Christian Bouchet. Bouchet, despite his personal interest in Evola, believed that bringing him into politics fostered pretentious inaction, making listless, psychorigid personalities believe they were heroes and intellectuals. In 2008 Baillet ultimately published a manifesto, *Pour la contre-révolution blanche* (For the white counter-revolution), with a negationist press. In it he maintains that "our only chance for survival depends on the emergence of a new human type of the white race, in the civilizational and ethnic wars taking shape."[54] In view of such a gross simplification, we can only wonder what thirty years of mobilization based on a philosophy as complex as Evola's have ultimately accomplished. That is a structural problem of the new right: not only does it no longer attract many intellectuals, but some of those who did participate have ended up professing a white affirmationist doctrine with little to offer. That tendency, much more than the critiques from the leftist movements, has led people to think, wrongly, that the new right is nothing more than an enterprise skillfully conducted to update the classic theories of the far right by expressing them in euphemistic terms.

What Is the Identity of the New Right's Identity Movement?

As soon as GRECE became known beyond the circles frequented by its founders, it became the target of virulent criticism. That criticism came from Maurrassian and Catholic circles beginning in 1974 and later from the left. They all saw GRECE—with some reason at the time—as a neo-Fascism looking for a way out of the political ghetto, not through innovative thinking but through a tactic of dissimulation and double talk, in short, by disguising their ideas. All these criticisms were expressed by Pierre-André Taguieff in particular, in a milestone 1981 article, whose title was blunt: "The Nazi Legacy of the New Right."[55] The reality is more complex. The new right does have roots in the revolutionary nationalist movements, in the nonconformism of the 1930s, and in the German Konservative Revolution. But it is neither their direct heir nor their clone and cannot be reduced to them. It entertains ambiguities, then complains of the affinities attributed to it. Benoist condemns anti-Semitism, but *Éléments* published a feature article glorifying the rabble-rouser Dieudonné.[56] Benoist also condemns racialism, but GRECE translated and disseminated the writings of Sigrid Hunke, a member of the Thule-Seminar who belonged to the Ahnenerbe (the SS's cultural institute) and wrote for its review *Germanien,* a number of whose illustrations can be found in *Le Partisan européen.* Éditions Pardès, meanwhile, offered translations of the Nazi raciological doctrinaire Hans Günther, with the purchase of two books from the "Révolution conservatrice" (Conservative Revolution) series, under the direction of Benoist. And so on. How are we to understand that phenomenon?

In the first place, we may consider the extraordinary classification essay published in the February 1999 issue of *Éléments,* which lists no fewer than thirty-six "families" on the right, each defined by a motto, a principal adversary, key authors, a symbolic era to which each appeals, the people each one admires, and each one's favorite films. The undertaking may appear rather comical to those who adhere to the topological criteria of political science. It is very pertinent, however, because it characterizes each movement on the right by its style, and the right is primarily a matter of style, an attitude toward life. From which of these families, then, does the new right borrow? A bit from the "personalist and communitarian right"; a bit from the "revolutionary nationals" and the "European federalists"; a bit from the "biohygenicist" right, and from the "regionalists" and "folkists" (Völkischen). What remains of that effort at revitalization? Simply—and this is not nothing—the irruption in intellectual debate of ideas that the new right played a role in disseminating and popularizing. These include an antimonotheism, which can also be found in Michel Houellebecq and Michel Onfray (but the defense of Evola appears to be a limit case: it was not taken up outside the far right except by Pierre-André Taguieff);[57] the acceptability of discussions about the respective share of the innate and the acquired in individual aptitudes; the rehabilitation, *contra* the Jacobin republican model, of religious or ethnic communities, or of communities in the sense of "subcultures" and networks, as Michel Maffesoli has studied them; the introduction into France of the American communitarians and of a number of studies on Carl Schmitt and Ernst Jünger; a rethinking of the economic positions of the right wing, in the direction of antimaterialism in the case of GRECE, ultraliberalism in the case of the Club de l'Horloge.

In addition, the members of GRECE and of the Club de l'Horloge put their stamp on the activities of the French National Front. It is true that, between 1976 and 1978, François Duprat managed to convince Jean-Marie Le Pen of the value of the slogan "a million unemployed is a million immigrants too many." But the proposal to establish "national preference" in all matters was theorized and given the seal of approval by Jean-Yves Le Gallou in 1985, in a book by that title written with the Club de l'Horloge.[58] The other contribution of the new rightists associated with Bruno Mégret is what the political scientist Alexandre Dézé calls "discursive euphemizing,"[59] which can be found in the training documents given to militants and developed by the general delegation. Far from dealing only with the questions of identity and immigration, that practice has the aim of appropriating republican referents. It led to an overhaul of National Front discourse, which, nearly twenty years before Marine Le Pen was elected president of the party, was supposed to implement its "de-demonization." Finally, the Mégrétists reconfigured the National Front's lexicon and ideas around the new right concept of "identity," a discursive rehabilitation strategy addressing ethnocultural themes that has proved to be effective.

As Bruno Larebière notes, however, "the penetration of the new right's ideas was stopped short by the 1998 crisis, with the departure of the cadres and militants the new right had trained. Its influence on National Front doctrine is now zero, and Marine Le Pen's 'full sovereignism' and 'republican' obsession are in fact diametrically opposed to the ideas the new right developed."[60] In a 2011 interview for the bimonthly *Flash,* whose principal writers are Bouchet and the radical anti-Zionist polemicist[61] Alain Soral, Benoist said he approved of the National Front's shift toward the "prominent critique of economic liberalism and the power of money," before adding that he "had never voted FN" and disavowed "its very Jacobin critique of 'communitarianism'" and "a critique of 'Islamization' that in my view appears increasingly to be replacing the critique of immigration," which he himself formulates in the name of the "right of peoples."[62] The FN is thus not a transposition to the political field of the new right worldview: it borrows (simplified) readings from the new right, while leaving aside anything that might invalidate metropolitan French nationalism and the old plebiscitary foundations of the "national right."

Europe-wide, the new right has had the merit of allowing many exchanges of texts, ideas, slogans, and reflections, which fostered the production of a common culture of Continental nationalists. During the summer solstice in 1992, for example, a London meeting attracted representatives of Third Way, *Scorpion,* the Islamic Salvation Front (Algeria), the Islamic Defense Council of Europe, *Orion* (an Italian review with which Claudio Mutti and the former leaders of Terza Posizione are associated), Nouvelle Résistance, the Ulster Movement, and the anti-Zionist American rabbi Mayer Schiller. Benoist, who was initially expected, sent his regrets. The minutes of the meeting specify that differences in appraisals were recorded, but that there was complete agreement about "the revival of grassroots communities, the establishment of liberated microzones, and a solidarity among all those who resist the New World Order, which could be summed up in the statement 'think globally, act locally' "[63] (a formulation inspired by Jacques Ellul). That definition of a minimum commonality is not without substance: there is a desire for the European organization of a space, albeit plural, where the new right would share its notion of the world with militant organizations. Finally, the new right has at the very least taken root in a lasting manner as an intellectual project and will no doubt remain the only enterprise in the history of political ideas to develop a worldview from the ruins of the activist far right of the 1960s, though that effort has primarily produced a transnational subculture.

4

Religious Fundamentalism

It is a common belief that a structural link exists between Catholic fundamentalism (also called "Catholic integrism") and the far right. The faithful of the different Protestant denominations are said to eschew extremism out of concern for freedom of conscience, their rejection of dogmatism, and their interest in individual rights. Yet populist, xenophobic, and nationalist parties are particularly well established in the Protestant countries of Denmark, Norway, and Switzerland, which suggests that the reality is more complex. In his pioneering study of the Konservative Revolution, Armin Mohler demonstrated the presence of a strong Protestant component in that intellectual movement, attributing it to the Lutheran conception of the authoritarian state, which follows from the two kingdoms doctrine (*Zweireichelehre*). He also pointed to the existence of a Protestant wing of the youth movements in the Romantic era (the *Jugendbewegung,* to which the Wandervogel belonged) and in the völkisch movement. The authoritarian interpretation of Protestantism may also explain the values that influenced the leader of the Swiss Union Démocratique du Centre, Christoph Blocher, the son of a pastor, or the vice president of the Hungarian MIÉP (Justice and Life Party), Lóránt Hegedüs Jr., a Calvinist minister. These are individual cases of militancy, however: it must be said that there is not a single case in Europe of a far-right political party declaring a Protestant identity—although, in 1987–1989, John Taylor, a member of the European Parliament representing the Ulster Unionist Party, belonged to the Group of the European Right under the leadership of the French National Front. That membership, however, can no doubt be attributed primarily to the position Taylor had taken against the European Union. We should therefore not think that no Protestants embrace the far right: they vote for it in various cases, but there is no ad hoc organization. The social demand exists, but not the specific political offering that would indicate a Protestant national phenomenon. The most interesting case of an organization espousing Protestantism, which converged with a fundamental nationalism of Maurrassian inspiration, was the Ligue Vaudoise (Vaud League) in Switzerland. An influential group founded in the mid-1920s by the lawyer Marcel Régamey (1905–1982), it was based on a Protestantism that gave a central place to predestination in order to denounce egalitarianism, and conceived of the Reformation not as favoring free will but as returning to the early church.

In any event, the question of the link between faith and extremism tends to lead back to Catholicism. But the words used to describe that link are somewhat confusing. "Integrism," "fundamentalism," and "traditionalism" are terms often used to evoke a system of beliefs and religious practices that denies the basic principles of liberal political systems: free will, democracy, individual rights. It is worth considering to what extent these three intellectual attitudes may translate into a commitment to the far right within the political space. Countries such as Poland and Spain have a certain Catholic national tradition (that is, Catholicism forms the underpinnings of nationalism there), and yet the real center of activity is France, even though that country is so secularized that none of these movements could achieve a partisan political form. Furthermore, the secularization of Western European societies accelerated after 1945: the proportion of citizens affiliated with a church and, even more important, the number of voters who cast their ballots based on the political views of their church, has been continuously dropping. But that has not stymied militants who reject the Maurrassian imperative of "politics first" in favor of an antimodernism that is at once theological, liturgical, cultural, and political.

One Faith, Several Paths

Émile Poulat, a historian and sociologist of religion, dates the first appearance of the term "integrist" to 1880s Spain,[1] when the lawyer and legislator Ramón Nocedal established the Partido Católico Nacional (National Catholic Party), better known as the Partido Integrista Español (Spanish Integrist Party). Within Carlist royalism, Nocedal—inspired by the antiliberal positions of Pius IX's *Syllabus of Errors* (1864)—fought modernity head on, in such a manner that his actions earned him a condemnation from Pius X. Yet that pope, in his encyclical *Pascendi Dominici Gregis* (1907), condemned the "errors of modernism," a current that sought to reconcile faith with reason and the scientific discoveries of the previous century. A network of prelates and laymen, run from Rome by Monsignor Umberto Benigni, was then secretly organized within the church, to bring together "integral Catholics" and root out any deviation from doctrine. This was called the *Sodalitium pianum* or the "Sapinière" (fir plantation) network.[2] Pope Benedict XV ordered it dissolved in 1921, primarily because of its methods: the network's trademarks were denunciations by informers and a permanent attitude of suspicion. It is important to understand that integrism is not a zealous conception of Catholicism that would therefore raise no concerns for the papacy. Integrism is a problem for the Vatican because it asserts the immutability of tradition, rejecting adaptation hic et nunc. It is inseparable from an ecclesial practice that finds the solution to social problems in the Gospel. Integrism maintains that a past moment of the institution is its eternal model, that there is only one orthodox response to a question, and it is inscribed in the past.[3] Monsignor Marcel Lefebvre (1905–1991), a key figure in integrism, exemplifies this view: he challenged the ecclesial arguments raised against him on the grounds that they belonged to a modernism condemned by Pius IX. He sacralized the encyclicals written by the popes from Pius VI to Pius XII, believing they constituted a "supreme authority and no doubt even the guarantee of infallibility" by which to judge the present actions of the church and of men.[4]

Despite papal opposition, the antimodernist tendency has never ceased to exist. Furthermore, the progress of Christian democracy, then the emergence of progressive Catholicism, as well as the church's slow but inevitable opening to the modern world—leading to the Second Vatican Council (1962–1965)—resulted in a backlash by those who called themselves "integral Catholics," and whose adversaries denigrated them as "integrists." For the far right and Catholic integrism, the period between 1945 and 1956 was a time of reorganization. Several groups and reviews created at that time were part of the intellectual legacy of Action Française,[5] whose founder, Charles Maurras—under the influence of Abbé Cormier—had himself returned to the Catholic faith during his time in prison. For example, until 1952 Abbé Georges de Nantes wrote the religious column for *Aspects de la France* (the successor to *L'Action française* in 1947), which Pierre Boutang had pioneered in that newspaper. The editors of *Pensée catholique* were recruited for the most part from the former students of Reverend Father Henri Le Floch at the French Seminary in Rome. Father Le Floch was in fact relieved of his duties in 1927 because of his sympathies for Action Française, and it seems he greatly influenced another of his seminarists, the future Monsignor Lefebvre.[6]

In 1946 Jean Ousset (1914–1994), taking up the doctrinal work already pursued under the Vichy regime by the Jeune Légion, founded the Centre d'Études Critiques et de Synthèse (Center for Critical Studies and Synthesis) and began to publish the review *Verbe*. In many ways, this center, which in 1949 would take the name Cité Catholique (Catholic City), was a continuation of the Sapinière network, minus the secret organization. For a long time, every issue of *Verbe* included its manifesto, which explained that its task was "the formation of an elite through the organization of a close network of working groups." It proved to be highly appreciated in military circles. In fact, during the time of the Algerian War, the ideas of Cité Catholique made inroads among officers, particularly those stationed in Algeria and those assigned to Colonel Charles Lacheroy's Cinquième Bureau (Fifth Bureau), also known as the Psychological Warfare Office. Lacheroy, a theorist of "revolutionary war," along with Colonel Roger Trinquier and others, made it clear to the army that the control of civilians had become essential: henceforth, every war was a total war, which "takes souls as well as bodies and makes them bow to obedience and the war effort." Especially after 1956, the army made it easy for Cité Catholique to infiltrate it, finding consistent, effective doctrinaires in the group who had no qualms about using psychological warfare methods. Cité Catholique groups multiplied in the ranks.[7]

If there was a high demand for these troops in the army, it was because, after the battle of Dien Bien Phu, a number of officers attributed the French defeat in Indochina to the army's lack of psychological preparedness and its ignorance of Communist ideology and strategies. The rout of a conventional army by means of guerilla warfare, they believed, could only be explained by the conditioning of the population, the basic tenet underlying the people's war fought by the Viet Minh. These officers had never before evaluated the full impact of propaganda on a conflict's outcome. They were in search of an ideology as coherent, exhaustive, and effective as Marxism, one that would be a rampart against "subversion." A very coherent worldview took shape: the Christian West versus godless Communism, which sought to wipe out the "natural order." Advocacy of the rights of the colonized peoples was said to be only a subversive tool in that eschatological confrontation. Jean Ousset's *Pour qu'Il règne* (His kingdom come), published with a preface by Monsignor Lefebvre, set out to promote a "Catholic doctrine of political and social action." It provided the doctrinaires of countersubversion with a theological and ethical justification for two practices at odds with the French military tradition: torture and activism. A true "national security" doctrine was the result. It was successfully exported, to Latin America especially.

It was also in that context that one of the main lay thinkers of integrism appeared: Jean Madiran (1920–2013), a veteran of Action Française who was awarded the *francisque* by Marshal Pétain personally.[8] A member of Cité Catholique, he presided over the far-right Catholic weekly *Rivarol,* but walked away from it when Lucien Rebatet joined on. He launched *Itinéraires* (1956), a review of major importance for anticonciliar thought, then participated in the creation and production of the daily newspaper *Présent*. A Dominican oblate, he remained an ultramontane and refused to follow the Lefebvrists at the time of their schism from the Catholic Church.

In 1963 Cité Catholique took the name, intentionally irreducible to an acronym, of Office International des Oeuvres de Formations Civiques et d'Action Doctrinale selon le Droit Natural et Chrétien (International Office for the Works of Civic Organizations and Doctrinal Action Consistent with Natural and Christian Law). With Vatican II, the political battle of the integrists moved inside the church. The end to the "teaching of contempt" for the Jews[9] eliminated a powerful tool in the legitimation and propagation of anti-Semitism. For those marked by anti-Judaism, it entailed a profound rethinking of their views. Although some of Cité Catholique's members or sympathizers were favorable toward Israel, inasmuch as it embodied a national rebirth and the reestablishment of a people's roots, the Vatican's lack of recognition for that state (diplomatic relations with Israel were established only in 1993) sometimes led indirectly to an anti-Zionism mixed with anti-Judaism. It seems that Abbé Pierre's support for the anti-Zionist, negationist book by Roger Garaudy should be understood in that light.[10] The analysis of Vatican II conducted by many right-wing extremists is perfectly rendered in the brochure published on the subject by *L'élite européenne,* a review that grew out of the Occident movement and played a role in the founding of Ordre Nouveau. The titles of the various parts speak for themselves: "Secret Societies," "Secret Societies and International Jewry," "Ecumenicism Seen through Synarchy," "The Aggiornamento Seen through Synarchy," and so on.[11] Vatican II resulted in a marginalization of extremist views within the church, but its advent revived conspiracy theories, which had had the merit of providing infinitely malleable material that transcended the ideological currents themselves. In 1936, for example, the traditionalist thinker Léon de Poncins and the Polish writer Emmanuel Malynski had co-authored the classic *Guerre occulte: Juifs et francs-maçons à la conquête du monde* (The occult war: Jews and Freemasons in conquest of the world), which inspired Julius Evola.[12] This was a fringe culture to be sure, but one with a large capacity to redeploy and aggregate various themes and diverse political projects.

One movement in particular demonstrates that capacity for thematic permutations: Oeuvre Française (OF). Founded in 1969 by Pierre Sidos, that Pétainist group had the originality of sending out signals that were both Fascist and Catholic white affirmationist. Anti-Judaism was persistent in the movement, which was also anti-Zionist and negationist. In short, the worldview of Oeuvre Française was an all-encompassing anti-Semitism. A monolithic organization, it was called a "cult" by its enemies within the far right. In 1980 the police determined that the organization could be dissolved, by virtue of the laws against private militias; they advised the government to keep it under surveillance.[13] The Ministry of the Interior considered breaking it up in 2005. The vulnerability of small groups vis-à-vis the law, combined with the appeal of Jean-Marie Le Pen's legacy, led the OF to become part of the National Front in 2007. Jean-Marie Le Pen and Pierre Sidos personally negotiated the integration of the two groups. Nevertheless, in 2011 Marine Le Pen noisily ousted the FN cadres who were members of the OF. The two men, Yvan Benedetti and Alexandre Gabriac, were, to cap it all off, supporters of her rival, Bruno Gollnisch. The peripheries were thus instrumentalized in the party's internal rivalries: Marine Le Pen ended up weakening both the Catholic national and Fascistic tendencies in her party, though

Sidos claims that the OF has continued to infiltrate the FN since then.[14] The outbursts of violence that occurred on the fringes of La Manif pour Tous (LMPT), and especially, of the Printemps Français marches in France beginning in 2012, led to the dissolution of the OF. They also allowed Marine Le Pen and Florian Philippot to proclaim that the FN was a republican party with no relation to that "far-right" radical faction, the only one, according to them, that deserved that designation. Ultimately, the episode raises the question of how to deal with intransigence in the twenty-first century.

The Institut Culturel et Technique d'Utilité Sociale (ICTUS; Cultural and Technical Institute of Social Utility, established in 1981) and Civitas (founded in 1999 by those who broke away with the Fraternité Sacerdotale Saint-Pie-X [FSSPX; Priestly Fraternity of Saint Pius X]), are both organizations in the tradition of Cité Catholique. With them, the self-designation "integral Catholics" tended to disappear, in favor of the much less pejorative "traditionalists" or "traditional Catholics." There is in fact a permanent ambiguity relating to the two concepts. "Integral Catholics" are proponents of the invariant nature of tradition, which, within the specific context of Catholicism, includes not only scripture but its interpretations by the fathers and doctors of the church, the councils and popes. According to supporters, these constitute an unchanging store of knowledge. Tradition obviously concerns dogma but also the liturgy, catechism, and, in general, the church's attitude toward the world.

There are subtle differences between the integrists and the traditionalists, but the core belief is the same: that the scope and nature of the church's message are collapsing under the weight of those whose guiding principle is to adapt the institution to the times, at the risk of watering down or even changing the basic tenets of the faith. The integrist has often been considered a doctrinaire, the traditionalist someone who is nostalgic for the outward forms of worship. It is more accurate to define them as belonging to the same family, with a common view of its history (the "break" introduced by Vatican II), but who diverge on how best to manage the inheritance.

Integrists want to roll back the conciliar reforms—the acceptance of religious freedom (and the end of the "teaching of contempt" for Judaism), the promotion of ecumenicism and collegiality. They want Mass to be conducted following the so-called Saint Pius V Tridentine rite. They differ from traditionalists not in what they demand from the church but in their mentality. Among other things, their view is more political, which leads them to call for a link between secular and spiritual powers. In France, which is so strongly marked by the quarrel between the church and the republic, that demand generally places the integrists on the right and far right, but a right-wing integrist is not inevitably a Catholic national in the manner of Cité Catholique. The French Dominicans, for example, condemned Cité Catholique, calling it the apostle of a "reactionary and authoritarian politics . . . favoring the past over the present, authority over freedom."[15]

Furthermore, the integrists are not content to demand a return to a time before Vatican II; they also call into question the truly Catholic nature of the conciliar church. The most radical even embrace "sedevacantism," the claim that the chair of Saint Peter is vacant. That doctrine was theorized in 1979 by Monsignor Guérard des Lauriers, who believes that, at least since the promulgation of the 1965 conciliar deliberations on religious freedom, Pope Paul VI and his successors do not possess divinely assisted pontifical authority.

Sedevacantism is an attempt to respond to an apparently insoluble contradiction: If the pope is infallible, how can he publicly teach heresy? The answer is that, though the chair of Saint Peter is materially filled, the one who occupies it must no longer be considered the legitimate pope. In France, about twenty religious organizations embrace that view. The principal sedevacantists in that country are the Institut Mater Boni Consili, the Société de Saint-Pie-V, and the Union Sacerdotale Marcel Lefebvre. Also worthy of note among those who criticize Vatican II is the integrist group known as the Contre-Réforme Catholique (Catholic Counter-Reformation; CRC), founded in 1967 by Abbé Georges de Nantes, who had been suspended from the church in 1966. The CRC developed branches in Quebec and in Belgium, where it was supported by *Nouvelle Europe Magazine*. Abbé de Nantes nevertheless rejected the option of schism and, beginning in 1975, chose to add a political movement: the Phalange Catholique Royale et Communautaire (the Royal and Communitarian Catholique Phalanx). The group is monarchist, but it maintains that, in an interim phase, a "dictatorship of public safety," inspired by the Franco, Pétain, and Salazar regimes, is acceptable. Its ideological foundation is an anti-Semitism that embraces conspiracy theories: Communism, Freemasonry, and globalism are said to be the fruits of Jewry, a "racial power that is the enemy of Christianity." The movement has had a certain impact. Its review had a circulation of 40,000 at its peak, and the group recruits from military circles, among other places. For several reasons, however, it faced a crisis beginning in 1985. First, despite being a Thomist theologian, Abbé de Nantes shares with the Adventists an inclination for eschatological prophecies, and these have not come true. Second, whereas his core followers looked kindly on the rise of the FN, the priest preferred Jacques Chirac over Jean-Marie Le Pen in the 1988 presidential election. Subsequently, he violently opposed the Lefebvrist schism. Finally, he chose to defend the Naundorffist theory (namely, that Louis XVII did not die in 1795 but disguised himself as Karl Wilhelm Naundorff, whose descendants would thus be the most legitimate pretenders to the throne). Considered a sect by Rome, the CRC was denied permission to participate in the transfer of Louis XVII's heart to the Basilica of Saint-Denis in 2004.

Another designation has recently gained currency: "tradismatic" (a contraction of "traditionalist" and "charismatic"). It reflects the fact that some European Catholic traditionalists have joined the charismatic movement, whose base has typically been rooted in American religious culture. The charismatic revival was approved and encouraged by the Catholic Church as of 1975, and its dynamism prompted traditionalists to establish ties with it. These "tradismatics" were an essential driving force behind La Manif pour Tous (LMPT) beginning in 2013, around Monsignor Dominique Rey (among others), who became known to the general public in 2015 when he invited Marion Maréchal-Le Pen to a symposium organized by the diocese of Toulon-Fréjus, long a meeting place for the right. The charismatics' ability to communicate, to become part of secular society, and to organize small active groups was essential in transforming the LMPT from a mere conservative protest to a true social movement. The militant offshoots of the LMPT have spread from one rightist movement to another, bringing with them a very antiliberal notion of conservative human ecology, but one suited to the times.[16]

The tradismatics and LMPT, knowing how to claim their place within modernity, were able to succeed where the integrists had failed in 1989. The integrists had believed they could build up popular opposition to the celebrations surrounding the bicentennial of the French Revolution. Their embrace of that theme demonstrates the extent to which they were a countersociety: they had trouble putting forward an analysis of social representations that was in touch with reality. In January 1989 a ragtag meeting at the Mutualité assembled Restauration Nationale (National Restoration, a successor to Action Française), the Parti Nationaliste Français et Européen, and the FSSPX. The tone was set by François Brigneau, former member of the Milice and a former vice president of the FN, when he declared: "No one has ever said so, but the *cocarde* is the yellow star turned inside out."[17] These opponents of the republic were expecting to attract a million demonstrators on August 15: in the end, between 7,000 and 10,000 integrists and / or far-right militants showed up.[18] The lesson is clear: antimodernity in the church leads to an antipolitical attitude. However coherent reactionary modernism and conservative revolution may be as intellectual paths, a strictly reactionary posture is purely a matter of aesthetics in an age when the political is the work of the masses.

Integrism in the Context of the National Front

The FSSPX, founded in Switzerland by Monsignor Lefebvre in 1970, is the chief integrist faction. Lefebvre, a bishop and missionary, belongs to the group of prelates who refused to endorse Vatican II reforms, which they considered a break with the teachings of 2,000 years of Catholic tradition. As he explains in one of his writings, Lefebvre "refuses to follow the Rome of the neomodernist and neo-Protestant tendency, which clearly manifested itself in the Second Vatican Council and in all the reforms that have emerged from it"— especially the liturgical reform, episcopal collegiality, interdenominational dialogue, and above all, religious freedom, which grants "the same right to truth as to error."[19] Hostile to ecumenicism, which he often conflates with syncretism, Lefebvre wishes to restore the church's role as a state religion and its missionary calling, and he proposes the Franco, Salazar, and Pinochet regimes as models. Identifying the origin of contemporary ills in the French Revolution, he believes that its advent can be explained by a joint conspiracy on the part of Freemasonry, the spirit of the Enlightenment, and the "progressive" clergy. Here he is inspired by Barruel and another eighteenth-century conspiracy theorist, John Robison. His young disciples, published in the nonschismatic newspaper *Présent,* also profess an anti-Judaism both religious and economic, seeking to demonstrate the "Jewish" origin of liberalism and Communism and, in any case, going further than preconciliar anti-Judaism, which was strictly theological. In 2002 the traditionalist Catholic Bernard Antony still maintained that "present-day politics is thus marked by the tenebrous alliance of stateless capitalism and international socialism, which one gradually discovers if one takes an interest in the question."[20]

Lefebvre's combative integrism attracted the attention of the mass media, thanks to the occupation of the Église de Saint-Nicolas-du-Chardonnet beginning in February 1977. That church became the central site and media focus of the faithful of the FSSPX, though its

Maison Généralice (principal seminary) was located in Bavaria. In 1999 Saint-Nicolas-du-Chardonnet became the center of activities for Civitas, run by the Belgian Alain Escada. From the start, Civitas attempted to establish ties within the far-right network, for example, with Projet Apache, young members of the Bloc Identitaire in Paris. But its cultural and moral rigidity, its mode of conduct as a countersociety walled off from the world, have not favored the success of their actions. The organization did not feel many affinities with Marine Le Pen, even fewer with Frigide Barsio, the staunch militant opposed to same-sex marriage, whom it avoided as strenuously as possible during LMPT.[21] But the FSSPX has hardly confined itself to its Paris bastion: it runs a network of 300 unregulated private schools, and it has developed a global network—it moved into Hungary shortly after the fall of the Iron Curtain—though it remains better organized in Western Europe. That geographical expansion continued at the time of the schism, because the three bishops Monsignor Lefebvre and his disciples consecrated before being excommunicated were an American, a Frenchman, and a Swiss.

Until then, integrism had remained on the fringes of the political organizations, publishing doctrinal reviews. In that sense, there is a logical continuity between Civitas and its predecessors. Nevertheless, the rise of the FN changed the game plan for the integrists committed to the Maurrassian legacy of political involvement. In order to gain new adherents, the FN incorporated into its discourse invocations of Joan of Arc and the "France of cathedrals," and it identified national culture with Christian culture. The rapprochement between the FN and traditionalists / integrists occurred in three stages: in 1980–1981 the Centre Charlier was established, under the leadership of Romain Marie (pseudonym of Bernard Antony); in autumn 1980, the first French Friendship Day was held in Paris, with Jean-Marie Le Pen and many Catholic national groups in attendance; and in May 1981, the FN, the Contre-Réforme Catholique, the Amis du Colonel Chateau-Jobert, and the royalists paraded side by side. In addition, the monthly magazine *Présent* became a daily newspaper in

November 1981. It was run by a staff that included Romain Marie, François Brigneau, and Jean Madiran. Still sold on the newsstands, though most of its readers are subscribers, *Présent* supports the FN and is very close to the Comités Chrétienté-Solidarité (Christianity-Solidarity Committees), another of Romain Marie's creations. In 1984 Romain Marie, who had joined the leadership of the FN, created the Alliance Générale contre le Racisme et pour le Respect de l'Identité Française et Chrétienne (AGRIF; General Alliance against Racism and for Respect for French and Christian Identity), which has sought to intervene in legal proceedings involving "anti-French" or "anti-Christian" racism, a concept renamed "Christianophobia" in 2005. Christianophobia was introduced into the Vatican's official discourse with Benedict XVI's address to the diplomatic corps in 2011.[22] It also entered the discourse of international organizations: the declaration of the second World Conference against Racism in Durban, South Africa (2009), speaks of the struggle against "Islamophobia, anti-Semitism, Christianophobia, and anti-Arabism"; and the Organization for Security and Co-operation in Europe (OSCE) held a conference on the subject in Rome on September 12, 2011.

Présent remains strongly marked by a preconciliar understanding of Judaism; it battles the progressive clergy and any expansion of cultural liberalism. On the Jewish question, its staff has acknowledged that it popularized the theme of a Jewish lobby opposed to the FN. In 1986 *Le Monde* published a press release from B'nai B'rith, an American-based, para-Masonic international Jewish and Zionist organization, which asked the political right to keep its pledge not to ally itself with the FN. *Présent* then launched an obsessive campaign denouncing "the diktat of B'nai B'rith," asserting that politicians on the right must have taken an oath in the organization's lodges. B'nai B'rith was later accused of being the perfect symbol of the Jewish lobby and of being the "motherhouse," the issuer of orders, of the antiracist movements. During the 1988 French presidential campaign, *Présent* published a brochure on the matter, with instructions to "ensure its ever-increasing dissemination"; it declined to accept orders of fewer than fifteen units. Seventy thousand copies of the brochure are said to have been sold in that way. On this matter, the group was clearly in the vanguard.

Within the FN, as within the church, the objective of these Catholic nationals was to constitute a movement that had its own press, training organizations, and established doctrine—but there was no desire to create an autonomous Catholic national party. In that respect, it imitated the attitude of integrists in all the European countries where an organized far-right party exists. Nor did the Catholic nationals in France choose to break away from the church. Given that context, the classic question of the conflict between Catholics and pagans needs to be reframed. In the 1990s, it was very common to use the opposition between Catholic and pagan militants as an interpretive grid for understanding the internal divisions within the FN. A number of observers believed that the conflict was grounded in theology. In fact, however, the quarrel between Catholic nationals and paganist radicals was first and foremost political, continuous with the opposition between nationals and nationalists. The neopagans' modus operandi consists in large part of a permanent quarrel with the Roman Catholic Church in particular and with Christianity in general. For them, there is little difference between the "System" and "Judeo-Christianity," conceived in terms of what a Marxist analysis would call the "superstructure." Fabrice Robert indicated as much when he wrote in 1996: "Even as its spirit continues to be embodied in the dominant ideologies, Judeo-Christianity, having lost some of its force in its original (religious) form, remains formidable in its economic version, namely, liberalism."[23] One worldview is pitted against another. It is important to understand that, for the far-right neopagans as for the Catholic Church, paganism is not a matter of polytheism but of culture. In fact, Christian Bouchet, a revolutionary nationalist cadre who also holds a doctorate in anthropology and is a specialist in the problematic of esotericism, analyzes neopaganism as a multifaceted cultural phenomenon. He rightly points out that far-right neopaganism is nondenominational: it is an attitude more philosophical than religious.[24] It is true that Ásatrúarfélagið, a neo-pagan faith, is recognized by the Icelandic state as a religious organization; but the figures of French neopaganism, such as Pierre Vial and Jean Mabire, are intellectuals in the völkisch faction of the radical far right. The few attempts to construct a neopagan religiosity within the new right have hardly been conclusive and have remained marked by a Nordicist orientation. In short, neopaganism is a post-modern reaction within the context of a highly secularized society to what remains of Christendom, a sort of quest for a golden age, more fictive than founded on the historical truth of what paganism was, experienced more as a life aesthetic than as an inner faith. Far-right polytheism, in fact, is alien to the white populations in neo-pagan völkisch circles; for that very reason, however, it has been able to attract some new rightists. Such is the case for the far-right Indian tradition, which has been imported to the Western world. The Hindutva movement embodies the radical political version of Hinduism. It was spearheaded in India and in the Indian diaspora in Europe by the Rashtriya Swayamsevak Sangh and the Vishva Hindu Parishad. These groups, active in the United Kingdom, the Netherlands, and Germany, are nationalist and fiercely opposed to Islam. They follow a strictly communitarian and fundamentalist program. Both have elicited interest in far-right circles, primarily because of their anti-Muslim preoccupations and their appropriation of an Indo-European tradition. One of the chief propagandists of Hindutva in the Western world is a far-right Flemish militant, Koenraad Elst, the publisher, between 1992 and 1995, of the Flemish new right review *Teksten, Kommentaren en Studies*.

Consequently, within the National Front the dispute between the neopagans and the Catholic integrists is not a quarrel of faith but a politico-cultural conflict, which, in the far-right field, means in great part an aesthetic conflict. In fact, that conflict was originally free of the pagan element, which did not take shape as such within the FN before the creation of Terre et Peuple. The antagonism arose with Duprat's return to the FN in 1974, even though the atheist Duprat despised neopaganism. He and his friends were denounced by Catholic cadres for their Fascist views and, from the standpoint of Christian dogma, it was their totalitarian conception of the nation in itself that constituted a pagan object, not some Odinist form of worship.[25] At the same time, the Nouvelle Droite's social Darwinism and biological materialism antagonized the traditionalists. In 1979, for example, Jean Madiran claimed that the Nouvelle Droite, by virtue of its anti-Christianity, was either leftist or a conspiracy by the left to destroy the far right from within.[26]

The Catholic nationals once again trotted out a conspiracy theory during the regrouping of new rightists and revolutionary nationalists around Bruno Mégret. After the scission, that alliance was denounced as being the result of an infiltration of Freemasonry into the far right, aimed at destroying it and allowing the disintegration and de-Christianization of France. But it is also true that, at the time of the Mégrétist schism, Catholic nationals, who already had a considerable place in the leadership of the FN, added to it the place left vacant by their intimate enemies. There is an instrumental aspect to the much-touted distinction between Christians and neopagans: everyone capitalized on that controversy to brainwash the militant base about the opposing camp's "betrayal." When the two camps gathered around Jean-Marie Le Pen, they were able to consider a nationalist and political compromise first, setting aside the religious question, even though the radicals nicknamed Bernard Antony "the Ayatollah Cassoulet." In reality, according to the revolutionary nationalists, Marx's adage that religion is "the spirit of the bourgeoisie" can be applied to "Judeo-Christianity" but not to religions considered more true to tradition in René Guénon's sense of ancient wisdom.

That instrumental dimension can also be found in what has been called "de-demonization." The normalization strategy first came to light when the National Front presented a new face to society, which meant opposing the Catholic nationals. It was embodied in Marine Le Pen's moderate positions on abortion and seemed logically confirmed by her republican and secular references and by the fact that she was living with a man outside of marriage. She exhorted the Catholic nationals to leave the FN in 2004. That was not just double-talk. Indeed, to oppose the Catholic nationals is to be "on the left" within the far right, a posture that seeks not an alliance of the rightist movements but rather the "disintegration of the system"— such is the revolutionary nationalists' aim—or, in Marine Le Pen's case, the assumption of power. Opposition to the Catholic nationals is an easy way for the FN to differentiate itself within the far right by appearing more progressive. In that respect, the discourse of Unité Radicale was exactly the same as that of the Marine-Lepenists of Générations Le Pen (an association founded in 2002 by those close to Marine Le Pen) when they took the party by storm: in calling into question the "Jesus fanatics," Unité Radicale was able to assert its modernity and its adaptation to the popular masses. For Généra-tions Le Pen, the strategy was to be less "stuffy" (as opposed to the Catholic nationals) and to become "deracialized" (as opposed to the racialists and those who embraced identity politics), and to purge Lepenism of anti-Semitic provocations. For media observers, the public embrace of a secular line was an intelligible sign of "de-demonization" that allowed the FN to attack the Catholic nationals who supported Bruno Gollnisch. The secularism advocated by the revolutionary nationalists and by the Marine-Lepenists is thus a high-grade internal weapon to marginalize both the Catholic nationals and völkisch-leaning neopagans. It is truly a jockeying for position, but it is not only that. The polemics directed against the Maurrassians are also "positive critiques" in Venner's sense: the search for an effective mode in tune with its time.

In the self-representation of the revolutionary nationalists and of the Marinists, who in this case follow the same logic (well beyond the simple opposition between "radicalism" and "de-demonization"), that refusal has everything to do with their "leftist" identification. In fact, these militants, who think in terms of worldviews, see being on the "left" less as a social policy than as a topos. "The two main lines of identification in the duality between right and left were the line between secularism and Catholicism and that between Socialism and liberalism. [The left] embraced 1789, immortal principles, the Republic, secularism."[27] These markers have been used to give substance to the ideological oscillation that destroyed the reference points for the right/left demarcation. It is these elements that the revolutionary nationalist tendency,[28] then the Marine-Lepenists, have continually emphasized to find a position for themselves in institutional politics. Any understanding reached with the Catholic nationals, for example, entails a displacement along the right-left axis. When Carl Lang, having been purged from the FN, founded the Parti de la France (Party of France) in 2009, he adopted the principle of nationalist compromise and the FN's 1984 line. Marine Le Pen, by contrast, after a departure marked by her opposition to the Catholic nationals, attempted both to shatter the rightist movements and to co-opt leftist markers, refusing to support the Printemps Français movement. Clearly, the pro-Catholic marker requires that one choose whether to employ the method of nationalist compromise. And, since the schism of 1999, the FN is no longer a party of nationalist compromise. The question of neopaganism has also become inconsequential. Beyond the question of their personal spiritual journeys, the fact that cadres such as Christian Bouchet and Philippe Vardon now declare a marked attachment to a nonliberal Catholic faith shows that the countercultural aspect of paganism does not correspond to the dynamic of opposition to cultural liberalism around which the right is now organized.

Partisan Paths

The galaxy of extremist religious organizations is Catholic-centered. What is remarkable is that large segments of the Protestant electorate vote for far-right parties, at a rate higher than that among their Catholic fellow citizens. The explanation is provided by the political scientist Bernard Schwengler in his comparative study of the religiously diverse zones of the Alsace region (France), Switzerland, and the German state (*Land*) of Bade-Würrtemberg. Schwengler explains that Catholic voters in each of these regions have available political offerings that embrace Catholic identity: respectively, the French centrist parties, the Christlichdemokratische Volkspartei der Schweiz, and the Christian Democratic Union of Germany. Protestant voters do not have any such faith-based party, and they split their vote among the different parties in the running, which means they may choose the far right rather than a Christian democratic party. Schwengler points out that Protestants are more likely than Catholics to vote for the National Front in Alsace, for the Union Démocratique du Centre in Switzerland, and for the Republikaner in Germany.[29] Notwithstanding, two errors are often made regarding the relationship between the Protestant denominations and the far right. The first is to label as "right-wing extremists" Protestant parties that take their ideology from a fundamentalist reading of their tradition. These parties exist in the Netherlands, where the Staatkundig Gereformeerde Partij (SGP) represents a backward-looking segment of society. But that movement is not part of the far right: it has demonstrated its concern for parliamentarian discussion and freedom of conscience and does not promote ethnic discrimination.[30] In Switzerland, the Union Démocratique Fédérale, despite its support for the ban on minarets in the 2009 referendum, also does not belong to the far right but rather to the conservative religious right, whereas the Parti Évangélique Suisse (PEV) combines conservative values, a commitment to environmentalism, and relatively progressive views on socioeconomic questions. A second error is the occasional attempt to situate on the far right Protestant pressure groups linked to the ideology of the Moral Majority in the United States, such as the Christian Institute or the Conservative Christian Fellowship in the United Kingdom. The Moral Majority was, to say the least, a reactionary movement, some of whose members adopted positions that devolved from self-righteousness to virulent intolerance. Nevertheless, it was merely a pressure group close to the Republican Party and not a far-right faction. The same is true for the aforementioned British groups vis-à-vis the Conservative Party and the religious right vis-à-vis the Australian prime minister John Howard.[31]

Confusions of another kind arise regarding the Jewish far right, which in fact is not particularly religious. To understand that phenomenon, we need to take a detour by way of Israel. There, several far-right parties and movements display an ethnonationalist notion of identity and of the state, acknowledging their use of violence and their contempt for democracy. Nevertheless, Israeli far-right parties have an ethnic notion of Jewishness that does not always correspond to a religious ideology. Avigdor Lieberman's Yisrael Beiteinu (Israel Our Home), for example, is a strictly secular party; the Ichud Leumi (National Union) is a mix of religious national Zionism and secular nationalism and advocates population transfers. The Israeli nationalist parties have organized groups of activists within the large Jewish communities of European countries; the same alliance between religious Zionists and secular nationalists therefore exists in Europe as well. In particular, the so-called self-defense groups set in place after 2000 were usually formed by secular Jews. For example, the Jewish Defense League is composed of nonreligious militants who left the Likud youth movement (Betar). And in fact, Orthodox and Ultraorthodox clergy are not necessarily Zionists. The only serious (albeit very marginal) attempt to construct ties between the radical anti-Zionist far right and the Jewish far right involves Ultraorthodox anti-Zionist Jews who believe in the separation of the races and of religious or ethnic groups and who are opposed to Israel's very existence. As such, they are ready to build bridges with black separatists, fundamentalist Muslims, and white supremacists. The emblematic figure of that effort is the American rabbi Mayer Schiller, a professor at Yeshiva University in New York, whose first contact with the far right dates to his association with the British Third Way movement in the early 1990s. He summed up his thinking in an interview with the revolutionary nationalist magazine *Ulster Nation:* "There are two things that threaten the West. One is liberalism, which is the destruction of faith and values and culture. The other is multira-cialism or multiculturalism which is essentially a peaceful invasion and take-over of these countries."[32] That alliance never bore fruit, though some segments of the European far right have shown interest in the Jewish religious group Neturei Karta. London and Viennese members of that organization attended the negationist conference held in Tehran in 2006, while some French members have worked with the radical anti-Zionist agitator Dieudonné and held a meeting with him at the Théâtre de la Main d'Or in 2004. Their own organ-ization did not forgive them, and they were ousted. Seeking con-vergences in the name of anti-Zionism is one thing, but getting Orthodox Jews from the Eastern European tradition, often descen-dants of Holocaust victims, to admit that the extermination of the Jews is a "Zionist invention" simply defies reason.

That type of radicalism is not at work in the far-right Catholic movements. In the case of Ireland and Poland, the Catholic Church retains a strong influence on everyday life, and the most conserva-tive Catholic voters, even the extremists, vote by preference for an ordinary conservative party. Their vote is not an "antisystem" protest but rather an affirmation of the values shared and supported by a large part of the church hierarchy. Significantly, in the 2007 general elec-tion in Poland, the Liga Polskich Rodzin (LPR; League of Polish Families) lost its parliamentarian representation, the influential Radio Maryja having preferred Prawo i Sprawiedliwość (Law and Justice), the Kaczynski brothers' conservative party of Catholic inspiration, to the LPR. In addition, the conservative Catholics who want to influ-ence the political agenda, particularly on questions of social values or bioethics, have a tendency to form their own camp within or along-side a dominant party on the right. Such is the case in France for Christine Boutin's Parti Chrétien-Démocrate (Christian Democratic Party), associated with the Union pour un Mouvement Populaire (Union for a Popular Movement), and of the Arbeitskreis Engagi-erter Katholiken (Working Group of Engaged Catholics) within the German Christlich Demokratische Union-Christlich-Soziale Union

(CDU-CSU; Christian Democratic Union-Christian Social Union).[33]
That choice is probably based on church doctrine, which recommends
obedience to temporal powers, and on a rational grasp of political
power relations. Whereas the integrists are on the margins of church
institutions and more easily occupy the political fringes, conservatives
defend a more pragmatic approach. In addition, the political behaviors of citizens motivated by their religious beliefs vary depending on
the European society. For example, in Flanders, Catholics who attend
church regularly are less likely to have hostile feelings toward Muslim
immigrants than are occasional churchgoers.[34] The political scientist
Nonna Mayer has shown that, in France, the relation between
Catholic faith and the FN vote depends on a variety of factors: context (when the Catholic hierarchy expresses a negative opinion of the
National Front, as it did from 1988 to 1997, the FN vote among
Catholics was lower than average); degree of religious observance
(regular churchgoers were less inclined to vote for the FN than were
less regular ones, but fundamentalists voted en masse for the FN);
and region (Brittany and Vendée, for example, which have a strong
Catholic culture, are less receptive to the FN, though there has been
a certain shift there since 2012).[35]

In fact, within right-wing government organizations in Italy, Ireland, Spain, and Portugal, and also in Bavaria's CSU, the influence
of conservative Catholicism, especially on questions of morality, is
clearly higher than that of integrism. The structural weight of national Catholicism is particularly in evidence in Poland and Spain,
in the Slovak National Party, and within Forza Nuova in Italy, where
integral Catholicism forms the ideological underpinnings of nationalism. That cannot be reduced to the social influence of Catholicism:
political traditions do exist. Polish national Catholicism emerged in
the nineteenth century and was long embodied in Endecja (formed
from the initials "ND," for Narodowa Demokracja, National Democracy). For Endecja, Poland's identity was consubstantial with its ties
to the Roman Catholic Apostolic Church. The National Democrats,
an anti-Semitic, anti-Ukrainian movement hostile to all the national

minorities in Poland but nonetheless democratic, constituted the principal political force during the two world wars. Despite the repression it suffered after Marshal Piłsudski's coup d'état, the National Democratic tendency continued to be pervasive in Polish political culture. The LPR is beholden to it for its choice of national Catholicism rather than integrist Catholicism. As Daniel-Louis Seiler points out, "religion serves as an anchorage point for national identity, and Catholicism and the nation prove to be consubstantial with each other. In this particular case, there is no question of defending the integrity or Romanness of Catholicism, only its Polishness." That theologico-political notion is not limited to Catholicism, however, since it is comparable to the one defended in Hungary by the Calvinist Horthy.[36]

It is altogether significant that Lefebvrist integrism and sedevacantism made their appearance in Poland not in national Catholicism but on the radical far right, particularly in the fanatically anti-Semitic Narodowe Odrodzenie Polski (NOP; National Rebirth of Poland). The particular focus of that party is the denial of the criminality of Auschwitz, and it is very welcoming toward skinheads. In addition, the NOP was part of the clerico-Fascist International Third Position, founded in England by Roberto Fiore in 1989. Romanian reviews in the tradition of the Iron Guard were also associated with Fiore's organization.[37] Clearly, this is a case of a mutual polarization and hybridization of the fringes, which give them a coherence proper but also cast into relief the fact that they are countersocieties by nature. In Poland, being Catholic to the point of defying the church can be perceived by militants as a sign of their revolutionary character, but that stance has no influence on the electoral process.

In Spain, the situation proves to be even more clear-cut. The relegation of Fuerza Nueva and of the neo-Phalangist organizations to the margins demonstrates that the importance of integrist Catholicism for Spain's political identity does not produce the election results one would expect. The Partido Popular occupies the entire field of conservatism. Historically, theologico-political intransigence in Spain was related to the Carlist movement, and there is likely no equivalent elsewhere in Europe of the capacity of that counterrevolutionary movement to modernize itself and to survive after 1900. Carlism did not allow itself to be imprisoned in dogma and, beyond its counterrevolutionary imperative, was able to adapt, particularly by becoming involved, at certain moments and in certain territories, with the defense of charters that govern local rules and privileges. Nevertheless, despite Pius X's desire to see the Spanish Catholics engage in the political process, the constant divisions between Carlists and integrists, and the uncompromising extremism of the integrists, quickly led the church to acknowledge that there was no possibility of building a partisan force of its own.[38] Adaptability, localism, and a chronic tendency to splinter into subgroups can be found even in the swing to the left of one part of Carlism, which moved closer to theories of joint worker-management control after Franco almost liquidated the movement. That swing to the left is somewhat comparable to the development that, in France, led part of Action Française to found Nouvelle Action Française in 1971 (it became Nouvelle Action Royaliste in 1978, to indicate its full split from the original group).[39] But in that case, the royal pretenders of Bourbon-Parma themselves were divided between integrist Catholic right-wing extremists and Socialists. The traditionalist Prince Sixtus Henry of Bourbon-Parma, pretender to the throne of France, attempted to federate the Spanish Carlist movement beginning in 1986. Also linked to the traditionalist faction of the French FN, he defended "the Christian West" but lambasted American imperialism and took the side of the Baathist regime in Syria. Nevertheless, though Carlism may have been a movement with a popular base in the nineteenth century, in the twenty-first century it fits the mold of a countersociety.

In fact, national Catholicism, as the offering of a political regime, could not withstand the fall of the dictatorships on the Iberian Peninsula. On the European scale, however, the emergence—marginal but real—of an overt conservative movement whose first priority is the defense of the traditional values of Christian society is altogether worthy of note. This movement is particularly concerned with the family, the differentiation of gender roles, and the right to life from conception to natural death. In the European elections of 2014, that political family found its way onto various slates. Force Vie, the French slate headed by Christine Boutin (1.2 percent in Île-de-France), the Pro Vida of Portugal, the Irish Catholic Democrats headed by Nora Bennis, and the Germans of the Partei Bibeltreuer Christen (0.2 percent) tried their luck with little success. By contrast, the joint slate of the two Dutch Calvinist parties, ChristenUnie (CU; Christian Union) and the Staatkundig Gereformeerde Partij (SGP; Reformed Political Party), earned two seats in the European Parliament, with 6.8 percent of the vote. Little by little, that political family is becoming better organized: the CU and the SGP are now the mainstay of a European Christian Political Movement with the status of an EU party, and it has three representatives in the new legislature. That is only the electorally submerged part of a more far-reaching ideological movement focused on social values that calls into question the traditional hegemony of Christian democracy over the electorate of Catholic and Protestant believers. The "conservative May 1968" evoked by the political scientist Gaël Brustier is, from that standpoint, a sort of political Counter-Reformation whose shifting of lines is bound to continue.

5

The Populist Parties

Contrary to a widespread myth, in the last several decades Europe has not experienced a constant rise of populist parties that aggregate protests from the right and the left. Granted, the French National Front has been a "catch-all" party from its creation, its ambition being to "unite category-specific discontent," in the expression of François Duprat, its first ideologue. But the voter base and the ideology of populism are homologous: both are interclassist, and that puts the populist parties firmly on the right.

The word "populism" tends to wander from one camp to another, and its political meaning fluctuates. It first appeared in the nineteenth century in two countries, Russia and the United States, where the split between right and left was largely unknown. But the term had its moment of glory after World War II, with the Arab and especially the South American nationalist regimes. A particular alchemy was at work there: the cult of the charismatic leader, but in the absence of totalitarianism; the unification of various social strata into a legitimate hierarchy; the affirmation of a state that was not in the thrall of oligarchies; a nonimperialist nationalism; and so on. These regimes have often been called "Fascist" in polemical debates, but the above criteria clearly provide rational grounds for excluding them from that category. The label "national populist" was therefore invented to describe them. The first to make use of that term in France was undoubtedly François Duprat, who, borrowing Jean-Marie Le Pen's definition of his own National Front, praised the "national, social, and popular" Latin American right.[1] In fact, populism appeared as a factor in elections in northern European countries, particularly in the 1970s, as an expression of opposition to the welfare state. The 1973 success of the Danish Fremskridtspartiet, which received an unexpected 16 percent of the vote and became the second-largest political party in Denmark, before collapsing, can be taken as a watershed.

The concept of national populism, used to describe the reemergence of the far right in European electoral politics, became popular after Pierre-André Taguieff used it in 1984 to describe the historical filiation of the FN. By the 1990s the label "populist" had saturated the media and was used across the board, including as a means to delegitimize counterproposals to Euroliberalism. But being a plebeian is not enough to make one a "populist." Populists understand political change as decadence, from which only the healthy common people can free the nation by forming one national class from the different social classes and casting aside the "corrupt elites." In fact, the populist parties represent one of the most visible symptoms of the Western shift to the right as earlier defined, provided one understands that populism is a matter of style and is not programmatic. But populist organizations also shed light on the reactions of European societies to the modulations in political offerings.[2] Finally, after 2001, the transition from national populism to neopopulism presented a paradox, albeit a misleading one: the extension of liberal values to the far-right field, combined with a shift from a critique of the welfare state to a critique of multiculturalism.

Insiders and Outsiders

In 1969 Giorgio Almirante declared in his report to the central committee of the Movimento Sociale Italiano (MSI): "We stand before two different paths: an alternative to the system or an alternative within the system."[3] That was a question that had gnawed at the cadres on the far right for decades. How to get away from old-fashioned protest methods and participate in power without betraying oneself? How could radicals participate in an electoralist and liberal system when what they wanted was to change the world, humankind, and the state? The problem became even more complicated during the Cold War, because anti-Marxist countersubversive actions became more closely aligned with the repressive sectors of the state, which, at the same time, they sought to subvert.

For decades, bipolar geostrategic issues were the foremost horizon of the far right. When the French National Front was constituted in 1972, its aim was to "block the Front Populaire," that is, the alliance of Socialists and Communists, which some feared might tip the global balance in favor of the Soviet Union. Little was said about immigration, nothing at all about Islam. These "populist" questions were first raised by the right wing of the British Conservative Party in 1968, a year after the birth of the British National Front and, more to the point, two years after the Conservatives had lost the elections. In a resounding oration, known to history as the Rivers of Blood speech, MP Enoch Powell, a member of the Conservative "Shadow Cabinet," forcefully introduced the racial question into political debate, claiming that Great Britain would face civil war if it did not manage to control the flow of nonwhite immigration. Powell, though an economic ultraliberal, did not speak of the cost of immigration but rather of an ethnocultural incompatibility that necessitated the repatriation of the migrants. The impact his speech had is evidence of the modifications in social relations brought about by the end of industrial society. The tone he adopted was also of key importance. The Union Movement's campaign on the slogan "Keep Britain White" had in fact had little success, and the theme of the genocide of the white race by an immigrationist conspiracy, launched by Colin Jordan in England, had remained underground on the radical far right. The Tories, however, decided to isolate Powell and his themes, especially since they believed that such views legitimized and favored the British National Front, which attracted increasing numbers of votes until 1976.[4] Powell's approach was one of Duprat's models when he reflected on the possibility of finding a winning formula for the FN. Switzerland was another: immigration had given rise to xeno-phobic sentiments in that country, despite the opposition of the parties, trade unions, and churches. The basis of the strategy was to denounce immigration in social terms at a time of high unem-ployment, force the right to compete with the far right on that theme, and thereby certify that the far right was not extremist but simply one rightist movement among others. Once normalization had been achieved, the goal was to take power.[5] That line of thinking was validated by events. The political scientist Kai Arzheimer has analyzed opinion polls from 1980 to 2002 taken in the countries of the European Union. He demonstrates that attempts by the right wing of national governments to seize on the alterophobic themes of the far-right parties ultimately increased popular support for the far right.[6]

The autonomy of the far-right electoralist parties is thus an impor-tant question, as is amply indicated by the case of Italy. Almirante, tired of remaining on the periphery, attempted in the early 1980s to pro-mote the MSI's participation in the public space. It was his policy to engage in debates with the democratic political forces. But in 1986, a meeting of the MSI leadership outvoted him on a motion to move away from Fascism and seek a rapprochement with the government parties. Almirante resigned in 1987. Proponents of the hard line sup-ported Pino Rauti as his successor, while advocates of moderniza-tion chose Gianfranco Fini, who was elected to the leadership of the MSI with 53.6 percent of the vote. His plan for an Alleanza Nazio-nale (AN; National Alliance) had the primary aim of building a cartel of all the rightist tendencies, beginning with the construction of AN clubs. The MSI would occupy a central position in that cartel. Fol-lowing the abrogation of the proportional electoral system in 1993 and the founding of Forza Italia (FI) by Silvio Berlusconi in 1994, the MSI-AN concluded an electoral agreement with FI and obtained 109 deputies, 43 senators, and 5 ministerial portfolios.[7] The MSI was therefore ripe for a partisan reorganization: at the 1995 congress it changed its name (becoming the Alleanza Nazionale), its logo (the famous flame used by the New Order syndicate and later popularized by the FN), its bylaws, and its platform. The metamorphosis was post-Fascist in nature: with the accession to power, the party officially abandoned Fascism and condemned both it and the extermination of the European Jews. In 2003 Gianfranco Fini visited the Yad Vashem memorial in Israel and there unequivocally condemned anti-Semitism and the Fascist experiments, the Republic of Salò included. The AN shifted to the center right, even as the radicals around Pino Rauti kept the flame alive within the Movimento Sociale–Fiamma Tricolore (MS-FT; Social Movement–Tricolor Flame). The overt Fascism of that organization did not rule out compromise, however: the MS-FT, despite its electoral inconsequentiality, participated with the other rightist parties in the electoral alliance headed by Berlusconi. At the European level, the MS-FT contributed to the Alliance of European National Movements (AENM), presided over by Bruno Gollnisch, vice president of the FN. In addition to these parties, Jobbik (Hungary), the British National Party (Great Britain), the Front National (Belgium), National Demokraterna (Sweden), Svoboda (Ukraine), the Movimiento Social Republicano (Spain), the Partido Nacional Renovador (Portugal), the Bălgarksa Nacionalna-Patriotična Partija (Bulgaria), and the Vlaams Belang (Flemish Nationalist Party of Belgium) all took part, with various associational statuses. The AENM thus had no ideological or programmatic coherence, attracting movements with totally diverging views on the national question and on plans for Europe. Parties with respect for the law rubbed shoulders with out-and-out radicals. That prompted Marine Le Pen to withdraw her National Front, in order to achieve a populist alliance among the European parliamentarians of the Austrian Freiheitliche Partei Österreichs (FPÖ), the Dutch Party for

Freedom (PVV), the Italian Lega Nord, the Vlaams Belang, and the French FN (apart from Jean-Marie Le Pen and Bruno Gollnisch).

The Italian experiment shows perfectly well the difficult balance to be struck between contesting the "system" and participating in the electoral marketplace. The AN's realignment toward an administrative center right more respectful than Berlusconi of the laws and of decency in politics, spelled political death.[8] In 2009 the AN dissolved and joined Berlusconi's troops in the new Il Popolo della Libertà (People of Freedom) party, then split off in 2010 to form Futuro e Libertà per l'Italia (Future and Freedom for Italy). That group certainly contributed to Berlusconi's fall, but nothing remains of it now. Marine Le Pen has cited the Fini experiment many times as a counterexample: to join the system culturally is to disintegrate it politically; the far right attracts votes only if the parties maintain their subversive charge.

For a time, the Lega Nord was able to seize on populist aspirations. That party is the only European ethnonationalist movement to make reference to a space that has never existed in history: the northern Italian "Padania," a geographical notion predating 1914 but reinvented in the 1970s for political ends by the group Stella Alpina, from which the Lega also borrowed its symbol. The Lega Lombarda (Lombard League), founded in 1982, united with the Liga Veneta (Venetian League) to form the Lega Nord per l'Indipendenza della Padania (Northern League for the Independence of Padania) in 1989. The excesses of its leader, Umberto Bossi, noteworthy even by the standards of Italian political life, allowed it to make its mark as an antisystem party, but that did not prevent its voters from embracing the Padania plan. The adoption of a shirt—albeit green, not black—as a uniform revealed the transgressiveness of the Lega. It has nevertheless evolved from an independence movement to a movement in favor of autonomy, even as the league's elected representatives have learned to stop insulting southern Italians, so as to be able to nationalize the party. Having won nearly 20 percent of the vote in northern

Italy in the regional elections of 1990, it received 8.6 percent in the national elections of 1992. As of 2000, immigrants became the new targets of the league's disparaging remarks. The Lega's participation in the exercise of power alongside Silvio Berlusconi, the confusion caused among its electorate when it supported Slobodan Milošević during the Kosovo War (its voters considered him a Socialist dictator), the resounding failure of the 2006 referendum to federalize and presidentialize Italy (the Lega Nord's primary objective since 1999), and finally, various politico-financial scandals contributed to its decline and to Bossi's resignation in 2012.[9]

Matteo Salvini became the Lega's new leader. He set aside Padania to concentrate on strong opposition to immigration, Islam, the European Union, and the refugees who have been arriving in southern Italy since 2007. That strategy was a success, and the Lega increased its share of the vote from 4 percent in the legislative elections of 2013 to 13 percent in the regional elections of 2015. It has also managed to attract new media attention. The Lega's leader developed a more far-reaching discourse, calling into question neoliberal policy and austerity while attacking the church. He denounced religious charity directed at migrants as a weakness, given the war supposedly being waged between them and the Italians, and claimed that that weakness contributed toward "the Africanization of Europe." And finally, he asserted that his party was bringing into politics exasperated citizens who would otherwise resort to violence.[10]

In short, in the case of the Italian experiment, it seems that the electorate is rejecting both the neo-Fascist far right and the post-Fascist right in favor of anti-oligarchic and alterophobic offerings. Participation in institutions is not necessarily a guarantee of success, but the electorate has greater indulgence toward its elected officials than toward outsiders. One indication of this is how few complaints have been made against the French FN, even though, despite having thirty-five deputies between 1986 and 1988, plus one FN and one Rassemblement Bleu Marine (RBM) deputy since 2012, it has no legislative record. Voters know that a ballot cast for the far right gives them leverage on migration, national security, and identity questions. Positive election results for the populist far right, even without its participation in government, exert constant pressure to modify the laws in these areas. The issue is not whether this is a "protest vote" or a "vote in support": rather, a "lobbying party" is being used to turn an electoral organization into an alliance with the president.

These populist movements are still often conflated with forms of Fascism. This misunderstanding led to large "anti-Fascist" demonstrations in Europe, when the FPÖ became part of the Austrian government in 2000. The populists' actions turned out to adhere to strict liberal orthodoxy. Those of the minister of finance, Karlheinz Grasser of the FPÖ, were consistent enough with the Euroliberal canon to win him a place in the Christian Conservative Party. But the FPÖ, which in 1999 had received a record share of the vote, 26.9 percent, saw its share fall to 10 percent in 2002, having lost its credit among the working classes. That is because, having been chosen by 48 percent of skilled workers to "denounce scandals and injustice" (the most important issue for 65 percent of FPÖ voters),[11] it wasted no time, once it had achieved power, in throwing its support behind the dismantlement of the state and of the social gains undertaken by the social democrats and pursued by conservatives. When it once again became an opposition party, it experienced renewed success (21.9 percent of the vote in the legislative elections of 2013), which shows the extent to which an antisystem position is more tenable without power, and how much indulgence the electorate has for populists, which it does not always have for the rest of the political class.

That also explains the disastrous results that European movements outside France have had when they have tried to imitate Lepenism, taking it as a model and plastering it onto a different national reality. The Belgian Front National has never been anything but an empty shell. But what solution could Lepenism offer to the problem of relations between Flemings and Walloons? In Spain, many of the far-right movements have also attempted to copy a hypothetical French formula, a difficult choice in a country that has long had a very stable ethnic structure (granted, it had 300,000 Gypsies in 1994, but only 0.9 percent of the population is composed of immigrants and only 0.4 percent come from outside the European Union).[12] Political organizations can learn from successes abroad, but a model's unsuitability to national structures leads to a loss of autonomy for a political offering, resulting in failure. The increase of immigration to Spain, combined with the Catalan independence movement, led to the emergence in 2003 of a Catalanist, national populist, identity-based Islamophobic movement (the immigrant population of Catalonia had risen from 94,000 in 1981 to more than 689,000 in 2003). That movement, the Plataforma per Catalunya (Platform for Catalonia), developed ties with Terre et Peuple, the Bloc Identitaire (BI), the FPÖ, and Vlaams Belang; but, despite its desire to learn from the Euroregionalists and their modernist language, it managed to make inroads with voters only in a few sectors.[13] The splinter group that broke away from the Movimiento Social Republicano after its Soberanía y Libertad (Sovereignty and Freedom) congress in 2014—inspired by the Bloc Identitaire, it even adopted the Greek lambda, the logo of that organization's youth movement—is not destined for a brighter future. Spain's inability to establish a national populist movement can be attributed to two principal factors. First, the Partido Popular, a large conservative party, was founded (under the name "Alianza Popular") at the end of the transition to democracy, and it welcomed all the Francoist moderates, thus cutting off the oxygen from potential organizations, leaving them without cadres or ideological positions. Second, the memory of Francoism and its repression of Basque and Catalan identities makes it almost impossible to sustain a far-right organization, which becomes irrelevant given that ethnic autonomy is, precisely, the strongest nationalist dynamic.

Germany provides another example of the failure of national populism. There as well, living memory and a powerful conservative party are prominent factors. Nevertheless, some inroads have been made, particularly with the Republikaner (7.1 percent of the vote in the European elections of 1989). The party grew out of a split with the Christlich Soziale Union (CSU) in Bavaria in 1983, and its leader, Franz Schönhuber, chose the French FN as its model. His past as a member of the Waffen-SS was a major handicap to his normalization. A bourgeois party of long standing, the Republikaner had fairly significant results between the Rhine and the Alps. But when German reunification, which had been their number one issue, took place during a conservative chancellor's term, the German far right's constituency shifted to the eastern Länder and their working-class youth. Nevertheless, the poor showing of national populism in Germany does not indicate the absence of a popular nationalism. German newsstands currently carry the largest number of nationalist titles, which both cast into relief and construct the spread of nationalist sentiments. They include: *Deutsche Wochenzeitung,* stamped with an iron cross on the masthead and the equivalent of the limited-circulation *Rivarol* in France, minus religion; the *Deutsche Stimme,* organ of the Nationaldemokratische Partei Deutschlands (NPD); *Zuerst* and *Compact,* two Islamophobic and pro-Russian nationalist monthlies; *Junge Freiheit,* a glossy weekly in the tradition of the Conservative Revolution but one that disseminates identity themes; and *Der Landser,* a review made up of war stories and portraits of German soldiers. The problem of the German far right is that, though it has both a working-class arena and a radical arena, it is unable to produce a stable political movement that would ensure an electoral compromise.

One of the other models sometimes hastily adopted is the FPÖ, even though many of its features are specific to Austria. Its history can be traced back to 1949, with the founding of the Verband der Unabhängigen (VdU; Association of Independents), which allowed many former mid-level and low-level cadres in the Nazi Party to be reintegrated into politics. In 1945, 500,000 former Nazis had lost their voting rights. They were restored four years later, which brought the VdU into Parliament with 11 percent of the vote. The creation of the FPÖ itself dates to 1955–1956. It was originally run by former Nazis, such as the former state minister Anton Rheinteller and the former Waffen-SS officer Friedrich Peter. But the FPÖ rapidly moved in two contradictory ideological directions: on one hand, it was joined by genuine liberals who wanted it to play a role in the government coalition; on the other, extremists in the party continued to fuel a national German faction that claimed Austria was only a fictive nation, a part of Greater Germany. Between 1983 and 1986, however, the FPÖ participated in a government coalition with the social democrats, sowing confusion about the party's political identity. Jörg Haider, advocating a return to basic tenets, was able to take control of the organization. The German national tendency was silenced beginning in 1993, and the FPÖ's ideology was elaborated in its political program of 1997. That program is particularly striking for its orientation, both nationalist xenophobic and economically ultraliberal. On economic and social welfare questions, the Party of Freedom wanted "a complete deregulation of the economy to guarantee prosperity and stabilize the employment market." The liberal character of such proposals, the fact that Haider came out in favor of the country joining NATO and that his criticism of the European Union was confined to asking that it not encroach on Austrian sovereignty and not become a federal organization, were the guarantees of the FPÖ's respectability.

The party welcomed the internal reforms of the far right: Haider's chief adviser was for a long time the new rightist Andreas Mölzer, who contributed to *Junge Freiheit* and published *Zur Zeit*. Mölzer was a pragmatic adviser, and it was thanks to his analysis of the dearth of votes from Catholic segments of the population that the party downplayed its neopagan elements in favor of an identity politics with Christianity as its foundation. In 1994 Mölzer worked on the party's institutional proposals (reduce parliamentary power in favor of measures of direct democracy and strengthen the executive branch). At the same time, he imported elements that came directly from the GRECE of the 1970s, as well as the following passages from the FPÖ program: "We reject multicultural experiments, which bear within them social conflicts. . . . The various peoples and ethnic groups have the right to see that their fundamental rights are preserved and to develop their own identity in peace." He was able to reintroduce into political vocabulary the term *Umvolkung*, which the SS had used for its policy of Germanic racial dissemination in Slavic territory, turning it into an expression that designated the colonization and ethnic changes that immigration would bring.

Haider managed to compensate for the weakness of the FPÖ's social standing through his media savvy and a marked talent for sparking controversies. Like Jean-Marie Le Pen in the FN, Jörg Haider's strength lay in his capacity to maintain a balance between different tendencies, by means of his charisma.[14] That did not prevent internecine quarrels, however: Heinz-Christian Strache established an alliance with the German nationals, which led Haider and his close circle to break away and create the Bündis Zukunft Österreich (Alliance for the Future of Austria) in 2005. Its future, already uncertain, was thrown into disarray when Haider died in 2008. Strache took over the leadership of the FPÖ, preserving the basic tenets of the party, including opportunism, which in 2015 led him to establish an alliance with the social democrats in the state of Burgenland, as Haider had done in his stronghold of Carinthia. That did not change a thing in the party's socioeconomic orientation: it lambasted what Greece was costing the Austrian taxpayer. At the same time, like Marine Le Pen, it adopted a policy of condemning gaffes: the party got rid of Mölzer in 2014, after he called the European Union, among other things, a "conglomerate of niggers." Nevertheless, the source of the FPÖ's strength is also the source of its weakness: essentially, the electorate is tired of the lack of diversity in political offerings. That raises a complex question, which also arises regarding the history of the Italian MSI and the French FN: popular exasperation with the existing political offerings may produce a populist dynamic, but, once populists are elected, how can they manage to hold onto that subversive function and not be eroded in turn by the exercise of power? Can the transaction be successful if the populists obtain reforms not of treaties or the economy, but of immigration and multiculturalism? That plan of action seems to be relatively effective.

The most convincing example is provided by the Finns Party. Formerly the "True Finns," the organization changed its name in 2011 because its leader, Timo Soini, wanted to clear up an ambiguity: the gap between the elites and the common people was more important to the party than ethnic distinctions. The party portrays itself as antisystem, critical of the European Union, and anti-immigration (only 5 percent of the population are immigrants). It does not cultivate radicalism: it presents itself as Christian conservative in its social values, left of center on the question of social benefits. It also purports to be the champion of the "little people," the defense of whom entails a clear program: stop immigration, treat multiculturalism as a danger, and reduce to a minimum the right of asylum and even foreign development aid. The party's leader does not fit the mold: in a country that is 98 percent Lutheran, he converted to Roman Catholicism; champion of one of the few non–Indo-European peoples on the continent, he has an absolute passion for Ireland, birthplace of the Celts. The party, having earned one of the top three slots in the legislative elections of 2015, joined a government coalition of rightist parties. Timo Soini was awarded the Foreign Affairs portfolio. That anti-elitist Euroskeptic served alongside Olli Rehn, former European commissioner, who had become minister of finance, and two multimillionaire businessmen, the new head of the government and his minister of transportation. The party's discourse on social problems was swept aside in favor of the government's objective of a six-billion-euro budget cut, and anti–European Union nationalism was channeled into a stated refusal to "pay for Greece." That transaction between participation in the exercise of power and submission to Euroliberalism, legitimized by an identity-based and anti-immigration policy, appears to be a future path for other European movements. In France, Nicolas Sarkozy understood this in 2015, when he pressured the FN not on questions of identity, on which the right-wing movements can agree, but on an economic program he lambastes as being on the "far left." If the FN wants to make the transition from a party with excellent election results in the first round of voting to a government party, it has no other choice but to turn toward liberalism, with the risk it will lose its subversive charge. In short, the protest against the dismantlement of the welfare state, which the FN says ought to be preserved but with its largesse reserved solely for nationals, has turned out to be an excellent means to increase vastly its share of the vote. Conversely, to become part of government institutions, it seems it will have to make sure that that advocacy of social programs more or less coincides with national liberalism.

A National Liberal Critique

The liberal critique of the interventionist state predominates in Scandinavian parties. For example, the Norwegian Progress Party and the Danish People's Party embody a rejection of the egalitarian model set in place by social democracy, within a context of relative prosperity (Denmark) and even real wealth (in spring 2015, Norway's unemployment rate reached its highest level in ten years: 4.2 percent). The far right attracts the vote of those who reject any form of income redistribution. From the mid-1970s on, Danish and Norwegian societies developed a populism that very quickly moved from antifiscal and anti-elitist protest to ethnic nativism. From 2009 to 2011, the Danish People's Party assisted the center right government in achieving a majority. It received a great deal in exchange: Denmark now has the most restrictive laws in Europe on immigration. Marriage is not allowed between a naturalized Danish citizen and an alien who come from the same country, unless both are at least twenty-four years old (to avoid forced marriages), and family reunification is allowed only if "the reunified family's attachment to Denmark is stronger than its attachment to the native country." Danish Islamophobia is fueled by a radicalization of Islam in that country. Denmark was stunned to discover that al-Qaeda's affiliate Al-Shabaab had widespread support within its Somali population and that the Islamist movement Hizb ut-Tahrir was lining its pockets with money from immigrant Pakistanis and Palestinians (the same is true in Great Britain, where it primarily attracts college students and graduates). As of 2004, before the publication of the caricatures of Muhammad by the *Jyllands Posten,* a Dane, Mustapha Darwich Ramadan, was the executioner of the (Jewish) American Nick Berg, who was beheaded by the Iraqi branch of al-Qaeda. The far right situates itself within that context of tensions around identity questions. Nevertheless, it can also have a regulatory effect. In Sweden, the 1990s were marked by the proliferation of groups of young neo-Nazis, modeled on American White Power culture, some with a capacity for terrorist action (the Vitt Ariskt Mostånd), and by a huge increase in the number of musical groups belonging to the scene in question (250 in 1996). As Sverigedemokraten has become part of the electoral field, the number of actions by radical groups has decreased: 1,947 in 2008; 1,507 in 2009; 1,469 in 2010, and 1,274 in 2011, more than half of them attributable to the Svenskarnas Parti and slightly more than 400 to the Svenska Motståndsrörelsen.[15]

Transitional forms between radicalism and national liberalism may emerge. Such is the case for the Flemish Vlaams Blok. It originated in 1978 following splits in the Flemish nationalist party Volksunie, some of whose members did not agree to participate in a government coalition that was judged pro-Francophone. The Vlaams Blok openly embraces the Verdinaso of the 1930s, an ethnic nationalism leading to a Europe of ethnic regions, an overt inegalitarianism vis-à-vis individuals and peoples, and an extremely pronounced organicism, leading it to assert that the rights of the individual must be "subordinate to the organic whole." But that radicalism is tempered by support for the building of a European army and the notion of a single European market, protectionist against outsiders but altogether neoliberal within. Its voter appeal was confined to a few isolated groups in the 1980s, but the Vlaams Blok experienced strong growth from 1991 to 2004.[16]

That growth in its voter base was accompanied by a reformulation of its ideological lexicon. The party has sought to modernize its mode of expression and its themes to broaden its appeal, but without an ideological aggiornamento. It has increased communication with Catholic circles and the working classes. It is responding to a paradoxical situation: the more votes Vlaams Blok brings in, the more powerless it becomes. In 1989, all the Flemish political forces pledged to reject any agreement with Vlaams Blok. At the same time, the Belgian media ostracized xenophobic and racist organizations (a position that is no longer tenable, because of the importance of the Flemish question and the replacement of television by the Internet as a medium of reference for entire swathes of Western societies).[17] As of 2003, the cordon sanitaire was breached: politicians on the right reached out to Vlaams Blok, all the while asking it to prove it would behave responsibly. There are also fierce intellectual discussions around the possibility of bringing the party into institutional debates, since its marginalization in no way held in check its electoral appeal. In 2004 the Vlaams Blok attracted 23.2 percent of the vote in the European elections; in the elections to the Flemish Parliament, it had within a decade doubled the number of votes it received.[18] At the same time, however, three associations close to Vlaams Blok were condemned for being racist. In view of the legal and economic risks, in 2004 the party reestablished itself under a new name, Vlaams Belang (Flemish Interest). It set about translating its racist discourse into Islamophobia and now emphasizes its neoliberalism. At first, its shift of focus was well received (in 2006 it became the leading party in the province of Antwerp). Later, however, Vlaams Belang experienced a persistent drop in its electoral results, in favor of the Nieuw-Vlaamse Alliantie (NVA; New Flemish Alliance), which emerged from the collapse of Volksunie in 2001. That party offered a more bourgeois and governmental version of Flemish aspirations. The growing acceptability of Vlaams Belang as of 2003, combined with the impossibility of its participating in government institutions, led it to adopt a de-demonization policy. But that approach, which weakened its antisystem appeal among voters, ultimately favored the nationalist right. Thirty-two percent of those who had voted for Vlaams Belang in 2007 chose the NVA in 2010; and, between the European elections of 2009 and those of 2014, the proportion of the vote that went to Vlaams Belang dropped from 9.9 percent to 4.2 percent.[19]

The difference between the Vlaams Blok and Vlaams Belang is very slight, when compared to that between the MSI and Alleanza Nazionale in Italy. Nevertheless, François Duprat's adage that "the voter always prefers the original to the copy," which has proven true when the right imitates the far right, also appears to work in the other direction. The vagaries of populism underscore a golden rule: politics is a marketplace in which parties must present their offerings autonomously. The Briton Enoch Powell paved the way for the French National Front by launching a product that his own party could not deliver. In France, the FN was insignificant so long as it remained within the anti-Communism niche, a segment that could not turn a profit because the rightist government parties are more efficient in that area and very active. Nicolas Sarkozy stole away Jean-Marie Le Pen's voters in 2007 on the "value of work" issue, but they returned to the fold and voted for Le Pen's daughter in 2012 in response to her campaign on identity, immigration, and Islam. In short, shares of the electoral market cannot be redistributed solely through triangulation (a tactic that is itself often misunderstood by politicians and their communications advisers): maintaining an identifiable, autonomous offering is indispensable.

The neoliberal populist parties appear to have reached their high point in 2000, with the successes recorded that year by the FPÖ, the Union Démocratique du Centre (UDC, Switzerland), the Lega Nord, the Progress Party, the Danish People's Party, and the Fremskridtspartiet. At the time, these organizations embodied a national populist reaction, not within a context of economic recession but in a situation of growth—full employment or low unemployment. They contested the methods of the social democratic government and those of the liberal right, which had rallied behind the welfare state to a greater or lesser extent, but they accepted without reservations the democratic political and institutional process. They benefited from the proximity of the Eastern European countries that joined the European Union between 2004 and 2013 and from the socioeconomic problems raised before and after that process was complete. The movements in the Alpine countries resemble one another rather closely: they want to dismantle the welfare state and deregulate the economy; distrust globalized free trade and embrace the national interest; oppose certain forms of supernationality, particularly a federal Europe, but without opposing a potential Europe of regions; defend an ethnodifferentialist notion of national identity; reject immigration; and emphasize the particularity of Mitteleuropa, which is overlooked by the European Union.

That ideological foundation is solid enough to constitute a political brand identifiable by the voter on the political market, but it remains malleable enough to allow for readjustments, as the Swiss UDC has demonstrated. Its name in the German-speaking part of Switzerland is more explicit: Schweizerischen Volkspartei (Swiss People's Party). It came into existence in 1971 as a result of the rapprochement between two agrarian parties (the Party of Peasants, Artisans, and Burghers and the Democrats of Graubünden and Glauis). The UDC received 11.6 percent of the vote in the federal elections of 1979, then leapt to first place in 1999 (22.5 percent). The party is opposed to any international openness on the part of Switzerland, whether juridical, geopolitical, economic, demographic, or cultural, favoring a timeless Switzerland with conservative mores and entrepreneurial common sense. In opposition to the elites, the UDC wants to further shore up the system of popular sovereignty, by reducing representative democracy to a minimum in favor of direct democracy. Its three pillars are fear of integration, xenophobia, and economic ultraliberalism. The party accepts the principle of "balanced bilateral agreements" with the European Union, provided they are submitted to the people for approval, and in 2002 it campaigned against joining the United Nations. On immigration policy, its program is an exact replica of Haider's in Austria. Its treatment of radicals has evolved: in 1999, though the national UDC ousted the new right lawyer Pascal Junod, who had taken over its Geneva branch, no penalty was imposed on the anti-Semitic negationist Emil Rahm or the neo-Nazi Roger Etter (now in prison for murder). In 2009 a young militant was expelled for having participated in riots with radicals from the Partei National Orientierter Schweizer.

As in many other countries, the far right's success in Switzerland has moved part of the political debate to the right. But, with the rise to power of Oskar Freysinger (he now represents the Swiss People's Party at the National Council of Switzerland Parliament for Valais), it has also displaced the UDC's own center of gravity. Adopting the Islamophobic themes of the Dutchman Geert Wilders, the far right got behind the popular initiative that led to the constitutional ban on minarets in 2009, despite the opposition of the body politic. That success left its mark on the European far-right movements, including the French FN, which was in a weak position at the time. An electoral majority had joined with the populist far right against the "system," thanks to Islamophobia: that was an example the FN would not forget. Furthermore, the theme of the "republic of referendums," in existence since 2002, was clearly favored by that vote.[20] The neopopulist shift of the European far right resulted from a dual shock: the geopolitical crisis subsequent to September 11, 2001, and the socioeconomic recession that followed the 2008 financial crisis.

The Neopopulist Shift

The appeal to Islamophobia, which is at the heart of neopopulism, predates 2001. During the war in the former Yugoslavia, Serbia, accused of Nazism, claimed in its propaganda that it constituted an advance post against the Islamization of Europe, where an "Islamic Fascism" was seeking to implant itself. The Muslims had long been accused of planning a "genocide" of the Serbs. The former leader of

Organisation Lutte du Peuple, who portrays himself as Jean Thiriart's heir, was one of the first to gain a hearing for that argument
in Western Europe, in the newspaper of the Belgian Parti Communautaire National-Européen (European-National Communitarian
Party).[21] Because the Kosovo War was concomitant with the split
within the French FN, and because the radicals chose Bruno Mégret
over Jean-Marie Le Pen, during the European elections of 1999 the
Mégrétists' Mouvement National Républicain (National Republican
Movement) began to use an Islamophobic discourse, attributing the
problems of criminality to a violent Islamization. That new approach
led the anti-Zionist radicals to rethink their views on the relationship between, on one hand, a West encompassing Israel and, on the
other, the Arab Muslim world, which for them included the European populations from Arab Muslim countries. In 2000, the meeting
in Belgium between Filip Dewinter, leader of the Vlaams Blok, and
several leaders of the Jewish community in Antwerp confirmed that
a process had been underway for several years to form an alliance between the Flemish nationalist party and a community radicalized
by the large increase in anti-Semitic acts committed by young immigrants.[22] The same year, the Ligue de Défense Juive was founded
in France, where anti-Semitic violence had leapt from 37 percent of
all racist violent acts in 1999 to 82 percent in 2000.[23] This is the
French branch of the American Jewish Defense League (considered
a terrorist organization in the United States, like its equivalent in Israel, Kach), inspired by the racist rabbi Meir Kahane, who was as-
sassinated by an Islamist in 1990. Granted, the movement is limited
in scope, but the birth of an activist far-right group of Zionists, combined with the success at the time of an anti-Arab Internet forum
called "SOS Racailles" (SOS Scum) and the invitations by Jewish
associations to Islamophobic speakers from the radical far right,
marked a change: the wall that had separated the European Jews from
the far right since 1945 was trembling on its foundations. Bruno
Mégret sent clear signals to French Jews after September 11, 2001, but
without success, obtaining only 2.3 percent of the vote. Philippe de

Villiers (Mouvement pour la France, a group on the sovereignist and conservative right), on the advice of the former Mégrétist Guillaume Peltier,[24] took up the refrain of Islamophobia and the denunciation of the globalism of elites during the presidential campaign of 2007, but he had no greater success (2.2 percent of the vote).[25] As it happens, it was in a country with scarcely a far-right tradition, by a man who did not even belong to the far right, that neopopulism emerged.

Pim Fortuyn was from the intellectual left, and he proudly declared his homosexuality. The Netherlands, a multicultural country that embraces a liberal philosophy, no longer had a far right, its share of the vote having fallen to 0.6 percent in the legislative elections of 1998. And yet, by vigorously denouncing the so-called freedom-destroying presence of Islam, Pim Fortuyn experienced a meteoric rise: his Lijst Pim Fortuyn received 34.7 percent of the vote in Rotterdam in the municipal elections of 2002. He combined a charisma comparable to that of Haider and Jean-Marie Le Pen, an assault on the elites, and an open homosexuality that allowed him to pass for a progressive defending freedom against an Islam shrouded in darkness. He co-opted the debate on *inburgering* (the integration of immigrants by means of assimilation) launched by the rightist and leftist parties to affirm that, in a country governed by the terms of a fragile accord between Christian religious groups and secularists, a supplementary "pillar" of society—namely, Islam—could not be allowed to stand. Muslim immigration was accused of shattering *zerzuiling* (politico-administrative segregation, known in English as "pillarization"), on which the Dutch consensus had rested since 1917.[26]

Fortuyn was murdered by a far-left activist in May 2002. The country's emotional response fueled the success of the Lijst Pim Fortuyn in the legislative elections a few weeks later (17 percent), bringing it into the government coalition. Nevertheless, the party was unable to hold together without its founder and quickly disappeared. No matter: the Lijst Pim Fortuyn had demonstrated the possibility of new political practices, in particular, of a "national security hedonism" (to use the expression of Gaël Brustier and Jean-Philippe Huelin), which would require an alliance between liberal individualism and national security concerns. The criticism of Muslims did not take up the theme of Christian conservatism; rather, it defended the freedoms achieved by women, gays, and Jews.[27] These criticisms resonate perfectly with neoconservatism, which, having first gained momentum in the United States, has now spread to the West as a whole and regularly conflates Islamism and Nazism.

Geert Wilders is a Dutch politician, linked, precisely, to American neoconservative circles. He managed to perpetuate that dynamic in the Netherlands, clearly orienting it toward the far right, especially when the 2004 murder of the filmmaker Theo Van Gogh laid bare the country's cultural crisis. Yet despite his virulent denunciation of the European Union as a "Nazi State" and of Islam, the Dutch leader did not come from the far right. In the 1990s, he was the parliamentary assistant to the future European commissioner Frits Bolkestein, author of the "directive on services," an ultraliberal and a Europeanist. Wilders, himself an MP in the Volkspartij voor Vrijheid en Democratie (People's Party for Freedom and Democracy) as of 1998, did not leave the party until 2006, when he founded the Partij voor de Vrijheid (PVV; Party for Freedom), of which he is the only member, thus breaking radically with all established political forms. He has amplified his former mentor's distrust of non-European immigration, which he seeks to stop for a period of at least five years. He follows him in the desire to reduce the state's prerogatives but, styling himself the defender of the "average Dutchman," he fights against raising the retirement age and reducing tax deductions on individual retirement accounts. He wants to ban halal and kosher slaughter methods, minarets, dual nationality, the construction of new mosques, and the Quran. The rest of his program is organized around the opposition between the common people and the elites: the rejection of elected officials, a return to authority and moral values, national security, the introduction of popular initiative referendums and binding legislative mandates. He defends returning Flanders to the Netherlands (the proposal to establish a zone extending from northern France to the

Netherlands has been made repeatedly by the radical far right in that region). He portrays Israel as a "sentry of the West" and maintains very good relations with its former minister of foreign affairs Avigdor Lieberman (leader of the far-right Yisrael Beiteinu). The PVV, having won 15.4 percent of the vote in the legislative elections of 2010, joined the parliamentary majority but not the government, on a compact to support the economic austerity policy and the fight against immigration. Its later subpar performance (in the elections to the European Parliament, its share of the vote fell from 17 to 13 percent between 2009 and 2014) led the PVV to withdraw from that majority, and there is a real question about the line it will take in the future, in view of the threshold effect it suffered. Populist unrest on "way of life" issues nevertheless fuels a heated debate in Europe, as indicated by the ban on halal and kosher methods of slaughter in Poland (passed in 2013, lifted in 2014) and Denmark (2015).

The neopopulist shift was not a blow to the FN in France. After the mass demonstrations calling for the defense of the republic against the "threat" represented by Jean-Marie Le Pen's presence in the second round of the 2002 presidential election, the cadres surrounding Marine Le Pen (Louis Aliot, Marie-Christine Arnautu, and others) became convinced that the party had to initiate a strategy known as "de-demonization": the elimination of anti-Semitism, anti-Zionism, and racialism; the expulsion of radicals or their submission to the party line; the submission or expulsion of the Catholic national militants to make the FN less "stuffy" and less denominational; a greater emphasis on social programs; and a focus on proposals for a republic of referendums to counter the accusation of Fascism.[28] The process did not move forward without a few failures. In 2006 the FN publicized the writer Alain Soral's entry into its ranks. With the help of Philippe Péninque, former member of the Groupe Union et Défense, Soral launched Égalité et Réconciliation, an association to scout out ethno-religious segments of the population and hence to supply the FN with cadres of "diverse origins," which would supposedly allow for the party's normalization by neutralizing the accusation of racism.[29] But Soral's radical anti-Zionism and volcanic personality proved unmanageable. Rejected as the party's top candidate for the European elections of 2009, he stormed out. Having successfully retreated to Égalité et Réconciliation, he undertook a cultural battle that has had clear results. He flirts with demonization to the point of declaring himself a "National Socialist," though his absence of racialism defies comparison to Nazism. His books sell by the tens of thousands, his videos and those of his close friend the comedian Dieudonné have attracted millions of views. The Soral-Dieudonné duo reached an understanding with the Shia of the Centre Zahra (close to the Iranian regime and the Hezbollah) and their Parti Antisioniste (Anti-Zionist Party) to put forward an anti-Zionist slate in the European parliamentary elections of 2009 (1.3 percent of the votes in the district of Île-de-France, the only one where they were on the ballot). After some wavering, Égalité et Réconciliation gave up the idea of becoming a political party and ousted Duprat's disciples, who were hoping to turn it into a revolutionary nationalist party. In the end, Soral and Dieudonné, believing the FN had committed a betrayal and was espousing a pro-Israel position, created a new party, Réconciliation Nationale (National Reconciliation), in late 2014.[30] It was a risky wager because, under French law, so long as Dieudonné was putting on "comedy shows," he enjoyed a broader right to free expression than a politician would have. In any case, the pair remains at the center of a self-proclaimed "Dissent," which attempts to unite the radical French and Belgian anti-Zionists.[31]

Despite what intellectuals influenced by the right claim, the high visibility acquired by the growing social acceptability of anti-Semitism and the social incapacity to mount any resistance to it should not be perceived as a sign that France has become anti-Semitic because of the portion of its population that is of Arab Muslim descent and because of the leftist movements. These factors are important, but they are not the only ones. As the political scientist Nonna Mayer has demonstrated, anti-Semitic opinions, and the conjunction between anti-Semitism and anti-Zionism, remain largely confined to the far right; and, though they may seek legitimation through hatred of Israel, they are still governed by the anti-Semitic notions of Jewish money and power.[32]

Granted, the FN has sent out signals that it has taken its distance from anti-Zionism, which was once prevalent in the party. Marine Le Pen wished to be received in Israel, and Louis Aliot visited the country in 2011. Less than a pro-Israel position, this was an effort to obtain a marker that would allow them to neutralize the accusation of anti-Semitism and to move closer to the right wing of the French conservative party, where economic liberalism goes hand in hand with support for Israel. It is thus less a geopolitical notion than a political positioning on the domestic front. Marine Le Pen has been able to incorporate the neopopulist shift and the defense of women, gays, and Jews, by pointing a finger at phallocratic, homophobic, and anti-Semitic Islam. That has served to frame the FN as almost a gay-friendly party, though not without internal tensions, and the proportion of women in the party has grown tremendously (about four militants in ten are female, and the FN respects gender parity in choosing its candidates).[33] To scout out other segments of the population, the FN has reactivated the strategy of constructing peripheral sectors (already advocated by Duprat and applied by Mégret). For example, the Collectif Racine (Root Collective), launched in 2013, works the education sector. It is entrusted to a man formerly close to the Parti Communautaire National-Européen (PCN) and a follower of Thiriart, which is a sign that FN vice president Florian Philippot's group is not without its radicals. As in the Mégrétist era, these endeavors, for lack of earmarked capital, have for the moment not managed to fulfill their function.

Why Populism?

A vulgarization of the geographer Christopher Guilly's analysis of "peripheral France" has been widely used to explain the FN's growing electoral success.[34] The FN is said to be gaining adherents in the outlying suburbs, among members of the middle and working classes relegated to the geographical and political fringes of the gentrified metropolises. These sectors are seeking to avoid the social problems of the working-class zones that have large populations of Afro-Maghrebi descent. This is a France suffering from globalization, a France that Marine Le Pen, since the success of that view in politics and the media, claims she represents, calling it "the France of the forgotten" or "the France of the invisible."

One of the undeniable merits of that theory has been to shed light on the connections between urbanism, way of life, and electoral choices. But the territorial question is not valid only for the FN; it can also be found in the evolution of European populism. In fact, three root causes for the growth of these movements and three developments can be discerned, only one of which has to do with the question of living space (with its cultural and economic aspects). The first forms of populism had a radical foundation (in Austria, Flanders, and so on), which led in the direction of identity populism. The next incarnations were rooted in tax revolt (Denmark, Norway, and others) and moved toward an identity politics of prosperity that could even entail inter-European antagonism: in Luxembourg, the National Bewegong (National Movement) demanded that the French leave, while in Switzerland the UDC and the Mouvement Citoyens Genevois (Genevan Citizens Movement) targeted French who crossed the border to work. Finally, the most recent forms of populism originated in agrarianism (Switzerland, Finland, the Boerenpartij [Peasant Party] in the Netherlands before 1981, and others) and moved toward a hedonist national security liberalism. It may be noted that the French FN has managed to combine all three aspects, which no doubt explains in good part the particular nature of its success.

It is of the utmost importance that the role of peasant populations in protests against globalization has been replaced by that of urban populations. In the nineteenth century, the far right lambasted industrial society, which had replaced "traditional" society. In the interwar period, the far-right movements converged in their loathing of the urban milieu, which they accused of being the site of decadence and uprootedness, and the question of the peasantry played an essential role in the history of Fascism.[35] In the postindustrial era, the social imaginary still grants a place to the small farmlands of peasants, which are wholly irrelevant to the current social structure. And, with the theme of "sensitive neighborhoods," it still sees the city as the site of decadence. At the same time, the FN, to take one example, now portrays industrial society as a golden age, with a mythified representation of working-class unity. Everything comes together, however, to mark the decline incarnated by postmodern individualism, and the populist movements are critical of the rapid transformation of ways of life, seeing it as a consequence of either "Islamization" or "Zionism." In other words, the influence of populism can be explained in terms of postmodern behaviors (citizens believe they have the right to shop around for their ideology; they can make electoral choices without a judgment predetermined by history; they demand more direct democracy so as to be partners in the decision-making process; and so on), but that populism is directed against postmodernity. The "national narratives" that allowed the integration of the masses into industrial society in the nineteenth century have not been replaced by a narrative to rival that of populist ethnonationalism. In a globalized and uncivil society,[36] where citizens are no longer incorporated into the political realm through trade unions, parties, and churches, there is a demand for a protective enclosure. For the moment, the only path leading in that direction involves a critique of cultural liberalism and a demand for social authoritarianism.

The question of living space is not isolated, therefore, but is part of a larger whole. The political scientist Pascal Perrineau has proposed that it be considered one of five "fractures" that explain the advances made by the FN. The other four are: inadaptation to the globalized economy, a positive relationship to enclosure and authority, the shift to the right on social values, and disenchantment with the political.[37] Joël Gombin, also a political scientist, has shown that, since the European parliamentary elections of 2009, the FN vote has correlated with income inequality in urban areas: a surfeit of inequality leads to a disproportionate vote for the National Front, even in cities where household income is above the national average. The FN vote of workers in the northeast, so often cited to show the link between the National Front and the working classes, thus conceals the disproportionate vote by cadres in various parts of the same region. The FN manages to appeal to a social democratic electorate by portraying itself as a jab at Euroliberalism, but it continues to participate in the electoral marketplace on the right, where it presents itself as the best bet against cultural liberalism.[38]

The FN vote is thus built not on "a peripheral France" but on its success in linking various peripheries, some well off and with no direct contact with multiculturalism, others that combine direct contact with a high proportion of immigrants and low income level. Moreover, the FN's success since 2012 cannot be explained by the party's "de-demonization" and "swing to the left"—corresponding to a social demand from the working class and the pauperized middle class—unless several factors are omitted. In the municipal elections of 2014, various cities had far-right slates other than that of the FN: the deputy and mayor Jacques Bompard (Ligue du Sud) was reelected in the first round in Orange, and his movement received 49.35 percent of the vote in Bollène. The members of Oeuvre Française, newly disbanded by the state and whose campaign poster made reference to Dieudonné, attracted 11.49 percent of the vote in Vénissieux. Carl Lang's Parti de la France (PF) put forward ten slates: a former member of the "No to Minarets" slate received 14.61 percent of the vote in Ronchamp (Haute-Saône) and 24.66 percent of the electorate voted for the PF in the village of Ouzouer-sur-Trézé (Loiret). That election also showed that the FN vote was closely linked to turnout. In short, it was not a "protest vote" indicating the "despair of the working classes." Rather, the vote for the far right was related to politicization and a return to the voting booth. Even outside the FN, then, the far-right vote exists: it now meets a social demand.[39] Granted, the demand for authoritarianism and the unity of the state can find an outlet other than the far right. In 1958, when the Poujadist wave disappeared as suddenly as it had appeared, it was not because it was a "flash in the pan," as a classic analysis would have it. Nor had the tax issues and the Algerian question that motivated it disappeared. But General de Gaulle's accession to power and the replacement of the Fourth Republic by the Fifth satisfied the desire for order and authority.

At present, the distance taken from the political, economic, and cultural "center" is radicalizing the "peripheries," which are calling for their "integration" by means of a social hierarchy judged to be legitimate (the exclusion of foreign elements, among other methods). The FN economic program has not moved to the left: it rests in the first place on "national preference" and embraces greater intervention on the state's part, which belongs to an overall radicalization of the role it allocates to the executive branch. That conception has the advantage of ideological coherence, but its limits were revealed in the departmental elections of 2015. The subpar performance registered by the party (success in the first round, but no department-wide victory in the second) can be explained, to be sure, by the difficulty of fusing the different identity demands of electorates on the right, but above all by the rejection on the part of conservative voters of state interventionism.

Criticism of postmodern and postindustrial society, falling back on the disparagement of people from the Arab Muslim world living on European territory, remains one of the best resources for European populists. Nevertheless, finding a political form for that criticism remains a complicated matter. The writer Renaud Camus, previously known primarily in homosexual circles and for the controversy he created in 2000 when he deemed the number of Jewish participants in a public radio broadcast too high, has had great success with his admonition about the "Great Replacement" organized by a "replacist" power. The success of that umpteenth incarnation of a theme launched immediately after World War II (Camus has personally declared his indebtedness to Enoch Powell) can be explained by the fact that he subtracted anti-Semitism from the argument. Nevertheless, transforming that dynamic into politics has proved to be an arduous task. Having founded the idiosyncratic Parti de l'In-nocence, Camus launched NON (short for "No to the Change of People and Civilization"), which presented a slate of candidates for the European parliamentary elections of 2014 in the district of Languedoc-Roussillon but received only 0.04 percent of the vote. (The slate headed by Louis Aliot came in first, which indicates the FN's hegemony over the far-right electorate.) The German phenomenon Patriotische Europäer gegen die Islamisierung des Abendlandes (PEGIDA; European Patriots against the Islamization of the West) then emerged as a model to follow.

As of autumn 2014, particularly in Dresden (a city that is about 2 percent Muslim), PEGIDA has regularly managed to assemble several thousand people against "Islamization" (as many as 25,000 in January 2015). Here as well, the organization's postmodernity is clear: it uses social networks, demonstrators come from the educated middle class but include in their ranks members of the radical far right, anti-immigrant slogans are combined with those from the 1989 demonstrations that brought down the Berlin Wall, and so on. PEGIDA, campaigning on the themes of Islamization and more direct democracy, managed to win 9.6 percent of the vote in Dresden in the municipal elections of June 2015. The movement exerted a magnetic attraction on the sovereignist party Alternative für Deutschland (Alternative for Germany), founded in 2013, which had received 7.1 percent of the vote in the European parliamentary elections of 2014. That dynamic has proved difficult to transpose to other countries, because the versions of PEGIDA across Europe are for the most part limited to agitprop on social networks. But in France, Renaud Camus and Riposte Laïque (Secular Response) announced, just after the terrorist attacks of January 2015, that they were founding PEGIDA-France.

It did not take hold, because of the disastrous timing, the hegemony of the FN, and the decision by PEGIDA-France to form an alliance with Réseau Identités (Identities Network), composed for the most part of the Ligue du Midi, rather than with the Bloc Identitaire, by far the largest identity movement. On its own, the BI steered clear of that initiative, which threatened to destroy its relations with the FN during negotiations regarding RBM nominations.[40] In France, moreover, the disparaging of ethnic subcultures and Islam has for several years been altogether mainstream and does not require a "catalyzing agent" like PEGIDA. Ultimately, PEGIDA's success in Germany was linked to the absence of any organized national populist and anti-immigration electoral offering, whereas in France the natural outlet for opposition on principle to the presence of Islam is a ballot cast for the FN. The initiatives taken elsewhere in Europe to export PEGIDA have had no more success. PEGIDA Walloon-Brussels made the same bad wager as its French counterpart: it introduced itself to the public after a terrorist episode that traumatized the country, in this case the assault two days earlier by the Belgian special forces against a radical Islamist group. As in France, the consequence was a ban on demonstrations. The demonstration of PEGIDA-Vlaanderen, its counterpart in the Dutch-speaking part of Belgium, was banned by Burgermeister Bart De Wever, president of the Nieuw-Vlaamse Alliantie (NVA). A government party at the federal level that had managed to cut into Vlaams Belang's share of the vote, the NVA could not allow an initiative to prosper that had been launched by militants such as Hans Dubois, formerly of the nationalist groups Voorpost and Onderzoek, Documentatie en Informatie Netwerk (ODIN); Rudy Van Nespen, the Vlaams Belang representative for Deurne; the essayist Wim Van Rooy, fellow traveler of the Vlaams Belang; and his son Sam Van Rooy, former colleague of the Dutch MP Geert Wilders.

In conclusion, populist successes and failures do not indicate merely the crises of multicultural society. They also bring to light the demand for participation in the political process in societies where the educational level has risen considerably within a few decades, at the very moment when the European space has reached a postdemocratic phase. Nonetheless, it is not notions of equality or freedom that are mobilized, but rather the desire to feel one lives in a "community," that one stands together with those like oneself. The question of populism cannot be swept aside in the name of an open society and the adaptation to a globalized society. Its condemnation as a "Fascist threat to democracy" is a tremendous misinterpretation. When in power, populists do not abrogate fundamental freedoms: they exchange the renunciation of their social demands for anti-immigration policies. They thus bring their electorate into a politics that is interclassist thanks to them, one that ethnicizes Euroliberalism. Populism allows for the production of a historical bloc, in the Gramscian sense of that expression (a union of social forces moving beyond their particular economic interests to seize power), to the benefit of an ethnoliberalism. But it cannot produce a revolutionary phenomenon in opposition to ordoliberalism (originally, a German liberal strain that believed the state's social role was to maintain a normative framework that allowed free and not manipulated competition, which is now an internationalized political reality). The far right's participation or nonparticipation in government can thus be seen not as a threat to democracy but as a choice. If the sovereign people want Euroliberalism, but without demographic globalization, logic requires that rightist populism be integrated into the exercise of power, since it allows for the construction of a social consensus and the elaboration of an ethnoliberal policy, all the more so in that this far-right movement no longer engages in antisystem protest. But if the sovereign people believe that Euroliberalism is either negative or that it ought to be dealt with in concert with egalitarian humanism, logic demands that the populist far right be kept on the periphery of the institutions.

6

What's New to the East?

The Eastern European far-right movements have followed their own particular path. Glasnost, the new openness of the Soviet regime sought by Mikhail Gorbachev, allowed freedom of speech within limits beginning in 1985. Four years later, the Eastern Bloc collapsed. In spring 1991 the Baltic countries (Estonia, Latvia, and Lithuania) demanded their freedom, which led to an attempted coup d'état that summer in Moscow from conservatives—in this case, the Communists, which makes it abundantly clear that the eastern part of the continent must not be understood in terms of Western assumptions. The Baltic countries and Ukraine declared their independence. By Christmas, the Soviet Union no longer existed. A Commonwealth of Independent States (CIS) was established, and Boris Yeltsin was the new strongman in Russia. Eastern European societies were thrust into the difficult process of adapting to representative democracy and a capitalist economy. In that phase of new and rapidly spreading globalization, far-right movements arose to contest the "new world order" proclaimed by U.S. president George H. W. Bush and to reject the multipolarity inherent in that project. They also refused to accept the "end of history" announced by some liberal Western intellectuals. For them, that was synonymous with atomized postmodern societies, where the rules of the market turn human beings into commodities / consumers and exert an influence even in the realm of ethics and individual modes of behavior.

In 1993 President Yeltsin clashed with his legislature, a conflict that culminated in the bombing of the Russian Parliament in October. United against Yeltsin were the Communist Party of the Russian Federation (KPFR), under the leadership of Gennady Zyuganov; the neo-Stalinists of the Labor Russia movement, whose leader, Viktor Anpilov, supported a "united antisystem front" that incorporated the ultranationalist right; and the "national Communists" of the newspaper *Den,* published by Alexander Prokhanov. All of them joined with the groups that grew out of the Pamyat movement, an unstable mix of Orthodox mysticism, rabid anti-Semitism, and monarchism in the spirit of the Black Hundreds of the prerevolutionary imperial era. A new constitution gave extensive powers to the Russian president. He set a policy that both Communists and nationalists considered submission pure and simple to Western norms: national humiliation. The convergence of militants on both sides took the form of a National Salvation Front (NSF; 1992–1993). For the most part, however, the opposition worked to the advantage of Boris Yeltsin, who played the "it's-me-or-chaos" card, and extremist cadres proved expert at his game. It fell to Vladimir Putin, who came to power in 2000, to reconcile the nationalist aspirations of those nostalgic for the Soviet era and of advocates of neo-Eurasianist imperialism. That very specific context explains in great part why post-Soviet far-right nationalism is above all a geopolitics grounded in Russian exceptionalism, that is, the conviction that the country's mission transcends the historical break between the Russian Empire and the Communist era and is valid for the present and the future.

Aleksandr Dugin's neo-Eurasianism was the chief ideological innovation.[1] It combines Eurasianism in its original form (analyzing Russia as a unique civilization by virtue of its geographic location between East and West), new right theories, revolutionary nationalist views, esoteric and Evolian elements, and the legacy of German geopolitical thought of the 1920s–1930s (specializing in the theories of *Lebensraum*). This ideology has played an increasingly large role in Vladimir Putin's policy to redefine Russia's borders and, especially, in his efforts to build a politico-economic space, the Eurasian Economic Union, extending from Belarus to Kyrgyzstan and incorporating the emergent power of Kazakhstan, where Eurasianism is official doctrine.

In addition to the Eurasianist theme, several problematics specific to Eastern Europe need to be pointed out. First, the central question there is how to define the nation, ethnonationalism in this case being by no means limited to the far right. In that part of the continent, it is generally accepted that the nation is an organic whole comprising three aspects: ethnicity (hence the problem raised by the Gypsy, Albanian, and Serb diasporas), historical nation, and religious community.[2] The religion in question is usually Catholic or Eastern Orthodox, but some Lutheran ministers are also very involved with the far right, such as Lóránt Hegedűs Jr. in Hungary, within the Jobbik movement (Alliance of the Young on the Right–Movement for a Better Hungary), founded in 2003. That conception is inadmissible from the standpoint of the West, which generally views citizenship as being contractual. Furthermore, many irredentist movements and territorial disputes persist in Eastern Europe, often aftereffects of the Treaty of Trianon (1920), which broke up the Austro-Hungarian Empire and destroyed the balance, fragile but real, that provided relative security to minorities, including Jews. Mitteleuropa, the Balkans, and the former Commonwealth of Independent States are a mosaic of peoples and languages, which the relocation of borders after 1945 left vulnerable in some cases (particularly the former Yugoslavia) to ethnic nationalist movements. In retrospect, it is also striking that Communism, which evidently did not succeed in eradicating ethnic particularism and religious practices, despite its proclamations, also did not obliterate prewar ideological frames of reference. After the thaw, as if Marxism had simply been shrugged off, some political parties—nationalist or not—reappeared under their old names (the Romanian National Liberal Party; the Internal Macedonian Revolutionary Organization [VMRO]; the Croatian Party of Rights). Cultural associations (such as the Matica Slovenská in Slovakia), which had promoted the national language and national identity in a clearly ethnonational spirit since the mid-nineteenth century, also resumed their activities.[3] Finally, under the Communist regimes, radical nationalist movements had continued to exist or even emerged: in Poland, Maciej Giertych (b. 1936), future leader of the League of Polish Families and scion of a family of nationalist ideologues, was able to return from exile in 1962 and earn his university credentials. And the Catholic association PAX, a national democratic group dating to before 1939, openly continued its activities with the regime's consent. In Romania, likewise, Iosif Constantin Drăgan (1917–2008), a former Iron Guard sympathizer, became an influential businessman and was part of Ceauşescu's intimate circle, before founding the Liga Mareşal Ion Antonescu in 1990. True, there was a ruthless purge of pro-Fascist militants, and their movements had to relocate political and publishing activities to European countries (primarily Spain), the Americas (Canada, the United States, Argentina), or Oceania (Australia), where large numbers of them had taken refuge, but that does not mean that the patterns of thought of radical nationalism totally disappeared under Communism.

Russia: From National Bolshevism to Neo-Eurasianism

Pamyat (Memory), founded in 1982, was originally a cultural association. In 1984 it turned to denouncing the "Judeo-Masonic conspiracy" and "Zionism," and the following year gave a public reading of the *Protocols of the Elders of Zion*. Many associations appeared under the same name or variants of it, some maintaining that they ought to urge Russia to take the lead in the "Aryan world" in the battle against the "Zionists." Fanatically reactionary, Pamyat maintained that the USSR was merely a cover for Zionist power, which was perpetrating the "genocide" of the Russian people. Pamyat wanted to hark back to the time of imperial Russia and to protect both the genotype of the

Russian population and the Orthodox religion as an element of ethnic identity[4] (though there were also neopagan factions, part of the multi-faceted nature of the phenomenon). Given the scope of the protests, the Soviet authorities attempted to launch their own Pamyat, in an effort to reconcile nationalism and Sovietism. The Pamyat network has thus had Communist, liberal, and monarchist faces; some down-played anti-Semitism while others specialized in it.[5]

From the ranks of that network emerged the man who would mark the birth of a Russian neonationalism: Aleksandr Dugin, who since 1988–1989 has moved in Western European new right circles. Robert Steuckers introduced him to Ernst Niekisch's national Bolshevism and the ideas of Halford Mackinder on geopolitics. (Mackinder, a Belgian doctrinaire, was a new rightist who contributed to *Vouloir* and *Partisan Européen,* the first reviews to reintroduce Niekisch.)[6] Dugin borrowed from Niekisch the idea of fusing Germanic nation-alism and Russian Sovietism as a means to create a vast anti-Western space. Taking inspiration from Mackinder, Carl Schmitt, and Karl Haushofer, among others, Dugin established an opposition between Eurasian might, which is organicist and tellurocratic (i.e., land-based), and Anglo-Saxon might: mercantile, prodemocracy, and thallasso-cratic (i.e., sea-based). Dugin's Eurasia includes the former USSR, but also China, India, Turkey, and the Balkans.[7] His is an imperial project in the Evolian sense, an awakening of Aryan racial consciousness, including non-Caucasian offshoots, which will allow Christianity, Islam, Buddhism, and Hinduism to coexist in an organic society that federates well-rooted communities. By contrast, the "Americano-Zionist" order is said to be that of a homogenizing globalism.[8] In other words, in geographical terms, "Eurasia" designates the Asian and European continents combined; but in post-Soviet Russia, it is a political concept that posits the existence of a space both Slavic and Turko-Muslim. Control of that space would allow global domina-tion. Eurasia is said to have a unique cultural identity, supposedly grounded in a fundamental opposition between the spiritual values of Orthodox Christianity and Islam on one hand and the materialist, liberal, and decadent values of the West on the other.

A parallel can easily be drawn between Pamyat and the Spanish Círculo Español de Amigos de Europa (CEDADE)—and, in fact, Dugin's first book, even before it appeared in Russia, was published by Grupo Libro 88 in Madrid, under the title *Rusia, El Misterio de Eurasia* (1992). The neo-Nazi reference "88" is explained by the fact that the director of the publishing house was a former CEDADE cadre. Upon Dugin's return from the Groupement de Recherche et d'Études pour la Civilisation Européenne (GRECE) colloquium in 1991, he founded Arctogaïa (which translates to "Ultima Thule"), an association purporting to be the equivalent of GRECE. The Russian writer also founded the review *Elementy,* which allowed the Russian public to read the positions of Alain de Benoist and Steuckers, of Guy Debord and Gilles Deleuze, of Régis Debray, Jean Thiriart, Arthur Moeller van den Bruck, Oswald Spengler and Ernst Jünger, and of Julius Evola and Carl Schmitt, all with illustrations drawn from esoteric Nazism. Dugin became the principal writer for *Den,* the main organ of what is known as the "national patriotic" opposition, and he worked at the newspaper to transform pro-Soviet conservatism into revolutionary nationalism.[9] He said the Soviet experiment had demonstrated that Communism produced a better closed society than Fascism: the two should therefore realize a Hegelian synthesis to destroy "open society," the Western materialistic values imposed by globalization, and in that way build the last empire. He maintained that the USSR's collapse had modified the Russian identity paradigm and that the objective conditions for constructing the Eurasian empire had come together, especially given that Russian culture is fundamentally conservative revolutionary and organicist. The October Revolution, in his view, resulted from the awakening of the imperial Russian soul in the face of the monarchy's liberal decadence. The Dugin formula that best sums up his thinking is "the Third Rome, the Third Reich, and the Third International are elements that must be connected in the revolt against the modern world."[10] His views had an impact in Western Europe via the post-Soviet reconfiguration of the radical far right there.

In 1989 Christian Bouchet, secretary general of Troisième Voie, judged that his organization was faced with two possibilities: either constitute a tendency within the FN or break away from the reactionary milieu of the "nationals" and try to work within alternative, environmentalist, regionalist, and Muslim circles.[11] His central idea was to contest the National Front from the "left," to force Jean-Marie Le Pen to recognize a radical tendency as it had existed in the FN during François Duprat's time. When the president of the FN rejected that faction, the radical cadres were compelled to put a good face on their defeat. In 1991 they founded Nouvelle Résistance, an organization that vilified the FN and revived Ernst Niekisch, national Bolshevism, and the Union de la Périphérie contre le Centre (Union of the Periphery against the Center). Their promotion of a united anti-system front clearly influenced Alain de Benoist at the time.[12] In order to gain credibility with Jean-Gilles Malliarakis, who was in charge of Troisième Voie, Nouvelle Résistance contacted the movements in the Groupe du 12 Mars (March 12 Group), proposing a new international organization: the European Liberation Front (ELF). It was set in place much more quickly than anticipated: the constitutive congress of Nouvelle Résistance in fact mentioned, among its two-year objectives, the creation of a "representative European secretariat." The organization made it clear that all the groups with which Troisième Voie was associated had opted in.[13] The ELF advocated a Europe of ethnic regions and played up its leftism. Its Europe was Eurasian in its dimensions, all the more so in that Thiriart's views about the relations between East and West had clearly evolved. In working with the Spaniard José Cuadrado Costa, the Belgian theorist had moved toward the idea that only Russia could build Greater Europe. In 1983 he affirmed that it was the European nationalists' duty to prepare for the invasion of Europe by the Red Army, whose soldiers, once they had reached Dublin, "would once again find blue eyes and blond hair, as in Kharkov, as in Vladivostok."[14] In 1984, in the review of the Parti Communautaire National-European (PCN; Communitarian European-National Party), Costa introduced references to the Russian Eurasian movement of the 1920s. He believed that his views ought to be adopted by the Soviet Union, but his Greater European space was not open to China or India (among other places), his perspective being that of a Europe "from Dublin to Vladivostok."[15]

The ELF's national Bolshevism was combined with an adogmatic Evolianism, which likely played a role in acclimating Dugin's views, themselves very influenced—but not determined—by Evola. In fact, when Dugin went to Madrid to give a lecture in 2013, at the invitation of an adjunct of the Movimiento Social Republicano (MSR), he began with a long summary of sorts of Evola's *Fascism Seen from the Right,* espousing a radical antimodernism rather than proposing a conservative revolutionary critique.[16] In the summer of 1992, an ELF delegation (Battara, Bouchet, de Benoist, Michel, Schneider, Steuckers, Terraciano, and Thiriart) had been received for a week in Moscow. It held a meeting there, at which Thiriart declared that networks needed to be established "between the lucid elite of the former USSR and the lucid elite of Western Europe, to prepare for the departure, the expulsion, of the American occupier." The delegation held discussions with *Den,* Dugin, and the Anti-Zionist Committee. It was received by the editorial staff of *Soviet Russia;* Geydar Dzhemal, representative of the Islamic Renaissance Party of Tajikistan and a close friend of Dugin's; Egor Ligachyov; Gennady Zyuganov; the national-populist Vladimir Zhirinovsky (Liberal-Democratic Party of Russia); and Viktor Anpilov (Russian Communist Workers Party).[17] The "new convergences" advocated by the ELF led to the importation to Western Europe of the Russian label "Red-Brown," used by pro-Yeltzin forces to counter the "national patriotic" designation being used in the National Salvation Front. But within the ELF, there was no union of nationalists and Communists. There, as within the groups composing it in Western Europe, the "Red-Brown" alliance was in fact an alliance between the "right" wing (European nationalism of the völkisch strain) and the left wing (revolutionary nationalism) of the radical far right. The misunderstanding of that essential nuance is universal, and a number of authors have sought (and have thought they found) a hypothetical "Red-Brown conspiracy" ready to descend on liberal Europe. That articulation does not correspond exactly to the one proposed by Dugin. He is hoping for a political reorganization in which the extremes would, to be sure, join together in the battle against globalism, but not without an indispensable recomposition of Russian politics, to separate out the Eurasianists, who believe they share a common enemy with the Muslim fundamentalists (namely, the new world order), from the racist and Islamophobic pan-Slavics.[18]

In 1993 Dugin and the writer Eduard Limonov co-founded the National Bolshevik Front, later known as the National Bolshevik Party (NBP), which joined the ELF. The NBP called for a united revolutionary front of Communists and nationalists to oppose the Westernized system, and it defined itself as an "intermediary between Mussolini's Blackshirts and the Red Guards of the Chinese Cultural Revolution."[19] It was primarily a countercultural aesthetic, Limonov having adopted a futurist discourse extolling violence as an instrument for achieving human fulfillment. The group used the crossed hammer and sword of Otto Strasser's Schwarze Front, previously adopted by the ELF, as well as more provocative symbols (a Nazi flag with the swastika replaced by a grenade,[20] another where it is replaced by a hammer and sickle). Dugin had traveled in France, and Limonov also knew that country well. He had lived there and was a contributor to *L'Idiot international* (where he advocated the union of the Communists and the FN) and *Choc du mois* (where he served as a liaison between the radical far right and the FN), which would allow him to organize a meeting between Jean-Marie Le Pen and Vladimir Zhirinovsky. The 1993 elections marked the end of the national patriotic coalition: Zhirovsky's and Zyuganov's parties henceforth played their own cards, each skilled at using Dugin's neo-Eurasianist theories. The NBP adopted the project for a Greater Europe, advocating "the creation of an Empire from Vladivostok to Gibraltar on the foundations of Russian civilization," the Third Reich's objective as Joachim von Ribbentrop (foreign minister of Nazi Germany) had seen it, but this time for the benefit of Russia. The NBP found its style when the Siberian punk rock singer Egor Letov joined. The organization was clearly countercultural: at its headquarters, it offered lectures in philosophy, rock concerts, and contemporary art exhibitions. Its militants were fond of black shirts and paramilitary uniforms, threw eggs at elected officials, chained themselves together in public buildings, and so on. In 1998 Dugin broke away: he no longer defined himself as a national Bolshevik but took to calling himself a "Eurasianist" and a "geopolitician." Seeking to transform cultural capital into social capital, he became an adviser to the Communist president of the Duma. As for Limonov, he was arrested in 2001 and accused by the Russian justice system of possessing weapons, of having constituted an armed militia, and of planning a coup d'état in Kazakhstan. When he was released from prison, he reoriented the NBP toward the defense of fundamental freedoms, against Putin's authoritarianism. When the NBP was banned in 2007, Limonov moved closer to liberal circles, which supported a market economy and Western-style democracy. He was not purged of his radicalism in that transition from neo-Fascism to democratism, given the violent modes of actions adopted by the militants. And, in any case, liberalism is a peripheral phenomenon in Russia.[21]

In addition, when Dugin left the NBP, the European radical far right as a whole was in the process of reconstructing itself. In October 1993 the ELF ousted the PCN because of the reactionary turn the ELF imputed to it: contacts with the Vlaams Blok and the Front National Belge, and a proposal to adopt an Islamophobic campaign inspired by Serbian nationalism, around the slogan, "Europe will not be an Islamic Republic." By contrast, the ELF wished to join together with the radical Muslim groups. Synergies Européennes and the PCN henceforth collaborated with each other, and the members of the PCN discreetly registered the bylaws of the ELF with the French authorities.[22] The PCN launched a new newspaper, in which it said it was the European partner of the Russian National Communist Front. At the same time, Dugin was still participating in the ELF, all the while taking the line that Islamism was an instrument of the American order and that Europe and Islam were irreconcilable.[23] Three years later, in view of the troubles faced by Nouvelle Résistance, Christian Bouchet announced he would resign. He managed ongoing affairs until a congress he convened on November 30, 1996.[24] The PCN took the opportunity to go on the offensive and registered the bylaws of Nouvelle Résistance.[25] It announced that Nouvelle Résistance militants had ousted their leadership for "collaborating with the Lepenist reactionary forces" and had voted to merge with the PCN, because the ELF now belonged to a Black-Red-Green [Fascist-Communist-Islamic] front.[26] The ELF rejected the PCN and maintained its relations with Nouvelle Résistance, which was forced to rename itself "Cercles Résistance."[27]

The Nouvelle Résistance congress went forward. The decision was made to constitute Unité Radicale on the fringes of the FN, with a call for the unity of nationalists, whoever they might be, and an appeal to young skinheads. The ideological line was summed up as follows: "Less leftism, more Fascism!" The internal bulletin informed its subscribers that all the ELF groups had renewed their confidence in the leadership staff, and it mentioned the difficulty of managing a nationalist international, since the result of the congress was a shift of its line to the right. The logical conclusion was drawn: it was necessary to break ties with foreign groups aligned on the "left."[28] The ELF was relocated to Great Britain, and the general secretariat fell to Troy Southgate, a militant marked by the Codreanu saga. The priority given to the target community over ideological coherence is indicated by the name of the European newspaper—*Jeune Europe* (Young Europe)—that for a time the second ELF considered putting out in four or five languages, for a total of a thousand copies.[29] Some movements made only minimal adjustments: because the Spaniards of Alternative Europa had no national populist party with which to align themselves, they founded Alternative Europa–Liga Social Republicana and later the MSR. Like a number of other Western groups in the ELF, they promoted a Europe that includes Russia rather than advocating for Eurasia. Although the notion of empire was cultivated, ethnonationalist concerns did not permit them to fully adopt neo-Eurasianist theories.[30]

In late 1997, moreover, the ELF merged with the Committee for a Revolutionary Nationalist League, established in England. It then entered into permanent contact with the Liaison Committee for Revolutionary Nationalism, an organization that includes movements located in the United States, Canada, and New Zealand. Although the Web site of the American Front offers texts by Dugin, the ELF had clearly moved away from Europeanist thought and toward white affirmationism. The proof, if any is needed, that an ideological swerve raised few problems: the Paris meeting of September 19, 1998, which founded the new ELF, took place within the framework of the annual celebration of the National Front, supposedly its sworn enemy until then.[31] The Russian National Bolshevik Party remained a member of the ELF. In 1999 Southgate published a manifesto of the organization, oriented toward defending the white race against the Zionist conspiracy, which supposedly sought to cause the degeneration of the race and thereby ensure its own global domination.[32] That document and the line it adopted did not receive the support of the other groups. When Dugin became part of the Russian establishment and Unité Radicale was dissolved, the second ELF fell apart. Bouchet, who had constituted a radical network in France, launched a European geopolitical network with the Italians of Sinistra Nazionale, who published the daily newspaper *Rinascita*. That network purported to be a continuation of the ELF, and it published the very professional-looking review *La Nation eurasienne*. The Spanish MSR and the Belgian Nation movement established on their own a new international partnership, where they were joined in 2011 by the

Italian group Movimento Sociale Europeo (a splinter group of the MS-FT). The far-right Belgian group Nation, the Réseau Radical, and the Italians of Democratici Egalitari d'Azione participated at the meeting convened by the MSR in Barcelona on February 15, 2003, to oppose the war in Iraq. Nation, Rinascita, the Réseau Radical, and the Parti des Musulmans de France (Party of French Muslims) undertook a media campaign called "Human Shield Action to Iraq." Eastern and Western dynamics definitively parted ways at that point. In Western Europe, the radical far right had difficulty surviving the successes of populist movements and turned in on itself, adopting a Eurosiberian thematics that advocated a white and Islamophobic Europe. In Eastern Europe, the race to recapture power paved the way for an institutionalization of Dugin's theories, integrated into the aims of one circle (though not the innermost) of Vladimir Putin's power.

The Putin Era

To analyze Greater Russian nationalism as it now exists, one must keep in mind the dynamism of the Orthodox Church. Patriarch Kirill of Moscow and a number of foundations headed by oligarchs, such as the Saint Basil the Great Charitable Foundation and its financier Konstantin Malofeev, proclaim that Russia is restoring its ties to its eternal destiny by professing the ultraconservative values of the "true faith" against a decadent, materialistic, and ungodly Atlantic bloc. In that respect, the Orthodox Church plays an essential role in the legitimation of Russian actions in Crimea (which it sees as the cradle of Christian Rus', hence of Russia, somewhat the same way that the Serbs make Kosovo their national homeland) and in Ukraine. Along with the neo-Eurasianists and the nostalgic national Communists, the church sees the Kremlin's actions as a return to the timeless Russian Empire, to a mystic and intense patriotism. These views are attractive to a substantial proportion of Russians, who are convinced that the difficulties their country faces are explained by Western deceit. The Russian cultural climate readily fosters imperial nostalgia and religious fervor. There is thus great interest in books that rehabilitate Nicholas II and the leaders of the White émigrés and the White armies, Pyotr Wrangel, Anton Denikin, and Alexander Kolchak in particular. A cult of martyrdom has grown up around Nicholas II and the imperial family, correlated to anti-Communism and imbued with religious mysticism. This was demonstrated by the canonization in 2000, by the patriarchate of Moscow of the Orthodox Church, of the tsar killed by the Bolsheviks and of his family. It was his belief that, if Nicholas II did not correspond to the canons that define the "Christian martyr," he did represent one of the millions of "secular martyrs" killed by Communism.

Vladimir Putin occupies the political space of nationalism by virtue of his Caesarist exercise of power, which is assimilated to Russian popular messianism, and the efficiency of the social mechanisms that have produced his charismatic image, but also because the national patriotic political offering has become weaker. In the 2012 presidential election, Putin received 63.64 percent of the vote, Gennady Zyuganov 17.18 percent, and Vladimir Zhirnovsky 6.22 percent. Nationalism is therefore hegemonic. But though the populist right that Zhirnovsky represents has made significant inroads since 2000 (when it received 2.7 percent of the vote), it has lost considerable ground since the legislative elections of 1993 (23 percent of the vote). On a personal level, Zhirinovsky suffers from the unshakable reputation he acquired during the Yeltzin years of being a puppet of the Kremlin: the opposition he represents, it is said, is fabricated by the regime itself. No matter who is president, his Liberal Democratic Party of Russia (LDPR) causes an uproar, but in the Duma it votes for presidential programs. The state appears to use the LDPR as a means to freeze out part of the nationalist forces. Granted, the reliability of the electoral results announced in Russia has been called into question many times. But if Putinism does keep the vote on the far right contained, he also provides it with a benefit. The LDPR has been able to incorporate elements of neo-Eurasianism, advocating an economic and political union of the countries of the former USSR and a policy to integrate Ukraine, Belarus, Turkey, Afghanistan, and Iran into Russia. That party, though vigorously opposed to NATO, is the least anti-American organization on the Russian far right.[33] LPDR leaders are called "clowns" and "sellouts," and the immanent disappearance of the party is constantly being announced, but they still manage to express a Russian-style national populism: their violent denunciation of the elites, combined with loyalty to Putin's leadership, allow them to combine an antisystem subversive charge with integration into the system.

The Russian electoral system keeps the radical movements contained outside the institutions, while limiting the ability of emergent forces to express themselves. In fact, whereas all the parties represented in the Duma automatically have the right to put forward slates in subsequent elections, other organizations can compete only by submitting 150,000 voter signatures. In the 2011 legislative elections, only seven parties were in the running. The LDPR received 8.14 percent of the vote, acquiring forty representatives. One of its opponents had disappeared: Rodina (Homeland). That party was founded in 2003 by Sergey Baburin and the current vice prime minister (since 2011), Dmitry Rogozin, among others. According to some observers, its function was to take votes away from Zyuganov's Communist Party, thus shoring up Putin's power (in the 2003 elections, Rodina received 9 percent of the vote). After a showdown in 2005 failed to move the government's social policy in a social nationalist direction, Rodina adopted the position of supporting the person of Putin, but while embodying a form of national patriotic opposition to the government. Credited with a quarter of intended votes, it was unable to put forward a candidate for the legislative elections of 2005 because, as a result of its anti-Semitic and xenophobic propaganda, it was sanctioned by the justice system for inciting racial hatred. Baburin then left the LDPR with the majority of the MPs to found a competing party. For a time, Rodina was marginalized by the Kremlin for being too harsh in its criticism of the authorities, following its rapprochement with the Communist Party. But later, Rogozin was co-opted by Putin, who in 2007 named him ambassador to NATO in Brussels. There he presented Westerners with a fairly firm anti-Western nationalist line, especially on the question of missile deployment. He is often considered the spokesperson for the military-industrial complex. Rodina allied itself with other organizations within the Fair and Just Russia Party, which supposedly opposes Vladimir Putin but, in actuality, has shown itself to be conciliatory (the party received 4.2 percent of the vote in the 2011 legislative elections, after which Rogozin was named vice prime minister).

The Russian far right is very active outside the Duma. Nationalist pride and white affirmationism are its most common features. Alexander Barkashov's Russian National Unity (RNU), before it shattered into rival groups in 2000, brought together about 15,000 openly anti-Semitic and antidemocratic members, who demanded "the racial hygiene" of a "pure Russia." The black clothing they wore further underscored their desire to present themselves as a Fascist militia. In several cities, members patrolled with police officers, while in others they attacked Jews or immigrants. Since 2002 the judiciary has taken a series of legal actions against the movement—at a time when, after a long period of leniency dating back to the Yeltzin era, the Kremlin has begun to repress the skinhead movement. The principal groups that came out of that movement are the Russian National Socialist Party, Russian Resurgence, and the Slavic Union. The RNU has often used the swastika, while the Russian ultranationalist groups privilege anti-Semitism as formulated by the Hundred Blacks under the tsarist empire, then in its Hitlerian form. Nevertheless, some movements have taken a turn comparable to that of their Western European counterparts, choosing since 2001 to move from anti-Semitic hatred to the defense of Israel and hatred of populations of the Muslim religion.[34]

Aleksandr Dugin plays a totally different game. He has honed neo-Eurasianism into an instrument of the Russian elites and their European allies. With the publication of his book *Foundations of*

Geopolitics (1997), he became a key figure in the thinking of some ruling circles in Russia, at least until he was suspended from Moscow State University in June 2014. He had launched the Eurasia movement in April 2001 with the support of the Kremlin as well as Orthodox,[35] Muslim, Jewish, and Buddhist dignitaries. Eurasia put forward a platform on which neo-Eurasianism emerged as both a representation of the world and a geopolitics. The Eurasian empire does not disregard the Eurafrican legacy: in his philosophy of *Lebens-Raum* Dugin sees a "Eurafrican arc" on the horizon, made up of three centralized ethnocultural spaces (Europe, the Arab Muslim world, and black Africa) within a common "geo-economic zone."[36] Efforts to make Eurasia a political movement met with failure. As a result, greater emphasis was placed on the metapolitical approach, with the 2003 launch of the International Eurasianist Movement (IEM), set up as a nongovernment organization. This group has played many different cards: over and above its geopolitical expertise and its NGO status, the IEM is still a countercultural offering. Its symbol, for example, is the "chaosphere," which the "chaos magicians" themselves borrowed from the dark fantasy cycles of the English writer Michael Moorcock.

After Vladimir Putin reassumed the presidency in 2012, Dugin enjoyed favorable treatment from the Russia media. According to Dugin, Putin had turned toward the radicals because his power was being diminished by the liberals' protests, and he had to outmaneuver them. In 2012, in conjunction with Rodina, Dugin co-founded the Izborsky Club with some in the Russian president's intimate circle and with Orthodox hierarchs. Their intent was to counter the influence of the Valdai Club,[37] which was judged too liberal. The members of the Izborsky Club, however, have had some difficulty agreeing on whether or not Greater Russia and Eurasia are multiethnic: a minimal agreement was reached regarding the traditional character of Russia's multiethnicity and the rejection of migrants. On the question of moral reform, various authors in the club advocate the return of the political police or the creation of a Russian equivalent of the

Third Reich's Ahnenerbe.[38] Since 2012 Dugin has continually called for the invasion of Ukraine, to hasten the advent of the new order. He ardently advocates support by the Russian authorities for all the European far-right movements, in order to break up the Atlantic bloc. He suggests that Russia should champion conservative values and reject cultural liberalism (the position of gays in Russia has continued to worsen). Dugin, a major presence in the media since the beginning of operations in Ukraine, urged Putin at the time to suppress democracy and proclaim himself tsar, on the foundations of an ideological order, a mark of Evola's continued influence on the Russian doctrinaire's thinking.[39]

The clear advantage of Dugin's neo-Eurasianism is that it reconciles the two theoretical elements of Georges Sorel's thought: myth and utopia. Myth is a mobilizing force, while utopianism undermines direct action by allowing reformism to present itself as an advance toward the revolutionary goal. According to Dugin, Eurasia is both myth and utopia: every element of the East-West connection and every Russian imperialist movement can be legitimized by the Eurasian revolutionary horizon.

Neo-Eurasianism provides the European radical far-right movements with geopolitical concepts. For example, Jobbik, Dugin's Hungarian contact, is split between those who promote a greater Turanian alliance that would link Hungary to the republics of Central Asia, to Russia, Iran, and Turkey, and those who confine themselves to a relationship with Russia for ethnocultural reasons. But neo-Eurasianism also provides ideas to the institutionalized far right when it is in power. In 2014 Prime Minister Viktor Orbán affirmed that Hungary ought to turn to Eurasian countries that are undemocratic but successful in globalized economic competition, rather than toward the West, whose liberalism is synonymous with decline. Granted, his views did not have the same intensity as Jobbik's. But it was the prime minister[40] who flew the flag of the Pan-Turanian Union over the Budapest Parliament, seat of the Hungarian National Assembly during the Austro-Hungarian Empire. As for opposition parties, Marine Le Pen, even before she assumed the presidency of the FN in France, indicated her interest in a pro-Russian reorientation, inspired by her former adviser Emmanuel Leroy. A veteran of the Ordre Nouveau and an elected representative and paid official of the FN in the 1980s, Leroy has navigated between revolutionary nationalism and radical anti-Zionism. He also established ties with Dugin. In 2007 Leroy participated in the White Forum held in Moscow, alongside Guillaume Faye and a former member of the CEDADE, as well as the American David Duke, former Grand Wizard of the Ku Klux Klan, representative of the transatlantic perspective of white affirmationism.[41]

The inroads the FN has made have far greater importance for Moscow than those of other movements: France has a permanent seat on the United Nations Security Council, and France and Germany together are the mainstay of the European Union. Since Nicolas Sarkozy's defeat in 2012, a faction of the Russian government—with a level of approval on President Putin's part that is yet to be determined—has thus become massively involved in the French far right. Furthermore, former president Jacques Chirac's Union pour un Mouvement Populaire (Union for a Popular Movement) never failed to translate Franco-Russian friendship into government action. In December 2012 Marion Maréchal-Le Pen was received by the chairman of the Duma, Sergey Naryshkin, Putin's former classmate at the KGB training center. In June 2013 Marine Le Pen spent a week surveying the neo-Russian space, beginning in Crimea—prior to its annexation—with a seminar in which economics (finance?) seemed to prevail over politics. She followed that up with a visit to the Duma in Moscow, where she met the chairman of the Foreign Affairs Commission in Parliament, then the vice prime minister, Dmitry Rogozin, who represents the national patriotic camp. She delivered a speech at the State Institute of International Relations, which has trained the diplomatic elite since before the Communist era. And finally, she laid a wreath at the monument commemorating the French airmen in the Normandie-Niemen squadron, anti-Nazi resistance fighters who battled alongside the USSR. Marine Le Pen ended her trip with a reception at the Duma in Saint Petersburg. Each time, she reiterated her admiration for Putin's toughness. She also said she liked Russia, which fought the "new world order," supported the Syrian regime, and shared the National Front's social values. The Kremlin was equally appreciative of her: a Russian bank lent nine million euros to the FN in September 2014, and the leadership of Rodina also appears to have made gestures in that direction. The Russian attitude can be interpreted as a desire to have two irons in the fire in the political zone of right-wing France: with the republicans, whom Moscow may suspect of an Atlanticism and a liberalism on social values that is now too far advanced; and with the FN, an ascendant force that can be used to pressure the traditional right and which, at the same time, would seem to be more in sync with the Russian national patriotic project, antiliberal in its essence even when it adopts the form (very imperfect, in fact) of a market economy.

Also in September 2014, other, more radical European far-right movements positioned themselves vis-à-vis Russia, with, for example, the founding of the Alliance for Peace and Freedom (APF), headed by Italy's Roberto Fiore, which belongs to the tradition of the defunct National European Front (founded in 2004). In addition, an international conservative forum was held in Saint Petersburg in March 2015, under the aegis of Yuri Lyubomirsky, who is closely associated with Rodina and is the leader of the Right to Bear Arms group. Included in the APF as well are the German Nationaldemokratische Partei Deutschlands (NPD), Greek Golden Dawn, and Italian Forza Nuova. When an APF delegation was given permission to meet with Nikolaos Michaloliakos, president of Golden Dawn, imprisoned at Korydallos in Greece, the group of visitors included a Russian lawyer, Mikhail Kusnetsov. Moreover, the APF Web site published a speech by the Russian minister of foreign affairs on the Ukrainian question and an appeal to Europe to stop the "new American cold war and NATO's policy of confrontation." The question arises whether this is the umpteenth attempt by a radical movement to woo Russia, or if some Russian milieus have decided to use the APF as an influence channel, even though the political benefit would appear to be nil. When the APF encourages the construction of "a common Eurasian trade zone, from the Atlantic to Vladivostok," are we to understand that Russian Eurasianist circles are watching? In addition to the parties that form its hard core, APF has for the moment the support of only small groups: the French-speaking Belgians of Mouvement Nation; British Unity, founded by a former member of the European Parliament, Nick Griffin, after he left the failing British National Party; Democracia Nacional in Spain; the Cypriots of Ethniko Leiko Metopo; and the Swedish Svanskarnas Parti. Yvan Benedetti, leader of the dissolved Oeuvre Française, also made an appearance in Brussels during a meeting of the organization.

Granted, without at least the support of the Hungarian Jobbik, the APF would remain on the fringes, because of the institutional normalization of the national populist movements. But beyond that, it appears that Russian forces are becoming involved in all the far-right tendencies believed to promote a geopolitical reorientation in their favor. Even when these movements are not in a position to seize power, they are part of a "soft power" strategy.[42] When they are in power or close to power, they seek—in addition to subsidies no doubt—linguistic elements useful to them in building their international political program. Dugin must not be seen, therefore, as an occult master of Russian politics. He is not an intimate of Putin's, even less his intellectual guide. All involved draw from neo-Eurasianism what suits them, and every idea borrowed legitimizes the aura of the neo-Eurasianist project. But Dugin should also not be underestimated. In 2001, the CIA judged the mobilization around the plan for a Greater Russia fruitless and without a future,[43] but in March 2015 Dugin was placed on the U.S. list of persons responsible for the situation in Ukraine, even as his influence was waning.[44] He is a conduit for ideas between radical movements on opposite sides of Europe, and he represents the concerns of a large portion of the Russian people, who are asking how national destiny ought to be conceived in its irreducible specificity and not steamrolled by globalization.

In Russia's Vicinity

When Ukraine regained its independence in 1991, it did so with a nationalist movement that was not on the far right. Now an independent country, it finds itself with two national narratives competing with each other. To the south and east, the Ukrainian population largely identifies as Slavic and Orthodox and is deeply nostalgic for the old Soviet state that connected them to the Russians. That nostalgia has nothing to do with the Communist political regime but instead concerns pan-Slavism. The West is a foil, as this slogan, chanted during the demonstrations, expresses it: "Down with the capitalist ogres! Long live the union of Slavs!" To the west, the national narrative is founded on the victimization of the population by the USSR. Stalin's "Holodomor" (extermination by hunger) in 1931–1933, which killed about three million Ukrainians and which the Ukrainian Parliament called "genocide" in 2006, is part of collective memory. In that part of the country, Russia is considered a colonialist power, against which Ukraine ought to have defended itself throughout its history. The Soviet period is portrayed as a Russian phenomenon, the belief being that the Ukrainian people did not participate in the system. In all regions of Ukraine, nationalist values are combined with antitotalitarianism: one side praises the "patriotic Great War," during which the Soviets defeated the Nazis; the other rails against Communism, which is called the principal totalitarian system of the twentieth century. Neither camp has opted for a closed society, since one clearly chooses the West, the other the East.[45] That two-pronged nationalism explains the very heterogeneous nature of the Ukrainian far right: from the Ukrayinska Natsionalna Assembleya–Ukrayinska Narodna Samooborona (UNA-UNS; Our Ukraine–People's Self-Defense Bloc), which wants a pro-Western unitarist nationalist regime but one that is the "heart of the Slavic empire"; to Derzhavna Samostijnist Ukrayiny (Independence of the State of Ukraine), a group hoping for an ethnically homogeneous Ukraine, which threatens Russians with the prospect of internment camps should it take power.[46] In 2013 the UNA-UNS, the principal far-right movement before the Orange Revolution, participated in the founding of Pravyi Sektor (Right Sector), both a party and an anti-Russia militia.

The initial situation became more radical still with the Orange Revolution (which protested the widespread corruption and fraud associated with the presidential runoff election of 2004), then the occupation of Maidan Square in 2013–2014, followed by the intervention of pro-Russian troops and the incorporation of Crimea into Russia in March 2014. For the Russian side, Maidan Square was a "neo-Nazi" phenomenon: Svoboda (Freedom), a populist resurgence in 2014 of a neo-Nazi movement founded in 1991, and Right Sector were particularly singled out for blame. According to one survey, their presence was real but far from hegemonic: in 2014 Svoboda was present at 18 percent of the demonstrations, Right Sector at 6 percent.[47] Maidan Square was decorated with many symbols associated with the Organization of Ukrainian Nationalists (OUN), especially its most radical branch. Stefan Bandera, its leader, had in 1941 been placed at the head of the Ukrainian Legion, a unit integrated into the Wehrmacht (the OUN also had troops of partisans that fought both the Wehrmacht and the Red Army, however). Right Sector makes explicit reference to Bandera and was intent on using the Maidan Square occupation as a revolutionary project to establish a nationalist regime. Svoboda's influence has grown: its share of the vote increased from 0.36 percent in March 2006 to 10.44 percent in 2012 (it has thirty-seven MPs). The party is proving very active in co-opting those disappointed by the Orange Revolution. It is also attempting to take advantage of the Russo-Ukrainian conflict to gain a foothold within the state.[48] The ideological core of Svoboda is an ultranationalism indebted to Bandera and the writings of Dmytro Dontsov (1883–1973), which are anti-Communist, tinged with references to the Orthodox religion, anti-Russian, and anti-Semitic, in quest of a romantic and ethnic national myth.[49] In 2012 its electoral bastions reflected the geography of the OUN (it received between 31 and 38 percent of the vote in the regions of Lviv and Ivano-Frankivsk in Galicia). The Svoboda vote was at that stage primarily a protest against endemic corruption, against the interference of the oligarchs in political life, and against elites who lean either toward the West or toward the East, hence toward the outside world in any case. But Svoboda paid the price for its participation in the post-Maidan government coalition: the party received only 4.7 percent of the vote in the elections of October 2014. At the same time, the organization met with disappointment at the international level. When the FN deputy Marion Maréchal-Le Pen decried "the neo-Nazi militias," after her aunt Marine Le Pen ended the relations with Svoboda initiated by her father, the vice president of Svoboda sent a worried letter to FN cadres, in an attempt to rid the group of the "neo-Nazi" label.[50]

Right Sector, for its part, purged its ranks of neo-Nazi elements in 2014, and attracted 1.8 percent of the vote in the same elections, which is to say, 284,943 votes. Meanwhile, the Congress of Ukrainian Nationalists, a direct descendant of the OUN, disappeared from the political scene, having received only 8,000 votes. According to its newspaper, Right Sector managed to nationalize its influence the same year, with twenty-seven local branches. Extending beyond the OUN's territories—historically, the regions of Lviv, Ivano-Frankivsk, and Uzhorod—it moved into the south and east (though to a lesser degree), as far as the cities of Lugansk and Donetsk in Donbass. With mobilizing slogans such as "If not us, who? If not now, when?" Right Sector has developed an eleven-point program. Internationally, it seeks to open Ukraine to the outside world via the West and the non-Russian East and through cooperation within the Baltic–Black Sea region. Domestically, it seeks to bring about a regenerated state and a regenerated man, to fight corruption, and to establish a social market economy.[51]

The pro-Russian far right is in a different situation. There are local branches of Russian movements (the National Union and the International Eurasianist Movement, for example) and specific organizations, such as the Donetsk Republic political party, founded in 2005 by disciples of Aleksandr Dugin, who are now at the helm of a self-proclaimed state, the Donetsk People's Republic, which emerged in 2014 thanks to Russian support.[52] The neo-Eurasianist dimension of the boundary changes in Ukraine is underscored by the name suggested by the Izborsky Club for the union between the Donetsk People's Republic and the Luhansk People's Republic, namely, Federated States of New Russia (Novorossiya). Ultimately, however, the confederation took the name Union of People's Republics, which expresses greater nostalgia for the USSR. Given the way the various pro-Russian referendums have proceeded, we cannot ascertain the real support received by the various nationalist movements in different regions. That is because, since 2003, voting on these referendums has been "monitored" by international observers chosen from within the pro-Eurasianist movement, ranging from the Russian National Union to the Parti Communautaire National-Européen,[53] which now confines its activities to the glorification of the Belarusian regime and of the unrecognized states of Transnistria or Donbass.

Both warring parties in Ukraine make use of anti-Semitic arguments, often coupled with a radical anti-Zionism, claiming that the Jews are disloyal to the nation and that they work for the opposing camp—a claim that is probably intended to disqualify the camp being designated, supposedly "pro-Jew," more than the Jews themselves. Since 2013 many Russian media outlets have advanced conspiracy theories that play on all the anti-Jewish stereotypes. That anti-Semitism must not be overestimated, however: during the Ukrainian presidential election of 2014, Vadim Rabinovich, a candidate of the Jewish faith with dual Ukrainian and Israeli citizenship, won more votes than those of the Right Sector and Svoboda candidates combined.[54] He was then elected MP in 2014 under the banner of the Opposition Bloc, whose best results are in the regions with a large Russian population.

The Kremlin has continued to lambaste "the Fascist junta in power in Kiev," but it also denounces "Baltic Fascism," which has come back to life. For example, in September 2003 Dymitri Rogozin, then-chairman of the Commission of Foreign Affairs in the Duma, declared that "the Nazis have come to power in Latvia," which he called a "country of thugs." Vladimir Zhirinovsky threatened in 2004 to "destroy Latvia," claiming that commandos were ready to leave Russia to bomb the capitals of the Baltic countries. The same tension can be found on the Baltic side: Toomas Ilves, former Estonian minister of foreign affairs, declared that Russian-language speakers "are used by Moscow rather like the Sudeten Germans were used by Hitler."[55] It is true that, after it achieved independence, Latvia saw a revival of the Pērkonkrusts (Thunder Cross), a nationalist corporatist organization from the 1930s that sometimes used the swastika, and some elements of which collaborated with the SS. That resurrection has been confined to small groups, but the Pērkonkrusts was banned in 2006 for its terrorist violence.[56]

The essential problem lies in the relations existing between the Latvian majority (57.6 percent of the population) and the Russian minority (29.6 percent). There is a real feeling of animosity toward that minority, which finds expression in ordinary language: to designate the era when the country was part of the Soviet Union, the Latvian majority speaks of "Russian" rather than "Soviet" occupation. By law, Latvian is the only national language, and proper names must be "Latvianized." University education in the Russian language has been abolished. In addition, the law on nationality, adopted in 1994, made naturalization contingent on a fairly difficult and discriminating test focused on the language, history, and law of Latvia; the result was that, ten years later, only 78,540 people had been naturalized. Nearly 20 percent of those living in Latvia are not citizens and are ineligible for certain jobs. Conversely, Latvia adopted a new law on the right of asylum in September 2002 and a new law on immigration in May 2003, which the United Nations Committee against Torture recognized as representing significant progress.[57]

The Russian minority enjoys political freedom of expression. That has allowed them to be represented in the European Parliament by the coalition "For Human Rights in a United Latvia," which includes a number of former cadres of the Soviet Communist Party. After being renamed the "Latvian Russian Union," the coalition saw its share of the vote drop from 9.7 percent in the European parliamentary elections of 2009 to 6.7 percent in 2014. The Nacionālā Apvienība Visu Latvijai!–Tēvzemei un Brīvībai Party (NA/TB/LNNK; National Alliance–All for Latvia! For Fatherland and Freedom), a name adopted in 2010 after several parties merged, professes anti-Russian sentiments based on a visceral anti-Communism. It attracted 14 percent of the vote in 2014. TB/LNNK was a national-conservative party, which held the prime minister's seat in 1997–1998 and currently holds the portfolios of Justice, the Environment, and Culture. It is a proponent of the Latvianization of the country, especially from the linguistic standpoint, and was behind the 1998 referendum that restricted Russophones' access to Latvian nationality. It was the Guntars Krasts cabinet (TB/LNNK) that made March 16 a national holiday, to celebrate the Latvian Legion, a zealous autochthonous division of the Waffen-SS (the holiday was abolished in 2000, in response to the outcry of the European Union). This should not be construed as philo-Nazism per se: the Baltic (and Eastern European) right-wing movements equate Nazism and Communism, both in terms of their ideology (totalitarianism) and by virtue of their violation of national sovereignty. They consider collaborators anti-Communist patriots. The NA/TB/LNNK believes that present-day Latvia is a direct descendant of the country pre-1940, that is, of the personal authoritarian regime of Kārlis Ulmanis, who banned the local Fascists of the Pērkonkrusts. Significant ambiguities remain, however, as indicated by the integration into the coalition of Visu Latvijai, a small radical nationalist organization headed by Raivis Dzintars. It defends the idea that the proportion of ethnic Latvians in the country must be increased to 75 percent; participates in the annual Latvian Legion commemoration of March 16 in Riga; and, as a symbolic gesture, in 2010 elected Visvaldis Lācis (b. 1924), a veteran of the legion, to Parliament. Nonetheless, the coalition's general line is favorable to a Europe of nations. It is socially conservative and economically liberal, closer to an ultraright party than to Central European forms of ultranationalism. The Baltic organizations do not confine themselves to disparaging the Russians, however. The Order and Justice Party (Tvarka ir Teisnigumas) in Lithuania, the only Baltic country where populist parties are well rooted in parliamentary life, calls for more direct democracy against the oligarchic elites, who have supposedly sold out to foreigners; and the Liberals' Movement of the Republic of Lithuania (Lietuvos Respublikos Liberalu Sajūdis) takes an "antisystem" stance. Unlike Western organizations, these parties do not combine their denunciation of the profiteers "at the top" with disparagement of immigrants.[58] NA/TB/LNNK's criticism of the European Union is fairly limited in scope, because it is allied at the European level with the British conservatives.

Recomposition and Permanence in Central and Eastern Europe

After the transition from the former popular democracies to capitalist democracy, several new organizations emerged in Eastern Europe. Populist, ultranationalist, and xenophobic all at once, they quickly obtained parliamentary representatives and sometimes lent assistance to government coalitions, though the ideological coherence of the coalitions was not always obvious. (In Slovakia, for example, the Slovak National Party joined a cabinet run by the center-left populists of the Smer [Direction] Party, which, for that very reason, was suspended from the European Socialist Party.) These parties include:

the Slovenská Národná Strana (SNS; Slovak National Party), the Magyar Igazság és Élet Pártja (MIÉP: Hungarian Justice and Life Party), România Mare (Greater Romania), Ataka (National Union Attack) in Bulgaria, and the League of Polish Families (LPR) and Samoobrona (Social Self-Defense) in Poland. These parties have had various fortunes: some made inroads (Ataka, from 2005 to 2013), while others were marginalized (MIÉP; Czech Republicans; and România Mare, which had remarkable electoral success, then disintegrated during the legislative elections of 2008 and 2012). Still others have participated in the exercise of power: the SNS, the aforementioned Polish organizations, and briefly, România Mare, in 1993–1995. The Serbian Radical Party (SRS, which incorporated part of the Chetnik legacy) even had occasion to take on the role of government partner under the Milošević regime, when Vojislav Šešelj acceded to the post of vice prime minister, and to participate in militias carrying out the ethnic cleansing policy. Šešelj was detained from 2003 to 2014 by The Hague Tribunal; he was released in 2014 for reasons of health, and he returned to Belgrade. On March 31, 2016, he was acquitted on all charges.

How to define the programmatic orientations common to these organizations? They are clustered around certain notions: the rejection of elites; distrust of the Western social and economic model; the denunciation of Communism and of political liberalism; opposition to the construction of a united Europe; defense of the social strata that have gained nothing or have lost materially as a result of regime change; glorification of both the national past and of an exclusivist concept of the nation founded on ethnicity, religion, and language. At the same time, these forms of populism are clearly distinguished from their counterparts in the West, particularly by the near absence of any anti-immigration dimension, at least until the beginning of the migratory crisis currently under way. The notion of an internal enemy (the Roma, an ethnic minority associated with a territorial dispute, and the Jews) supplants that of the peril of immigration, though the result is the same: retreat into an ethnic identity. These themes have resonated in a context where a significant portion of the population faces major economic and social difficulties. The vote for the far right has been fueled by a deep dissatisfaction with the new elites who emerged in the transition to a market economy. Corruption, the inefficiency of public decision making, and the domination of oligarchs lead to a distrust of parliamentary democracy and to a certain nostalgia for the minimal material security offered by the Communist regime, in a context where the unreformed Communist parties have ceased to be a political offering (MIÉP received 0.58 percent of the vote; the Bulgarian Communist Party has only 1 MP; and the Komunistyczna Partia Polski has been reduced to a few hundred members).

The far right made its presence known in Bulgaria in the second round of the 2006 presidential election. Volen Siderov, the leader of Ataka (founded in 2005), made a surprise showing in the first round, coming in second with 21.5 percent of the vote, behind the departing Socialist president. He improved his results in the second round, winning 24.1 percent of the vote. Endemic corruption and the fears triggered when the country joined the European Union in 2007 favored the far-right candidate. His party knew how to channel the widespread racism directed at the Turkish and Roma minorities. On that occasion, Ataka was also able to wave the banner of anti-Semitism: during the campaign for the legislative elections of 2005, the party made posters showing a map of Bulgaria covered with Turkish and Israeli flags, to indicate that it considers the country occupied. During the war between Israel and the Hezbollah in 2006, the television station that serves as Ataka's mouthpiece, Skat TV, generally took the side of the Shia fundamentalists. The vote for Ataka occurred at a time when people were weary of the forced march toward the West, undertaken by the Bulgarian elites without any real debate, and reflexively embraced identity politics in the face of the pivotal role played by the Turkish Movement for Rights and Freedoms (MRF). Ataka denounced the Atlanticism of the elites, the loss of sovereignty imposed by the European Union, the plundering of the state in the name of reform, and the abandonment of the Bulgarians to an insecurity supposedly imputable to the Roma—all served up by a leader who acts like a Roman tribune, backed by the networks that grew out of the former Committee for State Security and the Communist Party. That alchemy was able to attract "an electorate in search of order, social protections, and a restored national pride." In a country clearly marked by an ethnicization of social divisions, that electorate is composed primarily of the losers in the transition to the market economy: workers and retired people but also the young, even college graduates. Most of these voters live in mid-sized cities and believe in an ethnically pure Bulgaria of the Orthodox religion, rid of its Turkish minority. The Turks always remind them of the disdained Ottoman Empire, which ruled Bulgaria with an iron fist until 1878.[59] That hatred is paired with Islamophobia: for a time in 2011, anti-Muslim violence by Ataka militants prompted the authorities to consider dissolving the party and also worried a portion of Ataka's voter base.

In 2013, when mass demonstrations against corruption and oligarchy shook the country, a government alliance was formed between the social democrats and the MRF, with the nonparticipatory support of Ataka. The support given to the left and to the Turks met with violent disapproval from the electorate, and the party's share of the vote in the European parliamentary elections of 2014 plummeted to 2.97 percent, compared to 11.96 percent in 2009. The results of the legislative elections that same year also indicate structural reasons for the vote: the concentration of the voter base near the borders suggests anxiety about the threat to Bulgarian identity: the strongest showing was in Montana Province (7.9 percent), on the border of Serbia and Romania; Yambol Province (7.9 percent), on the border with Turkey; and Kyustendil Province (6.8 percent), on the border with Macedonia and Serbia. The vote for Ataka in the eastern provinces, where the Turkish minority lives, was fairly low (around 4.5 percent). Granted, Montana Province has the highest proportion of Roma (12.5 percent), but they also constitute 11.8 percent of the population in Sliven Province, and there the Ataka vote fell to 5.9 percent. The Roma are unlikely to vote for a party hostile to them, which automatically lowers the number of votes Ataka receives; at the same time, their presence is not enough to mobilize anti-Roma support for the party. The elements that come into play are therefore not entirely interethnic in nature.

The case of Bulgaria sheds light on the overall structure of Eastern European electoral sociology. There, the far-right constituency seems to have three dimensions: first, a minority of young men, workers or unemployed; second, pauperized retirees, some of them nostalgic for the Soviet era; and third, peasants. The geographical breakdown shows that the peasant vote (concentrated in the area east of Poland and Slovakia, for example) stands in contrast to an urban constituency more supportive of liberal and social democratic institutions. It may also be noted that, after a wave of success in the 1990s and early 2000s, far-right populism seems to be receding. Is that the effect of a slow political normalization, in particular, a drop in the number of organizations represented in parliamentary bodies and a certain polarization? Is it the consequence of the emergence of new populist players (Smer in Slovakia) or of competition from the radicalized conservative right (the Kaczynski phenomenon in Poland, the evolution of Fidesz in Hungary)?

The question is all the more complex in that the situation in Central and Eastern Europe still displays characteristics that have become rare in Western Europe. Anti-extremist and antiracist laws are weak there or are not applied. A historical continuity between present-day movements and their pre-1940s precursors is openly acknowledged. The fall of Communism has allowed the return of some surviving exiles who were part of the Fascist movements and has given them a new opportunity to share their memories and disseminate their propaganda. In Romania, for example, the members of the Iron Guard (legionnaires) were able to return in the 1990s. The former legionnaire leader Ivan Dochev moved back to Bulgaria in 1991 and died there in 2005. And in Slovakia, the former leader of the Hlinka

Guard, Alexander Mach, was released from prison in 1968 and was pardoned by the Communist president, Ludvík Svoboda. That continuity is perfectly embodied in the Giertych dynasty.

The Giertych family entered Polish politics in the nineteenth century. It was active in the Endecja Party during the interwar period and currently heads the LPR. Roman Giertych, a high-ranking member of that party, joined the government in 2006 as minister of education. His participation in government affairs was followed by a defeat for the LPR in the legislative elections of 2007: it received 1.24 percent of the vote, compared to 7.9 percent in 2005. Samoobrona, which was also involved in the government, lost 10 percentage points, falling to 1.48 percent. Both parties paid the price for their overly anti-European stance and for the loss of autonomy of their political offering in a very authoritarian and reactionary government. Although Samoobrona opted for a more civilized discourse than the LPR, the party combined anti-German xenophobia—exiles are suspected of wanting to come back and reclaim their lands—and religious and populist anti-Semitism, in a country with scarcely more than 3,000 Jews who identify themselves as such, compared to 3 million in 1939. The instability of the Polish far right is all the more in evidence in that, following the collapse of these two parties, the Congress of the New Right took their place (7.2 percent of the vote in the European parliamentary elections of 2014), after a campaign in which its leader praised Vladimir Putin's strength, questioned whether rape was nonconsensual, and claimed that Hitler had no knowledge of the genocide.[60]

Transgenerational relations comparable to those affecting the LPR can also be found in Hungary, between the Horthy regime and the MIÉP, and in Slovakia, between the Hlinka Guard and the SNS. Nevertheless, the current parties clearly owe less to the inheritance of the Fascist movements than to the legacies of the national conservative regimes or movements. In Hungary, the successors of the Arrow Cross are a string of small groups to the right of Jobbik, each composed of a few dozen members. In Albania, the Balli Kombëtar

Shqiptar (National Albanian Front; 0.28 percent of the vote in the 2013 elections) makes reference to the conservative republican party Balli Kombëtar of the 1940s, which fought the Italian Fascists, then moved closer to the Third Reich in its conflict with the Albanian Communists.

Slovenia shows how the map of the far-right movements can be drawn up on the basis of historical references. Zmago Jelinčič's SNS, founded in 1991 (4 percent of the vote in the European parliamentary elections of 2014), is an ideologically hybrid party. It is xenophobic (anti-Roma, anti-Croatian) and "anti–gender [equality]" but firmly secular, by virtue of its opposition to the Slovensko Domobranstvo (National Slovenian Guard), which collaborated with the Nazis and the Italian Fascists, and to which the Catholic Church was linked. Monsignor Gregorij Rožman, archbishop of Ljubljana, was particularly implicated. The SNS cultivates the memory of the Slovenian partisans, which prompted those who embrace the ideological line of the National Guard to split off from it. They formed the Stranka Slovenskega Naroda (SSN; Party of Slovenian People), which received 0.35 percent of the vote in the European parliamentary elections of 2014. Nevertheless, both organizations defend the idea of a Greater Slovenia that would include a part of Austrian Carinthia, the Italian region of Trieste-Gorizia, and a smaller portion of present-day Hungary at its western extremity. But it is not World War II issues that mobilize passions. Slovenia, a country that is truly democratic and ethnically homogeneous, and which has never faced the ordeal of terrorism, nevertheless illustrates a typical case of the instrumentalization of xenophobia. A controversy erupted there in the first half of 2004, surrounding the planned construction of a mosque in the capital of Ljubljana. Of the country's two million residents, only a few tens of thousands are Muslims, most of them from the countries of the former Yugoslavia (Bosnia, Macedonia). They have been trying to obtain a place to worship since 1969. In December 2003 the municipality of Ljubljana agreed to the construction of what would have been the only mosque in the country. But a petition in opposition, initiated by a municipal councilor from the SNS, was signed by 12,000 citizens. This is Islamophobia in the strict sense of the term, with no plausible explanation in terms of the "clash of civilizations": the "moral panic" diagnosed by Gaël Brustier is truly at work in Eastern Europe as well,[61] and began long before the mass arrival of refugees in the summer and autumn of 2015 provided the far right with an argument.

In the case of Hungary, the plurality of the far-right movements, as it turns out, has provided them with a more effective scheme for destabilizing the cultural consensus of a young pluralist democracy than the mere domination of one populist party. Viktor Orbán, Hungary's prime minister from 1998 to 2002 and leader of the Fidesz Party (Civic Union, affiliated with the European People's Party, which unites all the major conservative parties), retook power in 2010, after a divisive campaign. He focused on the denunciation of the elites ("the oligarchs"), the sense of wounded national pride (Hungary is said to be a weak country that the outside world no longer respects), and, though this may seem paradoxical, nostalgia for a time when Communism ensured lifetime employment for all. That former Communist, now extremely wealthy, was able to return to power thanks to street unrest staged by the radical far right against the departing government. The radicals appear to have been directing these operations for the benefit of Fidesz. The demonstrators did not hesitate to parade with the flag of the Árpád dynasty, used by the Arrow Cross, which underscores the absence of a social memorialization process in Eastern European societies. The very existence of Jobbik is another such sign, given that its program is utterly unambiguous: it says it wants to "tell the truth about multinational big capital, the European Union, the International Monetary Fund, Israeli expansionism, and Gypsy criminality," and to grant Hungarian nationality to the Magyars abroad who live within the borders of pre-1920 Greater Hungary. Nevertheless, populist success appears to be beholden in the first place to the population's exasperation with the neoliberal restructuring policy imposed by the previous social democratic government. All the same, the Orbán government has by no means put a halt to the neoliberalization process in Hungary. Instead, it has combined it with an authoritarian practice and discourse that restrict fundamental liberties (various protests in Europe have resulted) and xenophobia, which became even more intense during the migratory crisis of 2015. The increasingly hard line of the Orbán regime has not contained Jobbik—far from it. It allied itself with the MIÉP in 2006, and together they won 2 percent of the vote. Jobbick has continued to make inroads since then, winning 20.39 percent of the vote in the legislative elections of 2014. The party has had particular success with voters under thirty, in mid-sized cities, and in the Calvinist northeast.[62] Jobbik is not a liability to Fidesz, which looks by comparison like a lawful and conservative party.

In Eastern Europe, moreover, groups to the right of the established parties are proliferating, a phenomenon manifested primarily by a fairly large neo-Nazi skinhead movement, generally gathered into Blood and Honour and Hammerskins networks. Above all, the question of nationalities, minorities, and irredentist movements persists. For example, the Sixty-Four Counties Youth Movement (HVIM), the MIÉP, and Jobbik want to reconstitute a Greater Hungary as it existed prior to the Treaty of Trianon (1920), which would therefore include portions of present-day Austria, Romania, Slovakia, Croatia, Serbia, and Ukraine. The Serbian Radical Party remains a proponent of Greater Serbia, hence of a confrontation with all the other former federated republics of Yugoslavia.[63] România Mare, like Noua Dreapta, is in favor of reconstituting the Greater Romania that emerged after World War I, which incorporated Bessarabia, Bucovina, and Transylvania. Currently, the concept of a Greater Romania also entails the idea of a "reunification" of Romania and Moldova. That so-called unionist plan is also defended in Moldova by the Blocul Unității Naționale, which mobilized several thousand people (30,000, according to the organizers) around that issue on July 5, 2015, in the Moldovan capital of Chișinău.

Noua Dreapta is a "national Christian [Orthodox] movement." It proclaims that its economic system is "distributionist," a popular label to invoke Socialist tendencies; it defends the "traditional family" and wants to bar former Communists from public service. Its principal enemy is *politicianismului* (politicianism), a term that the Iron Guard's Corneliu Codreanu used to designate "the [class] spirit, mentality, education fostered in the political parties and inculcated in the elements destined to form the country's ruling stratum."[64] He contrasted *politicianismului* to a disinterestedness devoted solely to the nation, which supposedly characterizes the legionnaire. The leaders of Noua Dreapta are Tudor Ionescu in Romania, Sergiu Lascu in Moldova. The movement's symbol is the Celtic cross against a green background, green being the color of the Iron Guard.

These various forms of irredentism lie at the confluence of national, ethnic, and religious demands. Even more than in the West, extremist nationalism in Central and Eastern Europe is centered around religion. Surveying the Paris Peace Conference of 1919, the future Conducător (Marshal) Antonescu wrote a memorandum listing the "nationalities" present, region by region: the Romanians, the Jews, the Magyars, the Germans, the Roma, and others. In short, he drew a portrait in which the term "nationality" referred to national, ethnic, and religious entities. Although confusing for Westerners, that view is consistent with common Eastern European representations. Democratic Romania, in fact, opted for a system wherein parliamentary seats are reserved for minorities: eighteen minorities were recognized following the election reforms of 2000, but the electoral threshold excludes Roma representatives.[65] The Slovak SNS continues to bow to the clerical state founded by Monsignor Tiso in 1938. The LPR in Poland is in great part a Catholic party, one that certainly has its problems with the Polish hierarchy but was able to count on the support of a large part of the rural clergy. For a long time, Radio Maryja, an ultraconservative radio station with anti-Semitic undercurrents, actively solicited votes for the party. But since the elections of 2007 it has chosen to support the Kaczynski brothers' Law and Justice Party.[66] A great deal of overlap exists as well between the Orthodox religion and Serbian, Romanian, and Greek nationalism: the far-right party that joined the Greek Parliament in 2007 is called LAOS, an acronym that means "people" in Greek but also "Popular Orthodox Rally."

The Eastern European far right has other dimensions specific to it that account for a large share of its attraction and which do not exist, or do not exist in the same form, in Western Europe. First and foremost, there is the question of anti-Semitism, including "anti-Semitism without Jews," an aspect already studied by Paul Lendvai in the early 1970s.[67] It is sometimes undisguised, as in Hungary, where the Calvinist minister Lóránt Hegedűs Jr. in 2004 called on his compatriots to "expel the Jews before they expel you."[68] Other characteristics of the East European far right have a particular intensity: anti-Roma racism; the notion of the unity of the Slavic peoples, or at least of a common destiny, to which, according to the ultranationalists, the Western path of pluralist democracy would not be suited.[69] It also seems that the charismatic dimension of party leaders (Corneliu Vadim Tudor in Romania, Volen Nikolov Siderov in Bulgaria, Vojislav Šešelj in Serbia) is more acute than in Western Europe, and one can say with certainty that the leaders' individual trajectories have the peculiarity of often combining a commitment to Communism in their youth with a later evolution toward the far right. This is not only because the exigencies of the Communist era meant that anyone who wanted a political career had to work "within the party" but also because certain commonalities between Communism and nationalism were already present, at least in Romania, Poland, and Russia. In the Ceauşescu era in Romania, the official ideology, even from an objective standpoint, deserved the label "national Communism" that Thiriart attributed to it, and the same can be said for Alexander Lukashenko's Belarus. Although the thesis of a meeting of extremes has no explanatory force in the case of Western European policy, Eastern authoritarian regimes were in fact able to produce an ideologically organicist framework.

Several factors can be advanced to explain the difficulty the Eastern European far right has had in becoming stabilized over the medium

term. One is the incorporation of nationalist and irredentist sentiments, anti-Roma discourse, and criticism of the European Union
into the discourse and practices of the mainstream parties. But
another factor worthy of note is the capacity of certain Eastern European political systems to allow new populist parties, on the right
(Ol'aNo in Slovakia), somewhat on the left (the Palikot Party in
Poland), or linked to an entrepreneur (Rolandas Paksas in Lithuania,
Tomio Okamura's Úsvit in the Czech Republic), to find expression
in practically every election cycle. That capacity produces unpre-
dictability, even instability. But with the weakening of the major
Western European ideological systems, namely, classic liberalism and
the social democratic tradition (except in the Czech Republic), it also
allows for the expression of a contestation of power that competes
with the far right.

In addition, "core constituencies" that have dwindled away in the
West occupy space in the political systems of Eastern Europe that
any ethnonationalist organization would like to capture: for example,
the agrarians (in Bulgaria, in Croatia with the Peasant Party, in Latvia
with the Centrist Party of Peasants) and the nonreactionary monarchists (National Movement for Stability and Progress, headed by
Simeon II of Bulgaria). In Poland, there is even an intellectually
consequential counterrevolutionary school that embraces an economically ultraliberal but Catholic monarchism: the Conservative-
Monarchist Club, under the leadership of the historian Adam
Wielomski, which functions as a metapolitical group (Janusz Korwin-
Mikke is a member) exerting an influence on Kaczynski's party and
those to the right of the right. It can be argued that these core constituencies, like the Communist Party of Bohemia-Moravia in Slovakia, contribute toward the diversity of the political offerings and,
in avoiding or delaying polarization, limit somewhat the space of the
far right.

It is important to point out, however, that political nationalism in
Eastern Europe is not limited to the far right. The history of the
"Eastern Bloc" and the colonial situation that the countries under So-

viet control endured provide a logical explanation for the presence of a form of nationalism that embraces several different tendencies.[70]

The European parliamentary elections of 2014 and the most recent legislative elections benefited the far right in Eastern Europe much less than they did the West. Neither the National Slovak Party (4.6 percent of the vote in the legislative elections of 2012, 3.16 percent in the European parliamentary elections), nor România Mare (1.2 and 2.7 percent of the vote, respectively), nor the Slovenian National Party (2.21 percent and 4.04 percent, respectively, in the legislative and European parliamentary elections of 2014) has seats any longer in the new European Parliament or in national parliaments. The League of Polish Families has been defunct since at least 2007, when it lost its parliamentary representation and public financing. *Pace* Western prejudices, Central and Eastern Europe are less auspicious for the success of these organizations than is Western Europe. Partisan systems have proven to be more flexible to the east, where new populist parties arise in almost every election cycle and capture the protest vote (e.g., OL'aNO in Slovaia, Dawn of Direct Democracy in the Czech Republic, Bulgaria without Censorship) and express criticism of Euroliberalism and postdemocracy but do not lay claim to the ethnic nationalist movements of the interwar period.

Conclusion: Might the Far Right Cease to Be?

The European far-right field has demonstrated a capacity to adapt to structural changes that no one in the postwar years would have suspected. Over the long term, from the nineteenth to the twenty-first century, it has proven with every geopolitical change that it is able to produce new models of militant and cultural action. In the short term, the progress of the far-right movements is attributable not so much to the overthrow of old ideologies in favor of new ones as to a lexico-ideological adaptation. This is perfectly illustrated by the example of the French National Front.[1] Some societies, however, appear impermeable to far-right politics, which can gain no foothold there. Why have some countries, which may have gone through economic crisis, which have opened themselves to multiculturalism, and whose political system is fairly obsolete, not seen the emergence of the far right? In Ireland, for example, the far right is confined to small groups. Only the Catholic Democrats, a pro-life, conservative, and anti-European party, occupy the political fringes. This conservative and moral right wing attracts less than 1 percent of the vote. That is because, in Ireland, nationhood rests on a general consensus embracing groups from the far left (Sinn Fein) to the right (Fine Gael and Fianna Fail). Ireland is a recent state (established in 1919) that had a Fascist, Catholic, and corporatist movement (the Blue Shirts, founded in 1933 and banned in 1936), which remained powerless so long as the Irish Republican Army monopolized revolutionary aspirations. The construction of the national state and the reference point of the war of independence are not a matter of debate: a movement that rejects the cultural foundations on which the political system is built, as the far right does, cannot acquire any leverage. Fine Gael absorbed the militant potential of the Blue Shirts, whose leader, General Eoin O'Duffy, had previously been their own. O'Duffy's transition to Fascism led him to adopt violent methods against political adversaries, who themselves were Irish Catholic nationalists. And yet, though the technique of preventive counterrevolution was able to respond to the antisubversive aspirations of large segments of society, attempts to construct a subversive far right have never borne fruit (Italy, by contrast, provides a full range of historical examples of such positions).

Other countries as well have no far right, and all of them seem to share a number of specific traits. Iceland is another recent state (founded in 1944) whose national narrative and popular culture are profoundly consensual and well rooted. Monaco, Liechtenstein, and Luxembourg are geographically small and prosperous constitutional monarchies. Their grassroots democracy serves to quell social tensions, and their wealth makes for a quiet political life. The national question, if it exists, cannot lead to the creation of a party seeking to take power on ethnicist foundations. In the case of Monaco, what could form the basis for demands by a far-right movement? The Constitution of Monaco stipulates that "priority of access to public and private employment is ensured to Monégasques," and the state's real property is by law available only to nationals. In fact, the absence of a populist far right that would contest the social order sheds light on the confusion frequently made between "popular" and "populist." The success of populist organizations cannot be interpreted as a demand for social welfare policies. What is being demanded is a social hierarchy judged to be legitimate: the exclusion of some entails the inclusion of others.

Far-right states took this principle to the ultimate extreme. Most were swept aside in 1945, the imperialism of the Third Reich having sealed their fate. Only the Iberian dictatorships survived, because Salazar and Franco chose not imperialism but autarky. According to the analyses of the historian of Communism Romain Ducoulombier, what made for the specificity and longevity of state Communism was neither totalitarianism nor internationalism: "The geographical, economic, and cultural enclosure of Communist societies was a common trait and a fundamental characteristic of their governance," and allowed the state apparatus to "fend off the intrinsic contingency and instability of modern individualism."[2] Although these regimes were fundamentally different in both their ideas and their actual existence, the same enclosure allowed the two Catholic national states of Spain and Portugal to endure. Yet Patrice de La Tour du Pin's poetic lines are apt here: "All countries whose legend is no more / Will be condemned to die of cold."[3] Salazarism and Francoism died because they forgot that this adage is also valid for countries that cease to have a history and that think they are happy because of it. It was their failure to project themselves into the future that led to their doom, and also, in the case of the Portuguese Estado Novo, the ineluctable failure of its attempt to save its empire by means of the colonial wars, all of which set in motion the process leading to the Carnation Revolution in 1974. The only far-right regime to have been established in post-1945 Europe was the Greek Regime of the Colonels, whose fate was sealed by its overthrow of Cyprus and the Turkish invasion that followed. The only system that held on until its leader's death was therefore Franco's, perfectly enclosed between the Pyrenees and the mouth of the Guadiana. Far-right states do not survive outside full enclosure, as Ducoulombier defines it. And Francoism did not survive Franco, because the prolonged success of that enclosure condemned the society to give up altogether.

The far right is also mortal in democratic states. Movements such as Poujadism in France and the Republikaner in Germany show that a radical change in the relations between state and society, their core project, proves fatal to them. Over time, the far-right parties generally suffer as a result of their participation, even indirect, in parliamentary majorities. Granted, the ordeal of political responsibilities is politically painful for all parties. But as we have seen, whatever the country, far-right parties face a particularly large backlash from the electorate. Once they have gone back to being the opposition, they seek to recover ground through a popular and xenophobic realignment charged with expressing the desire for legitimate social hierarchy. That tactic usually works and once again fuels a social demand for authoritarianism. The case of the Austrian FPÖ can serve as a prototype in that regard.

This mechanism appears to be explained by the autonomy of the political offering proposed; an inadequately differentiated far-right movement loses its magnetic attraction. The case of the Alleanza Nazionale demonstrates that the visibility of the far right can lead to political death. The example of Vlaams Belang shows that, when a party tips the balance toward institutional integration at the expense of its subversive charge, its very position in the institutional process may ultimately prove problematic. Nevertheless, those who believed they could deduce from that fact that radicalism was the proper path have little to show for their efforts. Only Jobbik and Golden Dawn have managed to maintain a high profile on the radical far right, in contexts very different from those of Western Europe. The radicalism of international organizations has also been a failure, either because they overinvested in the subversive element (such is the case for the European Liberation Front) or because they became part of the globalizing process (through projects to unite white nations, from that of the European Socialists to that of the apostles of Eurosiberia), whereas the far-right demand is built on reactions against the advances of globalization.

Granted, the current demand for authoritarianism in Europe is not simply a response to the financial crisis. But within the context of the swing to the right and the de-Westernization of the world since 1973, the geopolitical crisis of 2001 allowed neopopulism to thrive.

Not only does the West now know it is not alone in the world, but the capacity of radical Islamism to strike at the heart of every state and to dispute the legitimacy of democracy has caused a geostrategic crisis in Europe and a crisis in its self-esteem. The financial crisis of 2008 allowed national populism to successfully transform itself into full sovereignism. As we complete this book, the general public is discovering, through the dead body of the three-year-old Syrian refugee Aylan Kurdi, that the difficulties of southern Mediterranean refugees have set off a migratory crisis. At each stage of globalization, the far right finds resources for proposing the path of enclosure as a protective solution. With the combination of these two crises, the far right in Europe will not cease to be. Just as it is part of our history, it will play a role in our future.

Notes
Acknowledgments
Index

Notes

Introduction

1. With the exception of the journalist Catherine Fouillet, who titled her book *Moi, j'aime l'extrême droite* [I for one love the far right] (Paris: La Librairie française, 1982). As far back as 1940, the writer Lucien Rebatet, in his pamphlet *Les décombres,* defined his political family as that of the "nationals."

2. ["Caudillist": characteristic of a Latin American military regime founded on a cult of personality.—trans.]

3. Marc Crapez, "De quand date le clivage gauche / droite en France?," *Revue française de science politique* 48, no. 1 (1998): 42–75.

4. *Dialogue entre trois électeurs, ou la clef des trois opinions* (Paris, n.d.).

5. Augustin Barruel, *Abrégé des mémoires pour servir à l'histoire du jacobinisme* (London: Le Boussonnier, 1799), 248.

6. René Rémond, *Les Droites en France* (Paris: Aubier-Montaigne, 1982; 1st ed. 1954).

7. Stéphane Rials, *Le légitimisme* (Paris: Presses Universitaires de France, 1983).

8. Adam McKeown, "Les migrations internationales à l'ère de la mondialisation industrielle, 1840–1940," *Le mouvement social* 241 (2012): 31–46.

9. Quoted in Zeev Sternhell, *Maurice Barrès et le nationalisme français* (Brussels: Complexe, 1988; 1st ed. 1972), 163.

10. Alain de Benoist, *Vu de droite: Anthologie critique des idées contemporaines* (Paris: Le Labyrinthe, 2001), 277.

11. Pascal Ory, *Du fascisme* (Paris: Perrin, 2003), 287.

12. Louis Dupeux, *Aspects du fondamentalisme national en Allemagne* (Strasbourg: Presses Universitaires de Strasbourg, 2001).

13. Quoted in Michel Winock, *Nationalisme, antisémitisme et fascisme en France* (Paris: Le Seuil, 1990), 231.

14. André Encrevé, "Protestantisme et bonapartisme," *Revue d'histoire du XIXe siècle* 28 (2004): 111–131.

15. Philippe Burrin, *La dérive fasciste: Doriot, Déat, Bergery (1933–1945)* (Paris: Le Seuil, 1986).

16. Louis-Auguste Blanqui, *Instruction pour une prise d'armes* (n.p. [Nantes]: n.p. [Ars Magna], n.d. [1868]), 7; *Auguste Blanqui: Textes choisis* (Paris: Les Éditions sociales, 1971), 167.

17. Karl Marx and Friedrich Engels, *Manifesto of the Communist Party,* in *The Marx-Engels Reader,* ed. Robert C. Tucker, 2nd ed. (New York: W. W. Norton & Company, 1978), 488.

18. Michel Winock, "La culture politique des socialistes," in *Les cultures politiques en France,* ed. Serge Berstein (Paris: Le Seuil, 2003), 189–226.

19. Olivier Dard and Nathalie Sévilla, eds., *Le phénomène ligueur sous la IIIe République* (Metz: Centre lorrain d'histoire, 2009).

20. Michel Winock, "Populismes français," *Vingtième Siècle: Revue d'histoire* 56 (October–December 1997): 77–91.

21. Pierre-André Taguieff, "La rhétorique du national-populisme: Les règles élémentaires de la propagande xénophobe," *Mots* 9 (October 1984): 113–139.

22. See Eugen Weber, *Action Française* (Stanford, CA: Stanford University Press, 1982).

23. Ibid., 521.

24. Olivier Dard, *Charles Maurras* (Paris: Armand Colin, 2013), 236–245.

25. Philippe Beneton, "La génération de 1912–1914: Image, mythe et réalité?," *Revue française de science politique* 21, no. 5 (1971): 981–1009.

26. Stéphane François, *Au-delà des vents du nord: L'extrême droite française, le pôle Nord et les Indo-Européens* (Lyon: Presses Universitaires de Lyon, 2014).

27. Zeev Sternhell, *Ni droite ni gauche: L'idéologie fasciste en France* (Paris: Fayard, 2000).

28. Zeev Sternhell, *La Droite révolutionnaire (1885–1914)* (Paris: Gallimard, 1997), 562.

29. Ory, *Du fascisme,* 39.

30. Quoted in Schlomo Sand, "Les représentations de la Révolution dans l'imaginaire historique du fascisme français," *Mil neuf cent* 9 (September 1991): 35; François Duprat, *Les mouvements d'extrême droite en France de 1940 à 1944* (Paris: L'Homme libre, 1998; 1st ed. 1971), 256.

31. See George Mosse, *La Révolution fasciste: Vers une théorie générale du fascisme* (Paris: Le Seuil, 2003). The connection between Fascism and Jacobinism was established in Germany and Italy by conservative circles. Their error was to base the rapprochement on the question of ideology or practice rather than style.

32. Philippe Burrin, "Le fascisme," in *Histoires des droites en France,* ed. Jean-François Sirinelli (Paris: Gallimard, 1992), 603–653.

33. Philippe Burrin, "Le fascisme: La Révolution sans révolutionnaires," *Le Débat* 38 (January–March 1986): 164.

34. Roger Griffin, "Europe for the Europeans: Fascist Myths of the European New Order 1922–1992," *Humanities Research Centre, Occasional Paper,* no. 1 (1994); Pierre Milza, *Les Fascismses* (Paris: Imprimerie nationale, 1985), 281–284.

35. "Manifeste de Vérone," in *Manifestes pour une gauche fasciste* (n.p.: n.p, n.d. [1943]), unpaginated.

36. Louis Dupeux, *National-bolchevisme: Stratégie communiste et dynamique conservatrice* (Paris: Honoré Champion, 1979).

37. Armin Mohler, *La Révolution conservatrice en Allemagne, 1918–1922* (Puiseaux: Éditions Pardès, 1993; 1st ed. 1950).

38. Jean-Pierre Faye, *Langages totalitaires* (Paris: Hermann, 1972), 70–79.

39. Ibid., 16; Dana Arieli-Horowitz, "The Jew as 'Destroyer of Culture' in National-Socialist Ideology," *Patterns of Prejudice* 32, no. 1

(January 1998): 51–67; Jan Nederveen Pieterse, *Development Theory: Deconstructions/Reconstructions* (London: Sage, 2001), 39–40.

40. Jean Maze, *Le système* (Paris: Segur, 1951).

41. [Nationalist compromise: the provisional acceptance of the legitimacy of the secular republican nation, despite the belief that "monarchy is the regime that best corresponds to the requirements of history and the French temperament" (Charles Maurras). See the Action Française Web site, http://www.actionfrancaise.net/craf/?Le-compromis-nationaliste—trans.]

42. Raoul Girardet, "Notes sur l'esprit d'un fascisme français, 1934–1939," *Revue française de science politique* 3 (1955): 529–546.

43. Philippe Burrin, "La France dans le champ magnétique des fascismes," *Le Débat* 32 (November 1984): 52–72.

44. Jean-Louis Loubet del Bayle, *Les non-conformistes des années trente* (Paris: Le Seuil, 2001).

45. On the Dreyfusards who became collaborators, see Simon Epstein, *Les Dreyfusards sous l'Occupation* (Paris: Albin Michel, 2001).

46. Quoted in Jean-Louis Maisonneuve, *L'extrême droite sur le divan* (Paris: Imago, 1991), 31.

47. Philippe Burrin, *Fascisme, nazisme et autoritarisme* (Paris: Le Seuil, 2001), 261.

48. Quoted in Philippe Burrin, *La France à l'heure allemande 1940–1944* (Paris: Le Seuil, 1995), 42; Direction Générale de la Sûreté Nationale (DGSN), Direction Centrale des Renseignements Généraux (DCRG), *Partis et groupements politiques d'extrême droite,* vol. 1: *Identification et organisation des mouvements et associations* (January 1956), 4, Archives Nationales (AN), F7/15591.

49. DGSN, DCRG, *Partis et groupements politiques d'extrême droite,* 1:4; Renseignements Généraux de la Préfecture de Police (RGPP), "Les amis de François Duprat" (1989), 6, Archives de la Préfecture de Police (APP), GAD8 913.285; PET (Danish services), *"Kommissionens beretning bind 112. Den danske nazisme i efterkrigstiden, 1945–1989."* On the subversive problematic, see François Cochet and Olivier Dard, eds., *Subversion, anti-subversion, contre-subversion* (Paris: Riveneuve, 2009).

50. DGSN, DCRG, *Partis et groupements politiques d'extrême droite,* 1:4–6.

51. Correspondence between Michel Leroy and Dominique Venner, November 1958, minutes of Michel Leroy's interrogation, Tribunal de Grande Instance de la Seine, June 18, 1960, 2, AN, F7/5W267.

52. Dominique Venner, *Pour une critique positive* (Nantes: Ars Magna, 1997). Originally published as *Politique éclair: Hebdomadaire de l'élite française,* supplement to issue 98 (August 28, 1962), unpaginated.

53. *L'Esprit public,* August 1963.

54. Patrick Moreau, "'Socialisme national' contre hitlérisme: Le cas Otto Strasser," *Revue d'Allemagne* (July–September 1984): 485–498.

55. Joey Cloutier, "Ambition et polémique: L'activité anti-hitlérienne d'Otto Strasser à Montréal et la Révolution conservatrice, 1941–1943," *Cahiers d'histoire* 19, no. 1 (Autumn 1999): 57–86. The influence of the conservative revolutionaries, such as Oswald Spengler and Moeller van den Bruck, can also be found in Strasser.

56. Anne-Marie Duranton-Crabol, *L'Europe de l'extrême droite de 1945 à nos jours* (Brussels: Complexe, 1991).

57. Michel Tournier, "Les mots fascistes, du populisme à la dénazification," *Mots* (June 1998): 162.

58. With the exception of the engagement by Spanish volunteers in the Blue Division, including the future vice president of the Spanish government, General Agustin Muñoz Grandes, and a future participant in the failed putsch of February 23, 1981, General Jaime Miláns del Bosch.

59. Maurice Bardèche, *Qu'est-ce que le fascisme?* (Sassetot-le-Mauconduit: Phythéas, 1994; 1st ed. 1961), 52.

60. See Philippe Carrard, *Nous avons combattu pour Hitler* (Paris: Armand Colin, 2011), 33.

61. Enrique León and Jean-Paul Scot, *Le Nazisme des origines à 1945* (Paris: Masson et Armand Colin, 1997), 156.

62. Henry Rousso, *Pétain et la fin de la Collaboration: Sigmaringen 1944–1945* (Brussels: Complexe, 1984), 219.

63. Secret communication from the chief of police, head of general intelligence (RG) services of Lille, to the director of the RG, October 21, 1943, AN F7/15304; Marc Sueur, "Collaboration et Résistance dans le Nord et le Pas-de-Calais," *Revue d'histoire de la Deuxième Guerre mondiale et des conflits contemporains* 135 (July 1984): 24–25; Léon Degrelle, *Un appel aux Français! Aux armes pour l'Europe: Texte du discours prononcé à*

Paris, le 5 mars 1944, au palais de Chaillot par le SS-Sturmbannführer Léon Degrelle (N.p.: n.d.).

64. *Devenir* 1 (February 1944); 2 (March 1944); 3 (April–May 1944); 4 (June 1944).

65. *Contribution de la section économique du groupe "Collaboration" à l'étude des problèmes européens,* Paris, May 1941, 4.

66. Marc Augier, *Les jeunes devant l'aventure européenne* (Paris: Les Conférences du groupe "Collaboration," 1941), 28–33.

67. Duprat, *Les mouvements d'extrême droite,* 149.

68. Hammerfest, Norway, is said to be the northernmost city in the world. German troops destroyed it in 1944.

69. *La Jeune Europe* 1–2 (1942): 42–44; 3–4 (1942): 9–11; 7 (1942): 21; 8 (1942): 24.

70. A concept used by Urs Altermatt and Hanspeter Kriesi, *L'extrême droite en Suisse: Organisation et radicalisation au cours des années quatre-vingt et quatre-vingt-dix* (Fribourg: Presses Universitaires de Fribourg, 1995).

71. Alain Néry, "Nouvelle droite et droite révolutionnaire," in *Vu de haut,* ed. Institut Universitaire Saint-Pie X (Sainte-Foy-lès-Lyon: Éditions Fideliter, 1981), 61–71.

72. Gaël Brustier, *Le Mai 68 conservateur: Que restera-t-il de La Manif pour tous?* (Paris: Le Cerf, 2014).

73. Benoist, *Vu de droite,* xii.

74. Piero Ignazi, *L'estrema destra in Europa* (Bologna: Il Mulino, 1994).

75. Hans-Georg Betz, *Radical Right-Wing Populism in Western Europe* (London: Palgrave Macmillan, 1994).

76. Cas Mudde, "The Extreme Right Party Family: An Ideological Approach" (PhD diss., Leiden University, 1998).

77. Roger Griffin, *The Nature of Fascism* (London: Routledge, 1991).

78. Roger Eatwell, *Fascism: A History* (London: Chatto & Windus, 1995).

79. Except in an individual capacity, some elected officials and leading cadres of the FN having been active in groups of that type.

80. Emilio Gentile, *Facismo: Storia e interpretazione* (Rome: GLF Editori Laterza, 2002).

81. See Johann Chapoutot, *Le National-Socialisme et l'Antiquité* (Paris: Presses Universitaires de France, 2008).

82. After receiving 2.1 percent of the vote in the European elections of 1979, Fuerza Nueva collapsed, winning only 0.5 percent in 1982.

1. What to Do after Fascism?

1. Damir Skenderovic and Luc Van Dongen, "Gaston-Armand Amaudruz, pivot et passeur européen," in *Doctrinaires, vulgaristateurs et passeurs des droites radicales au XXe siècle (Europe-Amériques),* ed. Olivier Dard (Bern: Peter Lang, 2012), 211–230.

2. PET (Danish intelligence services), "Nazisme, foreninger," April 11, 1960.

3. The historian Stéphane François defines "racialism" as the theory of the inequality of the races and as an explanation of history in terms of the racial question. See François, *Au-delà des vents du nord,* 15.

4. Statistic cited in Corina Vasilopoulou, "Aube dorée, le choc," *Le Monde diplomatique* 134 (April–May 2014): 20.

5. Robert Solliers, "Que devient l'Allemagne aujourd'hui? Naissance et développement de la NPD (1964–1967)," *Revue d'histoire du fascisme* 5 (September 1974): 170–186.

6. Delphine Iost, "L'implantation du NPD dans les nouveaux Länder allemands," *Hérodote* 128 (2008): 87–102.

7. Alexandre Agadjanian, "Pluralisme religieux et identité nationale en Russie," *Journal on Multicultural Societies* 2, no. 2 (2000): 97–124.

8. *Le Nouvel Observateur,* June 13–19, 2002.

9. Valérie Igounet, *Robert Faurisson: Portrait d'un négationniste* (Paris: Denoël, 2012).

10. Deborah Lipstadt came out against his incarceration in an interview on the BBC on January 12, 2006, on the grounds that it made a martyr of him and garnered him media attention, a fact confirmed by, for example, the publication of an interview with him in the British daily *The Observer* on January 22, 2006.

11. For a perspective that includes the United States, see Jean-Yves Camus, "El negacionismo en el mundo occidental: Una pantalla pseudocientífica del antisemitismo," in *La Extrema Derecha en Europe desde 1945 a nuestros días,* ed. Miguel Angel Simon (Madrid: Tecnos, 2007), 223–248.

12. Central Intelligence Agency (CIA), "Net Project: Los Angeles," 1947, Freedom of Information Act (FOIA), 519cd821993294098d516f71.

13. Pauline Picco, "Extrême droite et antisémitisme en Italie: L'exemple du *Centro studi Ordine nuovo* (1955–1971)," *Laboratoire italien* 11 (2011): 17–52.

14. It includes a discussion of the views of Yockey and Thiriart, nationalists who will be considered in the following pages.

15. Pierre Milza, *L'Europe en chemise noire: Les extrêmes droites européennes de 1945 à aujourd'hui* (Paris: Fayard, 2002), 99–100; Francesco Ferraresi, "Les références théorico-doctrinales de la droite radicale en Italie," *Mots* 12 (March 1986): 14.

16. Pino Rauti, "Thèse de l'Ordine Nuovo" (1963), quoted in François Duprat, *L'ascension du MSI* (Paris: Les Sept Couleurs, 1972), 58–67.

17. Isabelle Sommier, *La violence politique et son deuil* (Rennes: Presses Universitaires de Rennes, 2008), 99.

18. CIA, "Alleged Role in Coup Plans of Valerio Junio Borghese," August 6, 1970, FOIA, 519a6b27993294098d511202; CIA, "The National Front: An Ineffectual Right Wing Organization Often Accused of Planning a Coup d'État," January 1971, FOIA, 519a6b27993294098d5111f3.

19. Fulvio Reiter, *Ordine Nuovo Verità e menzogne Riposta alla Commissione Stragi* (Rome: Settimo Sigillo, 2007), n.p.; Frédéric Laurent, *L'Orchestre noir* (Paris: Stock, 1978).

20. Luciano Cheles, "Le 'New Look' du néofascisme italien: Thèmes, styles et sources de la récente propagande de l'extrême droite parlementaire," *Mots* 12 (March 1986): 29–42.

21. Roger Griffin, "From Slime Mould to Rhizome: An Introduction to the Groupuscular Right," *Patterns of Prejudice* 37, no. 1 (March 2003): 27–50.

22. Étienne Verhoeyen, "L'extrême droite en Belgique," *Courrier hebdomadaire du CRISP* (Centre de Recherche et d'Information Socio-Politique, Brussels) 715–716 (1976): 34–35.

23. Fédération Internationale des Résistants, *Le néofascisme en Italie* (Vienna: Fédération Internationale des Résistants, 1971), 40–41.

24. Pierre Clémenti, *La troisième paix* (Fribourg: Éditions de la Jeune Europe, 1949), 54.

25. CIA, "The Fascist International," January 9, 1956, 5–16, FOIA, 519a6b28993294098d51133c.

26. *Le Monde,* October 30–31, 1949.

27. CIA, "The Fascist International," 8; on Duprat's international connections, see Nicolas Lebourg and Joseph Beauregard, *François Duprat, l'homme qui inventa le Front national* (Paris: Denoël, 2012).

28. *Le Combattant européen,* April 1946 and June 1946; René Binet, *Théorie du racisme* (Paris: Les Vikings, 1950).

29. Kevin Coogan, "Lost Imperium: The European Liberation Front (1949–1954)," *Patterns of Prejudice* 36, no. 3 (July 2002): 9–23; Jeffrey Kaplan, "The Post-War Paths of Occult National Socialism: From Rockwell and Madole to Manson," *Patterns of Prejudice* 35, no. 3 (2001): 49; *Le Prophète de l'Imperium: Francis-Parker Yockey* (Paris: Avatar, 2004); Francis Parker Yockey, *The World in Flames: An Estimate of the World Situation* (New York: Le Blanc Publications, 1961); Francis Parker Yockey, *The Proclamation of London of the European Liberation Front* (n.p. [Metairie, LA]: n.p. [Sons of Liberty], n.d. [197?]).

30. Roger Griffin, "Caught in Its Own Net: Post-War Fascism outside Europe," in *Fascism outside Europe,* ed. Stein Larsen (New York: Columbia University Press, 2001), 46–68. Nazism was also modernized by borrowings from Satanism and esotericism. In 1968 George Wallace, the segregationist presidential candidate, received 13.5 percent of the vote, the strongest showing of any independent candidate in forty-four years. The young people who supported him formed the very radical National Alliance.

31. *Le Viking,* January 1964.

32. In the early 1950s, he moved to Orsay, in the Essonne department of France, where he later died and where his ashes were scattered.

33. Pascale Sempéré, "L'européisme d'Oswald Mosley à travers ses textes fondateurs: Un projet de Grande Europe sur les traces du fascisme historique," *Miranda* 9 (2014), http://miranda.revues.org/5891.

34. "La Paneurafrique," *Les annales coloniales* 31, no. 6 (November 1930): 1; Étienne Deschamps, "Quelle Afrique pour une Europe unie? L'idée d'Eurafrique à l'aube des années trente," in *Penser l'Europe à l'aube des années trente: Quelques contributions belges,* ed. Michel Dumoulin (Brussels: Nauwels, 1995), 95–150.

35. Marco Antonsich, "L'Eurafrica des Italiens: La revue *Geopolitica* conscience géographique du régime fasciste," *Outre-Terre* 11 (2005): 487–488; Charles Bloch, *Le IIIe Reich et le monde* (Paris: Imprimerie nationale, 1986), 432.

36. Bernard Bruneteau, *"L'Europe nouvelle" de Hitler: Une illusion des intellectuels de la France de Vichy* (Monaco: Le Rocher, 2003), 94–99; Gérard Bossuat, *Faire l'Europe sans défaire la France: 60 ans de politique d'unité européenne des gouvernements et des présidents de la République française (1943–2003)* (Brussels: Peter Lang, 2005); Désirée Avit, "La question de l'Eurafrique dans la construction de l'Europe de 1950 à 1957," *Matériaux pour l'histoire de notre temps* 77 (2005): 17–23; Sempéré, "L'européisme d'Oswald Mosley."

37. Oswald Mosley, *La Nation Europe* (Paris: Nouvelles Éditions latines, 1962); interview with Strasser in *La Nation européenne,* January 15–February 15, 1967.

38. Pauline Picco, "Théoriser la violence politique à l'extrême droite en Italie," *Storicamente* 10 (2014), http://storicamente.org/picco-violence-droite.

39. CIA, "The Fascist International," 2; Ian R. Barnes, "Anti-Semitic Europe and the 'Third Way': The Ideas of Maurice Bardèche," *Patterns of Prejudice* 34, no. 2 (2000): 62; Joseph Algazy, *La tentation néofasciste en France 1944–1968* (Paris: Fayard, 1984), 294–295.

40. CIA, "Arrow Cross 'Hungarista Movement,'" November 1955, FOIA, 51966ec2993294098d509642.

41. DGSN, DCRG, *Partis et groupements politiques d'extrême droite,* 1:11–12.

42. Olivier Dard, *La synarchie ou le Mythe du complot permanent* (Paris: Perrin, 2012); Frédéric Charpier, *Génération Occident* (Paris: Le Seuil, 2005).

43. On Victor Barthélemy, see Nicolas Lebourg and Joseph Beauregard, *Dans l'ombre des Le Pen: Une histoire des numéros 2 du Front national* (Paris: Nouveau Monde, 2012), 23–63.

44. Anton Mussert had participated in the European Fascist meeting in Montreux, Switzerland, in 1934.

45. "Meeting of the Nationaal Europese Sociale Beweging (NESB) in Amsterdam, June 21, 1953," Archives Binnenlandse Veiligheidsdienst (BVD), A8-no.689-'53. Div.

46. Skenderovic and Van Dongen, "Gaston-Armand Amaudruz."

47. *Déclarations du Nouvel Ordre européen* (n.p., 1958), 1–3; Maurice Bardèche, *Le racisme, cet inconnu* (Waterloo: Le Javelot, 1992; 1st ed. 1960), 3–8.

48. Last issue consulted in Lausanne in January 2015.

49. In 1954 the delegation of the Phalange Française, paying a visit to the MPE, was led by Henri Roques (1920–1944), former member of the Chantiers de Jeunesse under the Vichy regime, who became the MPE's assistant general secretary. Henri Roques was also linked to the New World Order's *L'Europe réelle*. He became famous when, at the Université de Nantes on June 15, 1984, he defended his negationist graduate thesis under irregular conditions and before a committee of academics close to the new right.

50. *Fidélité,* November 1957.

51. *Fidélité,* April 1958.

52. The CIA's count in "The Fascist International," 2–5.

53. DCRG, "Les mouvements néonazis: La FANE et le Nouvel Ordre européen," *Bulletin mensuel confidentiel: Documentation-Orientation* (October 1968): 7, AN F7/15585.

54. Griffin, "Europe for the Europeans," 39; Jean-François Brozzu-Gentile, *L'Affaire Gladio* (Paris: Albin Michel, 1994), 227.

55. Philippe Vervaecke, "Sir Oswald Mosley et l'internationalisation du fascisme britannique, 1947–1966," in Dard, *Doctrinaires, vulgarisateurs,* 90; Patrick Moreau, *Les héritiers du IIIe Reich: L'extrême droite allemande de 1945 à nos jours* (Paris: Le Seuil, 1994), 55–56.

56. Stéphane François, "Un exemple de contre-culture nazie: Le cycle thuléen de Wilhelm Landig," in *Résistances souterraines à l'autorité et Construction de contre-cultures dans les pays germanophobes au XXe siècle* (Bern: Peter Lang, 2014), 71–86.

57. Before the war, this diplomat had belonged to the Movimiento Nacional-Socialista de Chile.

58. Stéphane François, *Les mystères du nazisme: Aux sources d'un fantasme contemporain* (Paris: Presses Universitaires de France, 2015).

59. An author as politically engaged as the German linguist Wolfgang Krause (1895–1970), who collaborated with the Ahnenerbe, admitted that the runic insignia were primarily an alphabet used to compose inscriptions that were either "purely profane" or a text "profane in itself [that] maintains relations with magic or the cult." See Wolfgang Krause, *Runen* (Berlin: De Gruyter, 1970).

60. DGSN, DCRG, *Partis et groupements politiques d'extrême droite,* 1:7.

61. Marlène Laruelle, "Alexandre Dugin, esquisse d'un eurasisme d'extrême droite en Russie postsoviétique," *Revue d'études comparatives*

Est-Ouest 32, no. 3 (2001): 99–100; Harvey G. Simmons, "The French and European Extreme Right and Globalization," Colloquium on the Challenges to the New World Order: Anti-Globalism and Counter-Globalism, University of Amsterdam, May 30–31, 2003, 37.

62. See *Les peuples blancs survivront-ils? Les travaux du Nouvel Ordre européen de 1967 à 1985 présentés par G.-A. Amaudruz* (Montreal: Éditions celtiques, 1987).

63. DCRG, "Le Nouvel Ordre européen," *Bulletin mensuel confidentiel: Documentation-Orientation,* May 1969, AN F7/15585.

64. Anti-Defamation League of B'nai B'rith, *Extremist Groups in the United States* (New York: Anti-Defamation League of B'nai B'rith, 1983), 258; and *RésistanceS* (Spring 1999). No mention is made of Palestinian representatives in the DCRG document, "Le Nouvel Ordre européen." By contrast, Amaudruz's contacts with the Nasser regime in 1967 are confirmed in the archives.

65. DCRG, "Le Nouvel Ordre européen," 3.

66. His identity and biography are still in doubt.

67. Stéphane François, "Jacques de Mahieu entre racisme biologique et histoire mystérieuse," *Politica Hermetica* 26 (2012): 123–132; Pierre-André Taguieff, *Sur la nouvelle droite* (Paris: Descartes & Cie, 1994), 129–130.

68. See, for example, the writings of the Parti Communautaire National-Européen or of the European Liberation Front.

69. Heinrich Kessemeier, *Fortsetzung des Lebens nach dem Tode* (Hamburg: Ideal und Leben, 1919); Cornelia Wilhelm, *Bewegung oder Verein? Nationalsozialistische Volkstumspolitik in den USA* (Stuttgart: Franz Steiner Verlag, 1998).

70. Eddy de Bruyne, "La SIPO-SD à Liège," in *Bulletin d'information* (Centre Liégois d'Histoire et d'Archéologie Militaires) 9, no. 1 (2004): 29.

71. Francis Balace, "Le tournant des années soixante, de la droite réactionnaire à l'extrême droite révolutionnaire," in *De l'avant à l'après-guerre, l'extrême droite en Belgique francophone,* ed. Francis Balace et al. (Brussels: De Boeck-Wemael, 1994), 137–140.

72. Révision Générale des Politiques Publiques (RGPP), "Le mouvement Jeune Europe," February 1965, 2, APP GAJ4.

73. Moreau, *Les héritiers du IIIe Reich,* 58–59.

74. *Combat,* December 13, 1966; Yannick Sauveur, "Jean Thiriart et le National-Communautarisme européen," *Revue d'histoire du nationalisme révolutionnaire,* n.d. [1978], 25.

75. Translations of the book sometimes appeared under suggestive titles, such as *¡Arriba Europa!* in Spanish (a reference to the Falange Española) and *Das Vierte Reich: Europa* in Germany (a reference to a future Nazi Fourth Reich of Europe).

76. *La Révolution nationale-européenne* (Nantes: Ars Magna, n.d. [1963]), 15–31.

77. Direction de la Sûreté Militaire, "Hiérarchie du mouvement néonazi Jeune Europe," May 7, 1963, APP GAJ4; DCRG, "Le mouvement 'Jeune Europe,'" *Bulletin mensuel confidentiel: Documentation-Orientation* (September 1965): 10, AN F7/15584; Sauveur, "Jean Thiriart et le National-Communautarisme européen," 59–60.

78. Riccardo Marchi, "As Direitas Radicais no Estado Novo (1945–1974)," *Ler História* 57 (2009): 95–110.

79. The official name of Giovane Nazione, established in 1963, was Giovane Europa. It resulted from a radical schism in the MSI and was associated with Stefano Delle Chiaie. Its newspaper published texts on the radical right: "Italians! After twenty years of pornocracy, we turn to you to return to the right path in the defense of our Race. Italians! Unite with us under our symbol, the Celtic cross, which represents Nazi-Fascism, being reborn in Italy today. . . . Europe: united, great, free, under the Celtic cross of European Nazi-Fascism. We shall prevail! Long live Mussolini! Heil Hitler!" Serge Dumont, *Les Brigades noires* (Berchem: EPO, 1983), 116.

80. Bureau de Coordination de l'Action Européenne, "Jean Thiriart," communiqué no. 2, Brussels, June 30, 1963, APP GAJ4; Pierre Milza and Marianne Benteli, *Le Fascisme au XXe siècle* (Paris: Richelieu, 1973), 350; Verhoeyen, "L'extrême droite en Belgique," 20–31; Moreau, *Les héritiers du IIIe Reich,* 401–402; Sauveur, "Jean Thiriart et le National-Communautarisme européen," 41–42, 89–93.

81. The new right had its origin in the reconstitution of Jeune Nation as the FEN, via the establishment of a network around its review *Europe-Action.*

82. RGPP, March 15, 1963; April 4, 1963; May 2, 1963; May 13, 1963, 2; and May 2, 1966 (APP GAJ4).

83. In opposition to the Occident movement, Thiriart wrote: "Occident, which the French right wing is so crazy about, is only this: the expansion zone of American slop. . . . We cannot stomach that Occident. And we cannot stomach the people who become their accomplices [and idolize the USA], the foremost Jewish state in the world." *La Nation européenne,* March 15–April 15, 1966.

84. Letter from the general director of SDECE (Service de Documentation Extérieure et de Contre-Espionnage), predecessor to the Direction Générale de la Sûreté Extérieure) to the prefect of police, November 17, 1964, APP GAJ4.

85. CIA, "Memorandum," January 10, 1953, FOIA, 519bdecd 993294098d5143f7.

86. See Moreau, *Les héritiers du IIIe Reich,* 278–281.

87. Ernesto Milá, "*La Nation européenne,* el ultimo proyecto de Jean Thiriart," *Revista de Historia del Fascismo* 2 (December 2010–January 2011): 152–174; *Le Monde,* March 23, 1967; *La Nation européenne,* September 15–October 15, 1966.

88. Gustavo D. Perednik, "Naïve Spanish Judeophobia," *Jewish Political Studies Review* 15, nos. 3–4 (2003): 87–110; CEDADE, *Thule, la Cultura de la Otra Europa* (Barcelona: Ediciones Bausp, 1979), 235–237; Rosario Jabardo and Fernando Reinares, "Démobilisation de l'extrême droite en Espagne," in *Pouvoirs* 87 (*L'extrême droite en Europe*) (November 1998): 116.

89. Xavier Casals Meseguer, *La tentación neofascista en España* (Barcelona: Plaza & Janés, 1998), 132–133.

90. That was one of the effects of the disintegration of the Groupes Nationalistes-Révolutionnaires de Base network after the 1978 murder of François Duprat, their leader and, at the time, the second in command in Jean-Marie Le Pen's FN.

91. The present-day Catalanist movement does not have a far-right orientation. It does not so much oppose globalization as wish to become part of it in an optimal manner, even while preserving its cultural sovereignty.

92. José Rodríguez Jiménez, "Antisemitism and the Extreme Right in Spain (1962–1997)," *Analysis of Current Trends in Antisemitism* (1999), http://sicsa.huji.ac.il/15spain.html; Christian Bouchet, "Yockey, le précurseur," *La Revue d'histoire du nationalisme-révolutionnaire* 1 (December 1998): n.p.;

Andrea Mammone, Emmanuel Godin, and Brian Jenkins, eds., *Mapping the Extreme Right in Contemporary Europe* (London: Routledge, 2012), 319.

93. Cercle Écologique des Amis de l'Europe, "Service de librairie par correspondance" (1980), personal archives.

94. *L'Europe combattante: Note d'orientation no. 3 du secrétariat général de Nouvelle Résistance* 9 (1992), internal document, personal archives. We will consider the ELF in Chapter 6.

95. In 1997 Ramón Bau founded the Círculo des Estudios Indoeuropeos, which aspired to be the successor to the CEDADE.

96. RGPP, white paper of May 15, 1966; APP GAJ4; Balace, "Le tournant des années soixante," 117; Bruno Garcet, "Jeune Europe: Souvenirs de la section de Louvain," *In Memoriam Jean Thiriart* (Charleroi: Machiavel, 1993), 35.

97. *Révolution européenne,* January 15–February 15, 1965.

98. The Comités Tixier-Vignancour were run by Jean-Marie Le Pen, who organized the only far-right campaign for the presidency of 1965. All the far-right factions participated (Victor Barthélemy, for example, was a member).

99. RGPP, "Le mouvement Jeune-Europe."

100. RGPP, "L'extrême droite," September 10, 1969, 77, APP GADR15; DCRG, "Le mouvement 'Jeune Europe,'" 23; DCRG, "Le mouvement 'Révolution européenne,'" June 1965, 2, AN F7/15584.

101. RGPP, "Le mouvement Jeune Europe."

102. Verhoeyen, "L'extrême droite en Belgique," 20–23.

103. Jean Thiriart, *La Grande Nation: L'Europe unitaire de Brest à Bucarest* (Nantes: Ars Magna, 1988; 1st ed. 1965), n.p.

104. *La Nation européenne,* October 15–November 15, 1966; and November 15–December 15, 1966.

105. *La Nation européenne,* January 15–February 15, 1967; and February 15–March 15, 1967.

106. *Jeune Europe,* January 3, 1964.

107. Jean-Yves Camus and René Monzat, *Les Droites nationales et radicales en France* (Lyon: Presses Universitaires de Lyon, 1992).

108. Laurent, *L'Orchestre noir,* 133.

109. *De Jeune Europe aux Brigades rouges: Anti-Américanisme et logique de l'engagement révolutionnaire* (n.p.: n.p., n.d.).

110. Luc Michel, letter to Nicolas Lebourg, October 14, 2004, personal archives. The term "Nazi-Maoist" was not always totally rejected by Freda; see *Giorgio Freda: Nazi-maoïste ou révolutionnaire inclassable?* (Lausanne: Comité de solidarité avec Giorgio Freda, 1978).

111. Franco Freda, *La désintégration du système* (Nantes: Ars Magna, n.d. [1969]).

112. *La Flamme* (March 1972 and September 1972); Yannick Sauveur, "L'organisation 'Lutte du peuple,' un mouvement national-bolchevik?," n.d., 3; Laurent, *L'Orchestre noir,* 182.

113. PLO, *Code du militant Lutte du peuple,* n.d., 2, internal document, personal archives.

114. See *La Flamme* (January 1972); *Lutte du peuple,* July 1973 and March 4–18, 1974; Joseph Algazy, *L'extrême droite en France (1965 à 1984)* (Paris: L'Harmattan, 1989), 150–151.

115. See Pauline Picco, "Franco G. Freda: Idéologue, éditeur, activiste," in Dard, *Doctrinaires, vulgarisateurs et passeurs des droites radicales,* 143–160.

116. *La Flamme* (January 1972; March 1972; September 1972); Yves Bataille, interview, June 21, 2004.

117. *Article 31* (June 1986; December 1986). Action Nouvelle Droite (New Right Action) came into being in 1972, having split off from the NPD: the NARO split off from it in 1974, and, a few weeks later, the NARO-SdV split off from the NARO.

118. DCRG, "Les mouvements néonazis: La FANE et le Nouvel Ordre européen (NOE)," October 1968, 1–6, AN F4/15585; *Notre Europe* (June 1968; August 1968; October 1968; January 1969).

119. Lebourg and Beauregard, *François Duprat.*

120. René Monzat, *Enquêtes sur la droite extrême* (Paris: Le Monde éditions, 1992), 102–104; Moreau, *Les héritiers du IIIe Reich,* 290–298.

121. *Notre Europe* (organ of the FANE) (February 1980).

122. Anne-Marie Duranton-Crabol, *L'Europe de l'extrême droite,* 170. The organization Were Di was formerly Occident Belgique (recognized by its French model, but not linked to it). The NDP was banned in 1988.

123. *Informations NR,* October 21, 1985, internal document, personal archives.

124. *TV Rapport d'acitivité mai 1986; TV Bulletin bimensuel d'informations,* January 10, 1987, internal document, personal archives.

125. *TV Bulletin d'information NR,* November 1987, internal document, personal archives.

126. Letter of July 18, 1989, personal archives.

2. White Power

1. World Union of National Socialists (WUNS), *Cotswold Declaration of 1962,* text available at http://nationalsocialist.net/cotswold.htm.

2. Pierre Milza, *Fascisme français: Passé et présent* (Paris: Flammarion, 1987), 353; *Article 31* (July 1985).

3. Kaplan, "The Post-War Paths of Occult National Socialism"; Jacques Delarue, *Les nazis sont parmi nous* (Paris: Le Pavillon, 1969), 54.

4. *Le Viking* (January 1964); Stéphane François and Emmanuel Kreis, "Le conspirationnisme ufologique," *Politica Hermetica* 19 (2005): 116–137.

5. Heléne Lööw, *Nazismen i Sverige 1980–1997* (Stockholm: Ordfront Förlag, 1998), 226; *Créativité* (bulletin of the French chapter of the World Church of the Creator) 1 (December 2001).

6. In the case of the Mongol movement Tsagaan Khass, its leader claims to have discovered Nazism thanks to its pervasiveness in post-Soviet Russia (*The Guardian,* August 2, 2010).

7. Report of the "anti-Semitism" commission of the Mouvement contre le Racisme et pour l'Amitié entre les Peuples (MRAP), March 1983 (archives of the MRAP).

8. Guillaume Faye, *La nouvelle question juive* (Chevaigné: Les Éditions du Lore, 2007).

9. Gildas Lescop, "'Honnie soit la Oï!': Naissance, émergence et déliquescence d'une forme musicale de protestation sociale," *Copyright Volume! Autour des musiques actuelles* 2, no. 1 (2003): 109–128; Bruno Cabanes, "Football et violence: Un très vieux couple," *L'Histoire* (June 1998): 26–27.

10. *Signal* 2, June 17, 2007. The name of the publication is, of course, a reference to the SS newspaper.

11. Armin Pfhal-Trauchber, "La scène skinhead," in *Extrême Droite et National-Populisme en Europe,* ed. Pierre Blaise and Patrick Moreau (Brussels: Centre de Recherche et d'Information Socio-Politique, 2004), 531–533; Moreau, *Les héritiers du IIIe Reich,* 267–270.

12. Its French branch, the Charlemagne Hammer Skins (CHS), was broken up in 1997, because its leader sent death threats to Jewish figures, after some of its members (in 1996) profaned a corpse they had dug up. The CHS was responsible for importing to France National Socialist Black Metal. A new branch emerged in Savoie. The movement now operates under the name Hammerskin Nation France.

13. See Anton Shekovtsov and Paul Jackson, eds., *White Power Music: Scenes of Extreme Right Cultural Resistance, Mapping the Far-Right* (London: Searchlight Magazine / Radicalism and New Media Research Group, 2012).

14. Věra Stojarová, "Paramilitary Structures in Eastern Europe," in *The Extreme Right in Europe: Current Trends and Perspectives,* ed. Uwe Backes and Patrick Moreau (Göttingen: Vandenhoeck & Ruprecht, 2011), 265–279.

15. Marlène Laruelle, "La xénophobie et son instrumentalisation politique en Russie: L'exemple des skinheads," *Revue internationale et stratégique* 68 (2007): 111–119.

16. Fabrice Robert, "La diffusion de l'idéal identitaire européen à travers la musique contemporaine" (master's thesis, Université de Nice-Sophia Antipolis, 1996), 49–51 (Robert is the current president of the Bloc Identitaire).

17. Jean-Yves Camus, "Les Skinheads: Une contre-culture néonazie," *La Pensée* 304 (October–December 1995): 127–138.

18. The idea that the Jews controlled Jean-Marie Le Pen arose because of the way Jean-Pierre Stirbois liquidated the neo-Nazis in the FN after Duprat's murder. The rumor spread that Le Pen's real name was Stirnbaum, which is untrue, but his mother's maiden name was Luchtmeyer (archives of the National Assembly, information kindly communicated by Romain Ducoulombier).

19. *Bêtes et méchants: Petite histoire des jeunes fascistes français* (Paris: Reflex, 2002), 174.

20. *Bulletin interne Troisième Voie* 3 (September 2011), internal document, personal archives.

21. See Commission Nationale Consultative des Droits de l'Homme (National Consultative Commission on Human Rights), *La lutte contre le racisme, l'antisémitisme et la xénophobie: Année 2013* (Paris: La Documentation Française, 2014).

22. *Tribune nationaliste* (organ of the PNFE) (April 1987).

23. Stéphane François, *La musique europaïenne: Ethnographie politique d'une subculture de droite* (Paris: L'Harmattan, 2006).

24. Simon L. Garfinkel, "Leaderless Resistance Today," *First Monday* 8, no. 3 (March 2003); Roger Griffin, "Fascism's New Faces (and New Facelessness) in the 'Post-Fascist' Epoch," *Erwägen Wissen Ethik* 15, no. 3 (2004): 287–300; *Résistance!* (May–June 1998); Kaplan, "The Post-War Paths of Occult National Socialism," 53–58.

25. Far-right movements are not always anti-Masonic, far from it. See Stéphane François, *À droite de l'acacia: De la nature réelle de la franc-maçonnerie?* (Valence d'Albigeois: La Hutte, 2012).

26. See Nicolas Lebourg and Dominique Sistach, "The Role of Underground Music in the Renewal of the French Radical Right Wing," in Shekovtsov and Jackson, *White Power Music,* 25–34.

27. *La lettre des adhérents du Bloc identitaire* 3 (2012): 1, internal document, personal archives. The voters clearly favored a right-wing protest: 32.64 percent did not want any candidate endorsement; 32.46 percent were for Marine Le Pen, 2.04 percent for François Bayrou, 1.66 percent for Frédéric Nihous, and 0.5 percent for "other."

28. Sofia Tipaldou, "The Dawning of Europe and Eurasia? The Greek Golden Dawn and Its Transnational Links," in *Eurasianism and the European Far Right: Reshaping the Europe-Russia Relationship,* ed. Marlène Laruelle (Lanham, MD: Lexington Books, 2015), 193–219.

3. The New Right in All Its Diversity

1. Jacques Marlaud (1944–2014) was president of the organization from 1987 to 1991. This quotation was taken from an interview published on December 9, 2008, by the Bloc Identitaire's site Novopress, available at http://esprit-europeen.fr/entretiens_marlaud.html.

2. See Richard A. Viguerie, *The New Right: We're Ready to Lead* (Falls Church, VA: Viguerie Company, 1981).

3. On the Australian "New Right," see Marion Maddox, *God under Howard: The Rise of the Religious Right in Australian Politics* (Crows Nest: Allen & Unwin, 2005).

4. *Éléments* 94 (February 1999): 10–23.

5. See especially Marco Tarchi, *Contro l'americanismo* (Rome: Edizioni Laterza, 2004).

6. Interview with Alain de Benoits for *Le Monde,* May 1992. In the end, the editors did not publish it. Full text at https://s3-eu-west-1.amazonaws .com/alaindebenoist/pdf/entretien_sur_la_politique_francaise.pdf

7. See Sofie Delporte, "Nieuw Rechts in Vlaanderen: Het gedachtegoed van het Nieuw Rechtse tidjschrift 'Teksten, Kommentaren en Studies' " (bachelor's thesis, Ghent University, 2002).

8. *Junge Freiheit,* March 23, 2005. The circulation of *Zur Zeit* is estimated at 10,000.

9. Riccardo Marchi, "A extrema-direita portuguesa na 'Rua': Da transição à democracia (1976–1980)," *Locus: Revista de história* 8 (2012): 167–186.

10. Jaime Nogueira Pinto, *Visto da direita, 20 anos de Futura Presente* (Lisbon: Hugin, 2000). The author, though very young at the time, had to go into exile after the fall of the Salazarist regime, and in fact never left the clerico-reactionary right, which has remained frozen in its nostalgia for the Estado Novo and the colonial empire.

11. Venner, *Pour une critique positive.*

12. Dominique Venner, "Printemps arabe et destin de l'Occident," *Jeune Nation* 19 (August 1959): 8–10.

13. Dominique Venner, "Qu'est-ce que le nationalisme?" *Europe-Action* 5 (May 1963): 51.

14. DCRG, "La nouvelle tactique d'Europe-Action," *Informations hebdomadaires,* December 3, 1964, AN 57/15573.

15. RGPP, "Après l'éclatement du Comité Tixier-Vignancour: Remous à l'extrême droite," 1966, APP GADR15.

16. *Flamme camp école,* July 21, 1966, internal document, personal archives.

17. Klaus Schönekäs, "La 'Neue Rechte' en République fédérale d'Allemagne," *Lignes* 3, no. 4 (1988): 126–155; Moreau, *Les héritiers du IIIe Reich,* 186, 243, 254–256.

18. Olivier Dard, "La nouvelle droite et la société de consommation," *Vingtième Siècle* 91 (July–September 2006): 125–135; Stéphane François, "La nouvelle droite et l'écologie: Une écologie néopaïenne?," *Parlement(s)* 12 (December 2009–January 2010): 132–143; Moreau, *Les héritiers du IIIe Reich,* 154–174.

19. Anne-Marie Duranton-Crabol, *Visages de la nouvelle droite, le GRECE et son histoire* (Paris: Presses de la Fondation nationale des sciences politiques, 1988), 155.

20. DCRG, "Le Rassemblement européen de la liberté," 139 (April 1968), AN F7/15584; RGPP, "L'extrême droite."

21. Alain de Benoist, in Alain de Benoist et al., *Le Mai 68 de la nouvelle droite* (Paris: Éditions du Labyrinthe, 1998), 13.

22. Duranton-Crabol, *Visages de la nouvelle droite*; Henry Coston, *Dictionnaire de la politique française* (Paris: La Librairie française, 1979), 333; Pierre-André Taguieff, "La stratégie culturelle de la 'nouvelle droite' en France (1968–1983)," in *Vous avez dit fascismes?*, ed. Antoine Spire (Paris: Montalba, 1984), 13–152; Maurice Rollet, "Nous étions douze," in Benoist et al., *Le Mai 68 de la nouvelle droite,* 135–139.

23. In Roland Gaucher, *Les nationalistes en France: La traversée du désert* (Paris: Roland Gaucher Éditeur, 1995), 226.

24. DCPJ, "Situation des mouvements d'extrême droite en France," March 29, 1968, 2, BDIC F8150/1; RGPP, note on the Association des Amis de François Duprat, June 1989, 6, APP GAD8 913.285.

25. *Socialisme européen* 0 (1967); (May–June 1968; September–October 1968; November–December 1968).

26. *Réalités socialistes européennes* (December 1968; February 1969).

27. DCRG, "Les Groupes de recherches et d'études pour la civilisation européenne," *Bulletin mensuel confidentiel: Documentation-Orientation* 160 (July 1970), AN F7/15585.

28. Taguieff, *Sur la nouvelle droite,* 64–105.

29. *MNR: Bulletin de liaison,* December 10, 1984, internal document, personal archives; *Libération,* November 25, 1985.

30. *Libération,* November 11, 1985.

31. *GUD-Jeune Garde Infos* (April 1986), internal document, personal archives.

32. A sort of völkisch proto-scout organization, the Wandervogel (migrating birds) was founded in 1896 and attracted several thousand young Germans (including the young Heinrich Himmler, Adolf Eichmann, Baldur von Schirach, and the like).

33. Milza, *L'Europe en chemise noire,* 225.

34. Verhoeyen, "L'extrême droite en Belgique."

35. Guillaume Faye, Pierre Freson, and Robert Steuckers, *Petit lexique du partisan européen* (Nantes: Ars Magna, n.d. [1985]), 7–8, 39. This brochure was distributed by Troisième Voie in France and by Forces Nouvelles in Belgium.

36. *Le Partisan européen* (Vendémiaire–Brumaire 1986 [*sic*]).

37. *Le Monde,* August 25, 1987. The episode is very unclear, with all the protagonists claiming they took the initiative for the break. The staff of *Éléments* now even claim that Guillaume Faye was never ousted from GRECE, despite the letter in *Le Monde,* and even though they claim to have no links to the racist far right.

38. Robert Steuckers, e-mail to Nicolas Lebourg, May 30, 2014. On the Spanish side, Juan Antonio Llopart and his comrades, having returned from Lourmarin, launched Alternativa Europa. Gilbert Collard, the current deputy of the Rassemblement Bleu Marine, a friend and associate of Thierry Mudry, was initially supposed to be a speaker at the summer university.

39. *De l'Atlantique au Pacifique* (February 1976).

40. See Aleksandr Dugin, *La Grande Guerre des continents* (Paris: Avatar, 2006).

41. Robert Steuckers, *Au fil de l'épée* 11–12 (May–June 2000): 4.

42. Guillaume Faye, *La colonisation de l'Europe, discours vrai sur l'immigration et l'islam* (Paris: Aencre, 2000).

43. In an interview published in March 2000 in *Area,* an Italian review closely associated with the Alleanza Nazionale and with members from the Nuova Destra, Alain de Benoist mentions Guillaume Faye's "highly racist positions," especially on the question of Islam.

44. It borrows the title of a review formerly under the direction of Ernst Jünger and Mircea Eliade.

45. Christian Bouchet, *B.A.-BA du néopaganisme* (Puiseaux: Pardès, 2001), 91.

46. Verta Taylor, "Social Movement Continuity: The Women's Movement in Abeyance," *American Sociological Review* 10, no. 1 (1989): 761–775.

47. *La Flamme,* liaison bulletin of the Europe Jeunesse scout movement, no. 1, July 15, 1976, personal archives.

48. Notebooks of the Haute École Populaire de Normandie, first session, August 1–7, 1993, n.p., personal archives.

49. Pedros Carlos González Cuevas, "Las *otras* derechas en la España actual: Teólogos, razonalistas y neoderechistas," *El Catoblepas* 103 (September 2010): 10.

50. Riccardo Marchi, "The Extreme Right in Twenty-first Century Portugal: The Partido Nacional Renovador," in *Right-Wing Extremism in Europe: Country Analyses, Counter-Strategies, and Labor-Market Oriented Exit Strategies,* ed. Ralf Melzer and Sebastian Serafin (Berlin: Friedrich Ebert Foundation, 2013), 133–155.

51. In *Le Monde,* August 25, 1987.

52. Roger Griffin, "Between Metapolitics and Apoliteia: The Nouvelle Droite's Strategy for Conserving the Fascist Vision of the 'Interregnum,'" *Modern and Contemporary France* (February 2000): 35–53. Roger Griffin believes that the participation by leftist authors in *Krisis* did not occur within the framework of rational exchange, but that these contributions established the baseline for decadence and announced a new era. There would thus be no cultural distance here between Alain de Benoist and Guillaume Faye's reinterpretation of conservative revolutionary principles regarding the existence of an "interregnum," where the role of think tanks would be to produce ideas for "after the chaos."

53. Nicholas Goddrick-Clarke, *Black Sun: Aryan Cults, Esoteric Nazism and the Politics of Identity* (New York: New York University Press, 2002), 69–70.

54. See Stéphane François, *La Nouvelle Droite et la Tradition* (Milan: Archè, 2011).

55. Pierre-André Taguieff, "L'héritage nazi de la nouvelle droite," *Les Nouveaux Cahiers* 64 (Spring 1981): 3–22; an article by the same author appeared in the review of the Mouvement contre le Racisme et pour l'Amitié entre les Peuples that same year: "Présences de l'héritage nazi: Des 'nouvelles droites' intellectuelles au 'révisionnisme,'" *Droit et liberté* 397 (January 1981): 11–21.

56. François Laurent Balssa, "Dieudonné, Molière et la nullité de l'art contemporain," *Éléments* 149 (October–December 2013): 28–31.

57. Pierrre-André Taguieff, "Julius Evola: Penseur de la décadence: Une 'Métaphysique de l'histoire' dans la perspective traditionelle et l'hypercritique de la modernité," *Politica Hermetica* 1 (1987): 11–48.

58. Jean-Yves Le Gallou and the Club de l'Horloge, *La préférence nationale: Réponse à l'immigration* (Paris: Albin Michel, 1985).

59. Alexandre Dézé, *Le Front national à la conquête du pouvoir?* (Paris: Armand Colin, 2012),9ff.

60. E-mail to Jean-Yves Camus, May 20, 2014. Bruno Larebière contributed, notably, to *Minute* and *Choc du mois* and participated in *Éléments* 154 (2015). He was a revolutionary nationalist militant and a member of the Bloc Identitaire, before distancing himself from the far right.

61. Radical anti-Zionism denies Israel's right to exist as a state, deliberately conflates Jews and Zionists, and considers all Jews the representatives, relays, agents, of the State of Israel.

62. *Flash,* January 27, 2011.

63. *Lutte du peuple,* July 1992. The preliminary list of speakers included three new rightists (Benoist, Steuckers, and Walker), one representative from Third Way, one from Nouvelle Résistance, and one from the Pan-African International Movement (a movement calling for the global emigration of blacks to Africa).

4. Religious Fundamentalism

1. Émile Poulat, "Intégrisme: Un terme qui vient de loin," *Croire,* November 2006, http://www.croire.com/Definitions/Vie-chretienne/Integri stes/Integrisme-un-terme-qui-vient-de-loin.

2. Émile Poulat, *Intégrisme et Catholicisme intégral: Un réseau international antimoderniste: La "Sapinière" (1909–1921)* (Paris: Casterman, 1969).

3. René Rémond, "L'intégrisme catholique: Portrait intellectuel," *Études* 370, no. 1 (January 1989): 99–100.

4. Xavier Ternisien, *L'Extrême Droite et l'Église* (Paris: Brepols, 1997), 173–179.

5. Raoul Girardet, "L'héritage intellectuel de l'Action française," *Revue française de science politique* 7, no. 4 (October–December 1957): 765–792.

6. Jacques Maître, "Le catholicisme d'extrême droite et la croisade anti-subversive," *Revue française de sociologie* 2 (1961): 106–116.

7. Madeleine Garrigou-Lagrange, "Intégrisme et national-catholicisme," *Esprit* 271 (November 1959): 515–543; Anne-Catherine Schmidt-Trimborn,

Charles Lacheroy: Discours et conférences (Metz: Centre de recherche universitaire lorrain d'histoire, 2012).

8. [*Francisque:* a medal of honor in the shape of a double-headed ax awarded under the Vichy regime.—trans.]

9. Jules Isaac, *L'enseignement du mépris* (Paris: Fasquelle, 1962).

10. Roger Garaudy, *Les mythes fondateurs de la politique israélienne* (Paris: Librairie du savoir, 1996).

11. *L'élite européenne: Signification et perspectives de l'Aggiornamento* (n.d.).

12. Stéphane François, *La modernité en procès* (Valenciennes: Presses Universitaires de Valenciennes, 2013), 161–162.

13. Ministry of the Interior, Office of Regulations and Litigation, note to the attention of the director, November 14, 1980, AN 19990426/5.

14. Dominique Albertini and David Doucet, *Histoire du Front national* (Paris: Tallandier, 2013), 310–319; David Doucet, "Pierre Sidos, ce pétainiste qui a voulu tuer de Gaulle," *Charles* 5 (2013): 106–130.

15. *La Vie intellectuelle* (August–September 1952).

16. Brustier, *Le Mai 68 conservateur,* 93–133.

17. [*Cocarde:* the cluster of blue, white, and red ribbons that was the symbol of the French Revolution and the First Republic—trans.].

18. *Libération,* January 23, 1989, and August 16, 1989.

19. Letter to the members of the Fraternité Saint-Pie-X, cited in *Itinéraires* (January 1975). Monsignor Marcel Lefebvre, *Un évêque parle* (Paris: Dominique Martin Morin, 1974), 196.

20. Bernard Antony, *Abécédaire politique et social,* supplement to the review *Reconquête* (April 2002): 87.

21. Kevin Geay, "'Messire Dieu, premier servi': Étude sur les conditions de la prise de parole chez les militants traditionalistes de Civitas," *Politix* 106 (2014): 59–83.

22. *Osservatore romano,* January 11, 2011.

23. Robert, "La diffusion de l'idéal identitaire européen."

24. Bouchet, *B.A.-BA du néo-paganisme.*

25. *Le Salut public* (November–December 1977).

26. Philippe Vilgier, *La Droite en mouvements: Nationaux et nationalistes 1962/1981* (Paris: Vastra, 1981), 147–148.

27. Michel Winock, "Le terrain vierge de la nouvelle gauche," *Le Banquet* 7 (1995): 81–88.

28. Not without a logic proper to itself: for example, Déat did not hesitate to see Jacobinism as the ancestor of Fascism.

29. Bernard Schwengler, "Le clivage électoral catholique-protestant revisité," *Revue française de science politique* 55, no. 2 (2005): 381–413.

30. Wim Fieret, *De Staatkundig Gereformeerde Partij, 1918–1948: Een bibliocratisch ideaal* (Houten: Den Hertog, 1990).

31. Maddox, *God under Howard.*

32. *Ulster Nation* 32 (July 2000).

33. *Junge Freiheit,* November 27, 2009.

34. Jaak Billiet, "Church Involvement, Ethnocentrism, and Voting for a Radical Right-Wing Party: Diverging Behavioural Outcomes of Equal Attitudinal Dispositions," *Sociology of Religion* 56, no. 3 (1995): 303–326.

35. Nonna Mayer, *Ces Français qui votent FN* (Paris: Flammarion, 1999).

36. Daniel-Louis Seiler, *L'Europe des partis: Paradoxes, contradictions et antinomies,* Working Paper, no. 251 (Barcelona: Institut de Ciències Polítiques i Socials, 2006).

37. Rafal Pankowski, "Right-Wing Extremism in Poland," *Friedrich-Ebert-Stiftung International Policy Analysis* (October 2012): 3–6; Michael Shafir, "Varieties of Antisemitism in Post-Communist East Central Europe," *Jewish Studies at the Central European University* 3 (2002): 184–185.

38. Feliciano Montero Garcia, "El Movimeinto católico en la España del siglo XX," in *Movimientos sociales en la España del Siglo XX,* ed. Maria Dolores De La Calle Valasco and Manuel Redero San Román (Salamanca: Ediciones Universidad de Salamanca, 2008), 173–192; Jordi Canal, "La longue survivance du carlisme en Espagne: Proposition pour une interprétation," in *La Contre-Révolution en Europe,* ed. Jean-Clément Marin (Rennes: Presses Universitaires de Rennes, 2001), 291–301.

39. Humberto Cucchetti, "De la Nouvelle Action française à la Nouvelle Action royaliste," *Pôle Sud* 42 (2015): 87–104.

5. The Populist Parties

1. François Duprat, *Le Néofascisme en Occident,* vol. 2, *Amérique latine,* supplement to *La Revue d'histoire du fascisme* 13 (November 1975): 25.

2. The European parliamentary elections are something of a special case in civic life, since they do not really mobilize the electorate. In what

follows, however, we use them regularly as an indicator, because they make it possible to compare voting results across parties.

3. Alexandre Dézé, "Idéologie et stratégies partisanes: Une analyse du rapport des partis d'extrême droite au système politique démocratique: Le cas du Front national, du Movimento sociale italiano et du Vlaams Blok" (PhD diss., Paris, Institut d'Études Politiques, 2008), 353.

4. Stéphane Porion, "Le National Front et Enoch Powell: 'L'un des leurs'?," in *À droite de la droite: Droites radicales en France et en Grande-Bretagne au XXe siècle,* ed. Philippe Vervaecke (Villeneuve-D'Ascq: Presses Universitaires du Septentrion, 2012), 323–352; Paul Jackson, "White Genocide? Postwar Fascisms and the Ideal Value of Evoking Existentialist Conflicts," in *The Routledge History of Genocide,* ed. Cathie Carmichael and Richard C. Maguire (New York: Routledge, 2015), 207–226.

5. See Lebourg and Beauregard, *François Duprat.*

6. Kai Arzheimer, "Contextual Factors and the Extreme Right Vote in Western Europe, 1980–2002," *American Journal of Political Science* 53, no. 2 (April 2009): 259–275.

7. Bruno Mégret took the opportunity to question the isolationism of Jean-Marie Le Pen's FN and to put forward the plan for an alliance with the right that included a de-demonization of the FN.

8. For an overview of Italian populism, Berlusconism included, see Marco Tarchi, *Italia populista: Dal qualunquismo a Beppe Grille* (Bologna: Il Mulino, 2015).

9. Christophe Bouillaud, "La ligue du Nord, de la périphérie au centre, et retour (1989–2004)," in Blaise and Moreau, *Extrême Droite et National-Populisme en Europe,* 311–336.

10. See the interview with him in *La Reppublica,* August 17, 2015.

11. Exit Poll, *Fessel-GfK,* Vienna, 1999.

12. Moreno Feliu, "La Herencia desgraciada: Racismo y heterofobia en Europa," *Estudios Sociológicas* 12, no. 34 (1994): 54.

13. Xavier Casals, "La Plataforma per Catalunya: La eclosión de un nacional-populismo catalán," *Working Papers* 274 (Barcelona: Institut de Ciènces Polítiques i Socials, 2009).

14. Patrick Moreau, "Le Freiheiltiche Partei Österreich, parti national-libéral ou pulsion austro-fasciste?" *Pouvoirs* 87 (November 1998): 61–82.

15. See Gustave Fridolin, *Blåsta! Nedskärningsåren som formade en generation* (Stockholm: Ordfront Forlag, 2009).

16. Hans de Witte and Peer Scheepers, "En Flandre: Origines, évolution et avenir du Vlaams Blok et de ses électeurs," *Pouvoirs* 87 (November 1998): 95–113.

17. Alexandre Dézé, "Entre adaptation et démarcation: La question du rapport des formations d'extrême droite aux systèmes politiques des démocraties européennes," in *Les Croisés de la société fermée,* ed. Pascal Perrineau (La Tour d'Aigues: L'Aube, 2001), 335–361.

18. Anne Tréfois and Jean Fanie, "L'évolution des partis politiques flamands (2002–2007)," *Courrier hebdomadaire du CRISP* 1971 (2007): 5–51.

19. *Le Soir* (Brussels), April 5, 2012.

20. In 2010, Oskar Freysinger came to Paris within the context of the Assises contre l'Islamisation de l'Europe (Annual Conference against the Islamization of Europe), organized by the Bloc Identitaire. It was from that moment on, it seems, that Marine Le Pen realized the mobilizing potential of Islamophobia and maneuvered to no longer be outflanked by the BI.

21. *Nation Europe* (January–March 1995); Xavier Bougarel, "Travailler sur l'islam dans la Bosnie en guerre," *Cultures et Conflits* 47 (2002): 49–80; Jacques Sémelin, *Purifier et détruire: Usages politiques des massacres et génocides* (Paris: Le Seuil, 2005), 33.

22. *Regards,* September 12, 2000.

23. Commission Nationale Consultative des Droits de l'Homme, *La Lutte contre le racisme, l'antisémitisme et la xénophobie* (Paris: La Documentation française, 2001).

24. Having become a powerful Sarkozyist, Peltier now heads one of the French conservative factions. He follows the "Buisson line" (named for Patrick Buisson, a veteran of *Minute,* who was the brains behind Nicolas Sarkozy's identity politics in 2012). He seeks to make the French conservative movement an equivalent of the Spanish Partido Popular, which covers the entire spectrum of the right wing (Patrick Buisson and Guillaume Peltier hardly take into account the fact that Spain does not have a two-round majority electoral system).

25. See Jean-Yves Camus, "L'extrême droite européenne et la Turquie: Le double fantasme de l'islamisation de la reconquête," in *Turquie, Europe:*

Le retour des nationalismes, ed. Füsün Turkmen (Istanbul: Galatasaray University; Paris: Harmattan, 2010), 73–92.

26. Thomas Beaufils and Patrick Duval, eds., *Les identités néerlandaises: De l'intégration à la désintégration?* (Villeneuve-d'Ascq: Presses Universitaires du Septentrion, 2006).

27. Gaël Brustier and Jean-Philippe Huelin, *Voyage au bout de la droite* (Paris: Mille et Une Nuits, 2011).

28. Sylvain Crépon, *Enquête au coeur du nouveau Front national* (Paris: Nouveau Monde, 2012).

29. Abel Mestre and Caroline Monnot, *Le système Le Pen* (Paris: Denoël, 2012), 84–87.

30. During that time, the Islamophobic organization Riposte Laïque (which emerged from the left but joined the far right, and sometimes works with the Bloc Identitaire) vigorously denounced the FN's pro–Arab Muslim betrayal.

31. See Rudy Reichstadt, *Conspirationnisme: Un état des lieux,* note no. 11, Observatoire des Radicalités Politiques (Observatory of Political Radicalism) (Paris: Fondation Jean-Jaurès, February 2015).

32. See Nonna Mayer, *L'opinion publique française n'est pas antisémite,* note no. 10, Observatoire des Radicalités Politiques (Paris: Fondation Jean-Jaurès, October 2014); Nonna Mayer, "Les opinions antisémites en France après la seconde Intifada," *Revue Internationale et Stratégique* 58 (2005): 143–150.

33. According to the FN's general secretary, 39 percent of militants are women (e-mail from Nicolas Bay to Nicolas Lebourg, November 5, 2013). On the militant registration rolls of Perpignan (the only city with more than 100,000 residents where the FN won the first round of municipal elections in 2014, with Louis Aliot at the top of the ticket), the proportion of women rose to 44 percent. See Jérôme Fouquet, Nicolas Lebourg, and Sylvain Manternach, *Perpignan, une ville avant le Front national?* (Paris: Fondation Jean-Jaurès, 2014). On the question of gays in the FN, see Lebourg and Beauregard, *Dans l'ombre des Le Pen,* 365–380. This discussion triggered a controversy on the subject following the feature article in *Minute* on January 2, 2103, within the context of opposition to the right of homosexuals to marry, even though Marine Le Pen had adopted Florian Philippot's neutrality on social issues.

34. Christophe Guilly, *La France périphérique* (Paris: Flammarion, 2014).

35. On the vagaries of Fascism in rural environments, see Robert O. Paxton, "Les fascismes: Essai d'histoire comparée," *Vingtième Siècle* 45 (January–March 1995): 3–13.

36. On the concept of "uncivil society," see Andreas Umland, "Towards an Uncivil Society? Contextualizing the Decline of Post-Soviet Russian Extremely Right-Wing Parties," Weatherhead Center for International Affairs, Working Paper Series 2–3 (2002).

37. Pascal Perrineau, *La France au Front* (Paris: Fayard, 2014).

38. See Joël Gombin, "Contextualiser sans faire de l'espace un facteur autonome: La modélisation multiniveau comme lieu de rencontre entre sociologie et géographie électorales," *L'Espace politique* (July 2014), http://espacepolitique.revues.org/3066; Joël Gombin, *Vote FN aux européennes: Une nouvelle assise électorale?,* note no. 9, Observatoire des Radicalités Politiques (Paris: Fondation Jean-Jaurès, September 2014); Joël Gombin and Sylvain Crépon, "Loin des mythes, dans l'isoloir," in "Manière de voir," *Le Monde diplomatique* 134 (April–May 2014): 61–66; Fourquet, Lebourg, and Manternach, *Perpignan, une ville avant le Front national?*

39. Joël Gombin and Nicolas Lebourg, "Le vote pour l'extrême droite est une façon de repolitiser l'élection," *Le Monde,* March 28, 2014, 25.

40. *Identitaires,* the review of the BI, evokes the "anti-Islamization social movement PEGIDA." *Identitaires* 22 (May–June 2015): 14. But that movement interests them less than the possible adoption of its themes by Alternative für Deutschland (AfD; Alternative for Germany). Hence, evoking the results of PEGIDA in the first round of the municipal elections, the members of BI expressed delight that they had surpassed those of AfD (4.8 percent) and concluded: "The leaders [of AfD] who argue for greater consideration of identity questions are right."

6. What's New to the East?

1. We borrow the term "neo-Eurasianist" from Marlène Laruelle, specialist in that movement. There are in fact many differences between the Eurasianism of the 1920s and that advocated by Dugin, not the least of them being that Eurasianism considered the Jews part of the Eurasian genius, whereas the neo-Eurasianist theorist sets up an opposition between the Slavo-Aryan Nordic race and the Jewish race.

2. That view of the nation explains, for example, why Hungarian prime minister Viktor Orbán declared, regarding the reception given to migrants: "It must not be forgotten that those who are arriving . . . are the representatives of a profoundly different culture. For the most part, they are not Christians but Muslims. That is an important question, because Europe and European identity have Christian roots." *Frankfurter Allgemeine Zeitung,* September 2, 2015.

3. For example, in 1992 Matica Slovenská published a hagiography of Jozef Tiso written by a Catholic priest, the Salesian Milan S. Ďurica. The Slovak Foundation was created in 1863, after its Serbian and Czech counterparts and before the Croatian and Slovakian versions. Their activity today is not confined to political action, even less to the far right.

4. *Pamjat' parle* (Nantes: Ars Magna, n.d.).

5. Vladimir Pribylovski, "Le mouvement Pamiat, 'école des cadres' du nationalisme russe durant la Perestroïka," in *Le Rouge et le Noir: Extrême droite et nationalisme en Russie,* ed. Marlène Laruelle (Paris: CNRS, 2007), 99–114.

6. Anton Shekhovtsov, "Alexander Dugin and the West European New Right, 1989–1994," in *Eurasianism and the European Far Right,* ed. Marlène Laruelle (Lanham, MD: Lexington, 2015), 37–38.

7. The notion of Pan-Turanism, that is, of an ethno-linguistic kinship of the peoples of Turkic descent resulting in a common political destiny, sometimes overlaps with Eurasianism. For example, the review *Turàn,* published in Istanbul, mentions the actions of Jobbik and its leader, Gabor Vona, in an issue whose cover displays a photograph of Turkoman volunteers in the Waffen-SS engaged in prayer. *Turàn* 13 (2011).

8. Laruelle, "Alexandre Dugin, esquisse d'un eurasisme," 94.

9. Markus Mathyl, "The National-Bolshevik Party and Arctogaia: Two Neo-Fascist Groupuscules in the Post-Soviet Political Space," *Patterns of Prejudice* 36, no. 3 (2002): 64; Roger Griffin, "Plus ça change! The Fascist Mindset behind the Nouvelle Droite's Struggle for Cultural Renewal," in *The Development of the Radical Right in France 1890–1995,* ed. Edward Arnold (London: Routledge, 2000), 237–252.

10. Aleksandr Dugin, interview with *Lutte du peuple* (October 1992); Aleksandr Dugin, "Métaphysique du national-bolchevisme," "Julius Evola et le traditionalisme russe," and "La Révolution conservatrice russe," in *Archivio eurasia,* a Web site associated with Synergies Européennes.

11. Christian Bouchet, *Troisième Voie-Année zéro,* 1989, internal document, personal archives.

12. For example, in *Éléments* (May 1992), Benoist appears to be repeating material from the editorials in *Lutte du peuple,* the organ of Nouvelle Résistance.

13. *TV Circulaire SG-8,* September 4, 1991; *Nouvelle Résistance SG-9,* September 23, 1991, internal documents, personal archives.

14. Sauveur, *Jean Thiriart,* A–J; the first version of the text dates to 1981. It is presented here in its augmented version of 1983.

15. José Cuadrado Costa, "Insuffisance et dépassement du concept marxiste-léniniste de nationalié," *Conscience européenne* 9 (October 1984).

16. See Anton Shekhovtsov and Andreas Umland, "Is Aleksandr Dugin a Traditionalist? Neo-Eurasianism and Perennial Philosophy," *Russian Review* 68, no. 4 (2009): 662–678; Aleksandr Dugin, "La Cuarta teoría política," Madrid, November 12, 2013, available on YouTube.

17. *Lutte du peuple* (September 1992); Laruelle, "Alexandre Dugin, esquisse d'un eurasisme d'extrême droite," 87.

18. *Lutte du peuple* (October 1992).

19. Alexandre Dreiling, "Les nationalistes radicaux russes en 1996–1997," in *Les extrémismes en Europe,* ed. Jean-Yves Camus (La Tour-d'Aigues: L'Aube, 1998), 316–317.

20. *Limonka* ("little lemon," a nickname for an antipersonnel grenade) is the title of Limonov's newspaper.

21. Véra Nikolski, "Le Parti national bolchevique russe: Une entreprise politique hétérodoxe," *Critique internationale* 55 (2012): 93–115.

22. Declaration no. 9253, November 10, 1993, Archives de la Sous-Préfecture de Valenciennes.

23. *Nation Europe* 1 (February–March 1994); 2 (June–July 1994).

24. Christian Bouchet, *Lettre ouverte aux cadres de Nouvelle Résistance,* August 16, 1996, internal document, personal archives.

25. Bylaws of the Association Nouvelle Résistance, September 2, 1996, Archives de la Sous-Préfecture du Raincy.

26. See "À propos du Front européen de libération et du PCN," and "Communiqué de presse de Nouvelle Résistance—10 novembre 1996," http://fel.nr.free.fr/propos.htm.

27. *L'Europe combattante* (October 1996), internal document, personal archives; *Tribuna de Europa* 2, no. 8 (December 1996).

28. *3e Congrès de Nouvelle Résistance: Motion présentée par le secrétariat général de l'organisation,* 4; *L'Europe combattante* (November 1996): 1–2, internal documents, personal archives.

29. *L'Europe combattante* (Summer 1997), internal document, personal archives.

30. *Tribuna de Europa* 2, no. 10 (May–June 1997); no. 12 (October–November 1997).

31. *La Lettre du Réseau* (November–December 1997; November–December 1998), internal documents, personal archives.

32. Troy Southgate, "Manifesto of the European Liberation Front," 1999, reproduced in Troy Southgate, *Tradition and Revolution* (London: Arktos, 2010), 125–132.

33. Anton Shekhovtsov and Andreas Umland, "Vladimir Zhirinovsky and the LDPR," *Russian Analytical Digest* 102 (September 26, 2011): 14–17.

34. "Russie: Information sur le parti politique appelé Unité nationale russe (Rosskoyé natsional'noyé edentistvo—RNE), y compris sa taille, son influence, ses activités et ses relations avec le gouvernement," Canada, Commission de l'Immigration et du Statut de Réfugié, Direction des Recherches, June 9, 2004, http://www.refworld.org/docid/41501c562a.html.

35. He belongs to the movement called Edinoverie (Unity in Faith), which follows the ancient rite of the Old Believers. The Orthodox Old Believers opposed the liturgical and doctrinal reforms introduced in 1666–1667 by Patriarch Nikon of Moscow. They were persecuted by the state (until 1905) and by the church, and most of them settled in the Urals and Siberia. They constitute a very fragmented movement, whose religiously radical elements are imbued with an eschatological spirit. Since the beginning of the nineteenth century, parishes that practice the old rite have associated themselves with the Orthodox Church of the Moscow Patriarchate. Dugin is linked to that church.

36. "La vision eurasiste: Principes de base de la plate-forme doctrinale eurasiste," *La nation eurasienne* 1 (June 2003): n.p.

37. That pro-Russian international forum, founded in 2004, advocates multipolarity. Its French guests have included, notably, Aymeric Chauprade, Jacques Sapir, and Marion Maréchal-Le Pen.

38. See Marlène Laruelle, "Novorossiya: A Launching Pad for Russian Nationalists," *PONARS Eurasia Policy* 357 (September 2014); Marlène

Laruelle, "A Nationalist Kulturkampf in Russia? The Izborsky Club as the Anti-Valdai" (forthcoming), kindly provided by the author.

39. See *Le Nouvel Observateur,* May 1, 2014.

40. Umut Korkut and Emel Akçali, "Deciphering Eurasianism in Hungary: Narratives, Networks, and Lifestyles," in Laruelle, *Eurasianism and the European Far Right,* 175–192.

41. See Camus and Monzat, *Les Droites nationales et radicales en France,* 469–470; Mestre and Monnot, *Le système Le Pen,* 55–58.

42. Soft power is a concept developed by the American Joseph Nye: states, alongside their hard power (military resources), possess a soft power grounded in the attraction exerted by their cultural activities in the broad sense. Nye recommends that governments conduct a strategy of influence in international relations by turning social representations in their favor by means of that soft power (the image of the United States produced by American cinema, the Confucius Institute network that promotes Chinese culture, and the theme of Francophonia are three possible examples).

43. *Le Monde,* June 8, 2001.

44. Marlène Laruelle, "Scared of Putin's Shadow," *Foreign Affairs,* March 2015, https://www.foreignaffairs.com/articles/russian-federation /2015-03-25/scared-putins-shadow.

45. Olha Ostriitchouk Zazulya, "Le conflit identitaire à travers les rhétoriques concurrentes en Ukraine postsoviétique," *Autrepart* 48 (2008): 59–72.

46. Milza, *L'Europe en chemise noire,* 380–382.

47. Anna Colin Lebedev, "Les Ukrainiens au tournant de l'histoire européenne," *Études* 3 (2015): 7–18.

48. Olha Ostriitchouk Zazulya, "Les dessous de la révolution ukrainienne: D'une contestation civique à une guerre identitaire," *Le Débat* 180 (2014): 3–16.

49. One of Dontsov's works is titled *The Spirit of Our Past* (*Douch nachyi davnynyi*; 1944). On its cover, it shows an Orthodox church, a sword, and the word "traditionalism."

50. Oleh Pankevych to the National Front, March 7, 2014, http://www .contre-info.com/lettre-de-svoboda-au-front-national-exclusivite-contre-info.

51. *Pravyi Sektor,* n.d. (2014); Right Sector propaganda leaflet, personal archives.

52. Anton Shekhovtsov, "The Spectre of Ukrainian 'Fascism': Information Wars, Political Manipulation, and Reality," in *What Does Ukraine Think?*, ed. Andrew Wilson (London: European Council on Foreign Relations, 2015), 80–86.

53. Anton Shekhovtsov, "Far-Right Election Observation Monitors in the Service of the Kremlin's Foreign Policy," in Laruelle, *Eurasianism and the European Far Right*, 223–243.

54. Irena Cantovovich, "Post-Soviet Region," *Antisemitism Worldwide 2014 General Analysis Draft* (Tel Aviv: Moshe Kantor Database for the Study of Contemporary Antisemitism and Racism, 2014), 17–21.

55. Radio Free Europe / Radio Liberty Report, October 10, 2003, by Kathleen Knox; *Baltic Times,* April 8, 2004; *EU-Reporter,* February 23–27, 2004, 14.

56. Céline Bayou, Jaroslav Blaha, Édith Lhomel, and Jean-Yves Potel, "Populisme et extrémisme en Europe centrale et balte," *Le Courrier des pays de l'Est* 1054 (2006): 27–43.

57. Report / CAT / C / CR / 31/3, February 5, 2004.

58. Ilze Balcere, "Comparing Populist Political Parties in the Baltic States and Western Europe," Working Paper, ECPR General Conference, Reykjavik, August 25–27, 2011.

59. Nadège Ragaru, "Ataka: Les raisons du succès d'un parti nationaliste radical en Bulgarie," note, CERI CNRS, 2005; Nadège Ragaru, "Ataka: Les gloires éphémères de la xénophobie? La redéfinition des frontières intérieures de la société bulgare," *Recherches internationales* 92 (October–December 2011): 69–80.

60. Quoted in Gilles Ivaldi, "Euroscepticisme, populisme, droites radicales: État des forces et enjeux européens," *L'Europe en formation* 373 (2014): 7–28.

61. In the tradition of the English sociologists Stanley Cohen and Stuart Hall, Gaël Brustier terms "moral panic" the disproportionate reactions of social groups to minority cultural behaviors.

62. Balázs Ablonczy and Bálint Ablonczy, "L'extrême droite en Hongrie: Racines, culture, espace," *Hérodote* 144 (2012): 38–59.

63. Tomislav Nikolić, the Serbian president elected in 2012, came out of the Serbian Radical Party, but he broke away in 2008 to found a pro–European Union party.

64. Horia Sima, *Histoire du mouvement légionnaire* (Rio de Janeiro: Dacia, 1972), 44.

65. Ion Antonescu, *Romanii, originea, trecutal, suferintele si depturile lor* (Bucharest: Saeculum, 1998 [1919]), 55; Oleh Protsyk, *Representation of Minorities in the Romanian Parliament* (Geneva: Inter-Parliamentary Union, 2010).

66. The current president of the party is former prime minister Jaroslaw Kazcynski (1949), whose twin brother, Lech, was president of Poland. In 2010 Lech Kazcynski died when the plane he was traveling in crashed during its descent toward Smolensk (Russia). The circumstances of that crash gave rise to multiple conspiracy theories in nationalist circles.

67. Paul Lendvai, *L'Antisémitisme sans juifs* (Paris: Fayard, 1971).

68. Since January 2002, the synod of the Hungarian Reformed Church has firmly condemned Hegedűs's various views and the presence of some ten religious ministers among the MIÉP candidates in the legislative elections of 2002.

69. President Vladimir Putin also uses that idea of Russia's "specific path," as does Gennady Zyuganov's Communist Party.

70. Mark Mazower, *Le continent des ténèbres: Une histoire de l'Europe au XXe siècle* (Brussels: Complexe, 2005).

Conclusion

1. Cécile Alduy and Stéphane Wanich, *Marine Le Pen prise aux mots* (Paris: Le Seuil, 2015).

2. Romain Ducoulombier, *Histoire du communisme* (Paris: Presses Universitaires de France, 2014), 4–5.

3. Patrice de La Tour du Pin, *La quête de joie* (Paris: Gallimard, 1933).

Acknowledgments

Books are collective ventures. Our thanks go out to Jean-Christophe Brochier, who edited the French edition of this one. The European far right constitutes a field of investigation for a number of researchers. Our exchanges with them provided food for thought for this book. Furthermore, journalists in France have for the last few years built up a set of resources that proved invaluable to us. Finally, the far right, too, has its intellectuals, able and willing to engage in analyses of their milieu with outside observers. We would therefore like to thank Manuel Abramowicz, Dominique Albertini, Graeme Atkinson, Uwe Backes, Francis Balace, Christian Bouchet, Xavier Casals, Humberto Cucchetti, Guillaume Daudin, Alain de Benoist, Renaud Dély, David Doucet, the staff of the review *Expo* (Stockholm), Christophe Forcari, Jérôme Fourquet, Roger Griffin, Jérôme Jamin, Steve Kayser, Bruno Larebière, Nonna Mayer, Abel Mestre, Caroline Monnot, René Monzat, Patrick Moreau, Cas Mudde, Emmanuel Négrier, Rafal Pankowski, Pascal Perrineau, Dina Porat and the Kantor Center for the Study of Contemporary European Jewry (Tel Aviv), Jonathan Preda, José Luis Rodríguez Jiménez, Alfred Ross, Michael Shafir, Anton Shevkotsov, Marco Tarchi, Andreas Umland, Philippe Vervaecke, and Eric Weaver. There are also militants who, without appearing by name in this book, provided information, documents, opinions, and eyewitness accounts. Without them, we would have found it impossible to understand the living operations of the milieu studied. We also thank two researchers who directed international programs related to the far right that gave rise to a specific set of writings: Olivier Dard (*Internationalisation des droites radicales Europe-Amériques*) and Marlène Laruelle (*European Fascism*). Naturally, our thoughts go out to the staff of *Charlie Hebdo,* who illustrated the earlier book we co-authored, and we pay special tribute to the victims of the attack of January 7, 2015, whose survivors battle on. Our thoughts are also with the team of researchers at the Observatoire des Radicalités Politiques (ORAP) at the Fondation Jean-Jaurès: Cécile Alduy, Joseph Beauregard, Gaël Brustier, Sylvain Crépon, Alexandre Dézé, Delphine Espagno, Stéphane François, Joël Gombin, Rudy Reichstadt, and Dominique Sistach. So too the foundation's staff, which keeps the ORAP running: Gilles Finchelstein, Laurent Cohen, Aline Grange, Alice Chatzimanassis, and Jérémie Peltier. Our thanks to Frédérique Le Bourg for proofreading the French edition. Thank you, Myriam, Lumael, and Ylan. To Annie-Paul, Liora, and Flora, and to Alex Derczansky (ZL), irreplaceable conveyor of memory and ideas.

Index

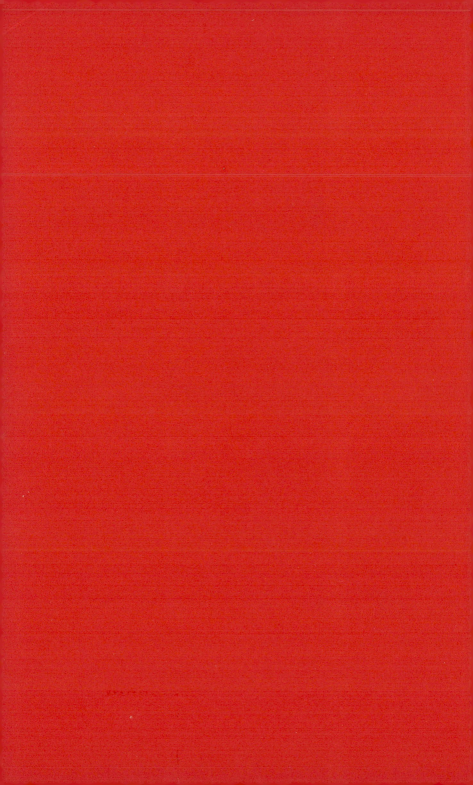